interactive policy making, metagovernance and democracy

Edited by
Jacob Torfing and Peter Triantafillou

ecpr PRESS

© Jacob Torfing and Peter Triantafillou 2011

Cover image © Jayson Gatdula

First published by the ECPR Press in 2011

Paperback first published by the ECPR Press in 2013

The ECPR Press is the publishing imprint of the European Consortium for Political Research (ECPR), a scholarly association, which supports and encourages the training, research and cross-national cooperation of political scientists in institutions throughout Europe and beyond.
ECPR Press
University of Essex
Wivenhoe Park,
Colchester
CO4 3SQ, UK

Typeset by ECPR Press
Printed and bound by Lightning Source

British Library Cataloguing in Publication Data
A catalogue record for this book is available from the British Library

Hardback ISBN: 978-1-907301-13-1

Paperback ISBN: 978-1-907301-56-8

www.ecpr.eu/ecprpress

ECPR – Studies in European Political Science

Series Editors:
Dario Castiglione (University of Exeter) and
Vincent Hoffmann-Martinot (Sciences Po Bordeaux)

ECPR – Studies in European Political Science is a series of high-quality edited volumes on topics at the cutting edge of current political science and political thought. All volumes are research-based offering new perspectives in the study of politics with contributions from leading scholars working in the relevant fields. Most of the volumes originate from ECPR events including the Joint Sessions of Workshops, the Research Sessions, and the General Conferences.

Books in this series

The Domestic Party Politics of Europeanisation: Actors, Patterns and Systems
ISBN: 9781907301223
Edited by Erol Külahci

Interactive Policy Making, Metagovernance and Democracy
ISBN: 9781907301131
Edited by Jacob Torfing and Peter Triantafillou

Perceptions of Europe: A Comparative Sociology of European Attitudes
ISBN: 9781907301155
Edited by Daniel Gaxie, Jay Rowell and Nicolas Hubé

Personal Representation: The Neglected Dimension of Electoral Systems
ISBN: 9781907301162
Edited by Josep Colomer

Political Trust: Why Context Matters
ISBN: 9781907301230
Edited by Sonja Zmerli and Marc Hooghe

Please visit www.ecpr.eu/ecprpress for up-to-date information about new publications.

| contents

| list of figures and tables

Figures

Tables

| list of abbreviations

BDI	German Industry Federation
BEPG	Broad Economic Policy Guidelines
BERR	Department of Business, Enterprise and Regulative Reform
BMU	The Environment Ministry
CBI	Confederation of British Industry
CDSEI	Comité du Dialogue Social pour les questions Européennes et Internationales
CFDT	Confédération Française Démocratique du Travail
CGT	Confédération Générale du Travail
COOP	Cooperative Union
COP	Conference of the Parties
CSO	Civil Society Organisations
DA	Confederation of Danish Employers
DECC	Department of Energy and Climate Change
DEET	Department of Employment, Education and Training
DEETYA	Department of Employment, Education, Training and Youth Affairs
DEEWR	Department of Employment, Education and Workplace Relations
DEWR	Department of Employment and Workplace Relations
DK	Denmark
DTI	Department of Trade and Industry
DWP	Department for Work and Pensions
EDF	Électricité de France
EES	European Employment Strategy
EPC	Empowered Participatory Governance
EPSRC	Engineering and Physical Sciences Research Council
ESRC	Economic and Social Research Council
ETUC	European Trade Union Confederation
EU	European Union
FI	Finland
FSC	Future Search Conference
GDA	Generic Design Assessment
HSE	Health and Safety Executive
IPC	Infrastructure Planning Commission
ISP	Inter-muncipal Strategy Plan
ISV	Interregionale Structuurvisie

JCP	Jobcentre Plus
JSA	Jobseekers Allowance
LO	Danish Confederation of Trade Unions
MCC	Municipal Contact Council
MEDEF	Mouvement des Entreprises de France
MILKO	the Dairy Producers
MP	Member of Parliament
NAP	National Action Plan
NATO (criteria)	Nodality, Authority, Treasure and Organisation
NDA	Nuclear Decommissioning Authority
NGO	Non-governmental organisation
NII	Nuclear Installations Inspectorate
NO	Norway
NPM	New Public Management
NRP	National Reform Program
OECD	Organisation for Economic Co-operation and Development
OFGEM	Office of Gas and Energy Markets
OMC	Open Method of Coordination
OND	Office of Nuclear Development
OST	Open Space Technology
PC	Provincial Council
PE	Provincial Executive
RDP	Regional Development Programme
RGP	Regional Growth Plan
RMC	Regional Management Committee
RTSC	Real Time Strategic Change
SBA	Swedish Board of Agriculture
SV	Sweden
TUC	British Trade Union Congress
UBA	German Environment Agency
UK	United Kingdom
UN	United Nations
UNICE	Union of Industrial and Employer's Confederations of Europe
VROM	Ministerie van Volkshuisvesting, Ruimtelijke Ordening en Milieubeheer
WoC	World Cafe
WTO	World Trade Organisation
ZLTO	Southern Agriculture and Horticulture Organisation

| acknowledgements

The first version of the chapters in this edited volume were presented in the eight panels of the section on 'Interactive Governance, Policy Innovation and Democracy' at the 5th ECPR General Conference held at Potsdam University, 10–12 September 2009. We would like to thank the academic conveners, the local organisers and the many participants who all contributed to the making the ECPR General Conference in Potsdam a successful and intellectually stimulating event.

We would like to thank the authors for their participation and their constructive cooperation in the process of revising the chapters to fit this edited volume and the anonymous reviewer who provided some very helpful comments to the chapters at an earlier stage.

We are also grateful for the financial support from the Danish Social Science Research Council that helped to make it possible to put together this volume despite the usual hassles of teaching and administrative tasks.

Finally, we are grateful for the active support and encouragement that we have received from the series editors.

Jacob Torfing and Peter Triantafillou
Center for Democratic Network Governance
Roskilde
June, 2011

| about the contributors

KEITH BAKER is lecturer in Politics, Department of Social Sciences, Northumbria University, United Kingdom. His research interests include the governance of complex technical systems, energy policy, public sector procurement and public-private partnering.

MARK CONSIDINE is Professor of Political Science and Dean of Arts, University of Melbourne. His research interests include public sector reform, local employment and economic development, network governance and policy design theory.

JURIAN EDELENBOS is Professor of Public Administration, Department of Public Administration, Erasmus University Rotterdam, The Netherlands. Scientific Director of IHS (International Housing and Urban Management Studies). His research interests include water governance, network management, citizen engagement, trust and control, knowledge co-production, and institutional innovation.

ANDERS ESMARK, Associate Professor in Public Organisation and Policy, Department of Political Science, University of Copenhagen, Denmark. His research interests include new forms of governance, Europeanisation and political communication.

TRINE FOTEL is Assistant Professor in Public Administration and Public Policy, Department of Society and Globalisation, Roskilde University, Denmark. Her research interests include local government reforms, regional policy and planning, democracy and interactive governance.

MIRJAM KARS, is a senior local government researcher. Her expertise and areas of interest include multi-level governance, the EU, international political economy, and the governance of utility sectors. Her research focuses mainly on European cooperation regarding utility sectors and its consequences for policies and actors at the European, national, and domestic level.

ERIK-HANS KLIJN is Professor in the Department of Public Administration at Erasmus University Rotterdam. His research and teaching activities focus on complex decision-making and management in networks, institutional design and Public Private Partnerships and branding and media influences on governance processes.

JOOP KOPPENJAN is Professor of Public Administration at the Erasmus University Rotterdam. He is senior staff member of the Netherlands Institute of Governance and member of Trail (The Netherlands research school of Transport, Infrastructure and Logistics). His research is focussed on governance of complex multi-actor situations.

PAUL KRUMMENACHER, founding partner and CEO of Frischer Wind, a company that is specialised in facilitating and mediating development and clarification processes in companies, institutions and government bodies and in the public sector in Switzerland.

JENNY M. LEWIS is Professor of Public Administration and Public Policy, Department of Society and Globalisation, Roskilde University, Denmark. Her research interests include power and ideas in the policy process, new forms of governance, and professions and disciplines.

LOUIS MEULEMAN is Research Fellow at the Free University, Amsterdam; senior lecturer Nyenrode Business University, Breukelen; director TransGov project, Institute for Advanced Sustainability Studies, Potsdam. National expert at DG Environment, European Commission. His research interests include metagovernance and sustainability (meta)governance.

SIMONA PIATTONI, Professor of European Union Politics, Department of Political Science, University of Innsbruck, Austria. Her research interests include multi-level governance, informal and personalistic politics, clientelism.

GERRY STOKER is Professor of Governance and Politics at the University of Southampton, UK and Director of the Centre for Citizenship, Globalisation and Governance. His research interests include: governance, anti-politics, civic engagement, welfare reform and behaviour change.

JACOB TORFING is Professor in Politics and Institutions, Department of Society and Globalization, Roskilde University, Denmark. Director of the Centre for Democratic Network Governance. His research interests include welfare reforms, network governance, collaborative innovation and institutional theory.

PETER TRIANTAFILLOU is Associate Professor in Politics and Administration, Department of Society and Globalization, Roskilde University, Denmark. His research interests include the exercise of power and freedom through welfare policies and new forms of governing in the public sector.

NICO VAN DER HEIDEN is Senior Project Manager, Centre for Democracy Studies Aarau, Switzerland. His research interests include deliberative democracy, foreign policy of sub-national units, federalism, and urban and agglomeration politics.

HAIKO VAN DER VOORT is an Assistant Professor of public administration at Delft University of Technology. He a Masters degree in Public Administration at Leiden University. He teaches organization theory and decision making theory at Bachelor and Masters level to professionals and elective students.

INGMAR VAN MEERKERK is PhD student, Department of Public Administration, Erasmus University Rotterdam, The Netherlands. His research interests include legitimacy of governance networks, complexity management, boundary spanning, citizen participation and institutional innovations.

ÅSA CASULA VIFELL is researcher in political science at Södertörn University, Institute for Contemporary History and Stockholm University, Department of Political Science. Her research interests include transnational democracy, Europeanization, public administration, and decision theory.

chapter one | introduction to interactive policy making, metagovernance and democracy

Jacob Torfing and Peter Triantafillou

This edited volume aims to deepen our understanding of how public policy and governance is produced and delivered in advanced industrial societies. A lot has been written over the years about the role and functioning of the formal institutions of government and how they contribute to public governance. More recently, the introduction of market principles in the public sector, triggered by the global tsunami of New Public Management[1] reforms, has also received much attention from public administration researchers all over the world. Therefore, this book has a different focus as it aims to highlight the role and impact of *interactive forms of policy making* that are facilitated by the formation of public forums, tripartite bodies, think tanks, governance networks, partnerships and strategic alliances. Interactive forms of governance are both supplementing and supplanting traditional forms of governance through hierarchical government and competitive markets and their role in producing, delivering and amending public policy is considerable. Although interactive policy making is far from being neglected by political scientists and public administration scholars, the growing importance of collaborative forms of governance in most Western societies calls for further studies of interactive policy making.

So far, the research literature has identified, described and evaluated interactive forms of policy making in different areas and at different levels of government (Heffen, Kickert and Thomassen 2000; Hajer and Wagenaar 2003; Marcussen and Torfing 2007). However, more *empirical studies* are required in order to understand the different forms of institutionalised policy interaction and how the interactive processes and policy outputs are shaped by the cultural and political context as well as by the social and political actors engaged in policy interaction. There is also an urgent need to address two unfortunate lacunas in the research literature on interactive governance: the role of metagovernance and the democratic implications of enhanced policy interaction.

First, there has been far too little focus on the question of how interactive policy making arenas are designed, managed and directed through *metagovernance*. Metagovernance can be defined as:

---

1.   New Public Management refers to a management philosophy introduced to modernise the public sector in the 1980s. The main hypothesis behind the NPM reforms is that more market orientation in the public sector will lead to greater cost-efficiency for governments, without having negative side effects on other objectives and considerations.

a reflexive and strategic attempt to govern interactive governance arenas without reverting too much to traditional statist governing tools based on command and control.

Metagovernance is necessary because interactive forms of policy making are just as prone to failure – though for other and different reasons – as the more traditional forms of governance through hierarchies and markets. However, the study of how interactive governance arenas are metagoverned has been systematically neglected by both the first wave of interactive governance theorists that claimed interactive policy making contributed to the hollowing out of the state (Rhodes 1997) and the second wave of interactive governance theorists that merely reasserted the primacy of government and reduced interactive policy making to a tool of modern governments (Bell and Hindmoor 2009). A more balanced account of the relationship between traditional forms of government and the interactive forms of governance will argue that governments are neither 'hollowed out' nor 'filled in' by the surge of interactive policy making (Matthews 2011). Instead, governments – their roles, institutional forms and interventions – are re-articulated and transformed by the proliferation of new and more institutionalised forms of interactive policy making. In order to harvest the gains associated with sustained policy interaction, governments at all levels are struggling to find ways of facilitating, managing and directing the interactive governance arenas without undermining their self-regulating capacity, and thus scaring off the non-governmental actors whose knowledge, ideas and resources are paramount to solving public policy problems. Further research on metagovernance is necessary in order to understand how governments and other resourceful actors are metagoverning interactive policy arenas and in order to assess the effects of different types of metagovernance for the production of public purpose through multilateral action.

Secondly, there has only been scant regard for the *democratic implications* of interactive policy making. In public hierarchies and public–private quasi-markets, the production and delivery of public policy is anchored in authoritative decisions taken by politicians who have democratic legitimacy because they are elected by the people and command a political majority in the elected assemblies. The politicians compete for office and it is possible to hold them accountable for their actions and inactions through public enquiries and regular elections. In interactive policy making, the questions about democratic legitimacy and accountability are more complicated. On the one hand, participation of relevant and affected actors in public policy making might enhance democratic input legitimacy as more people become actively engaged and more views and interests are accommodated. By the same token, learning-based negotiations of problems and solutions might augment democratic output legitimacy as the quality of public decision making is improved when different public and private stakeholders exchange knowledge, ideas and opinions. On the other hand, there are some clear democratic problems as the participants in policy interaction are often appointed rather than elected; participation tend to be biased in favour of well-organised and resourceful actors; the collaborative negotiations are frequently rather secluded; and the responsible actors are difficult to hold to account for the policy outputs and policy outcomes they are producing due to the absence of regular elections and the presence of monopoly interest representation.

However, evaluating interactive forms of governance on the basis of the traditional model of liberal representative democracy does not tell the full story about the democratic quality and impact of interactive policy making. As convincingly argued by Warren (2009), interactive governance holds a contingent promise for a further democratisation of a society that responds to the so-called 'democratic disenchantment' – evidenced by the decline in voter turn-out and party membership and the mounting distrust in elected politicians – by ensuring that those affected by public policies have a direct influence on these policies through engagement with relevant public authorities. Governance-driven democratisation seldom involves ordinary citizens as the participatory arenas are often captured by non-governmental organisations and private firms, and the democratisation process is not driven by the people, but rather advanced by administrative elites that recognise the need for the mobilisation of the knowledge, resources and energies of private actors. Elected politicians might occasionally participate in interactive policy deliberation, but most often governance-driven democratisation is de-linked from electoral democracy. Nevertheless, what is really interesting about governance-driven democratisation is that it brings into existence a number of dynamic and overlapping constituencies consisting of the intensely affected people that replace the static territorial constituencies on which traditional forms of representative democracy are based (Warren 2009). As such, it contributes to redefining the way we think of 'the people' in modern democracies. 'The people' is not just a relatively passive and predefined electorate consisting of many of individual wills, but it is also a number of collective wills that are actively engaged in the formulation and implementation of public policies by which they are intensely affected. With the increasing de-territorialisation of policy making, this contingent determination of the people becomes more and more important. The democratic implications of interactive policy making has been discussed and assess by a number of scholars (Sørensen and Torfing 2005a; Benz and Papadopoulos 2006; Klijn and Skelcher 2007) and some researchers have also addressed the 'demos problem' (Bohman 2005; Catlaw 2007; Keane 2010; Warren 2009). However, more research is needed in order to better understand when and how interactive governance may contribute to a democratisation of society.

It should be noted that the metagovernance of interactive policy making and the democratic implications of interactive governance are intrinsically linked. First, metagovernance can play a crucial role in realising the democratic potential of interactive governance. Although elected politicians, public managers and other would-be metagovernors often tend to give priority to the demand for effective governance, they can also enhance the democratic quality and performance of interactive governance arenas by ensuring inclusive participation, empowered decision-making and democratic deliberation. Second, the demands for democratic anchorage of interactive policy processes in elected politicians tend to emphasise the need for involving elected politicians in metagovernance of networks and partnerships rather than leaving it to public administrators or quasi-independent agencies with a delegated monitoring authority. As such, governance-driven democratisation seems to be conditional upon an effective metagovernance of interactive policy arenas.

Interactive policy making

Interactive policy making can be defined as:

> a relatively stable and institutionalised process of horizontal interaction that engages a plurality of public and private actors in the formulation and/or implementation of public policy.

The purpose of interactive policy processes may vary. As such, the purpose may be to exchange information among key policy actors; to facilitate consultation of and discussion with stakeholders; to generate an informed policy advice; or to engage relevant and affected actors in joint decision-making and coordinated implementation. The institutional designs of interactive policy arenas might vary accordingly and, thus, will tend to include open discussion forums, tripartite bodies, think tanks, governance networks, partnerships and strategic alliances.

There has been a significant rise in interactive policy making in the last few decades. While this trend does not necessarily imply the diminution of the role of hierarchical steering and market-based competition in public governance, the interactive modes of governance clearly provide an increasingly important strategic and political terrain for the governing of public issues. There has always been some degree of interaction between different public authorities and between public and private actors, both in the process of policy formulation and even more so in the implementation phase. This long-lasting tradition for interaction has been captured and described in different ways by classical theories of (neo-)pluralism, (neo-)corporatism and policy sub-systems. In this sense there is nothing new under the sun. Nevertheless, the increasing recognition of multiple resource interdependencies in public policy making and the growing belief amongst public and private decision-makers that collaborative interaction can help to improve public policy in increasingly complex, fragmented and multi-layered societies tend to spur policy interaction at all levels of government and in all phases of the policy process. It also tends to change the status of interactive modes of governance from an inferior supplement to an integral part of the tool box available to the central decision-makers. Last but not least, interactive forms of governance tend to become more formalised and institutionalised through the creation of governance networks, public–private partnerships and strategic alliances. With the exception of the elaborate systems of corporatism in Scandinavia, the Netherlands and Austria, interactive policy making has hitherto been relatively informal and not very institutionalised, but this now changing as the creation of formal and institutional arenas for negotiated interaction are gradually becoming an integral part of public governance. It is these quantitative and qualitative transformations of interactive governance that have stimulated the development of the new research paradigm that we hope to advance.

In a wide range of policy areas, elected politicians, civil servants, experts, private businesses, non-governmental organisations, individual citizens and other relevant and affected actors interact in the formulation and implementation of public policies (Marsh 1998; Heffen, Kickert and Thomassen 2000; Hajer and Wagenaar 2003; Marcussen and Torfing 2007; Kahler 2009). Local and regional planning, public health, education, social housing, labour-market policy, monetary regulation and international security increasingly depend on a more or less collaborative interaction between a plurality of public and private stakeholders. The interactive policy arenas are regulated by an array of governing technologies and procedural designs, which in various ways seek to stimulate, monitor and shape the interactive policy processes (Dean 1999). Such technologies and designs vary immensely from user-satisfaction surveys, balanced scorecard, and benchmarking over focus group interviews and relational contracts to user boards and citizen assemblies. Hence, interactive policy making both has an inter-subjective dimension and a more technical-administrative dimension, which mutually condition and shape each other.

In a time, with increasing expectations to and mounting pressures on the public services on the one hand and scarce fiscal budgets on the other, governments in many OECD countries have willingly engaged in interactive policy making and they often help to facilitate and promote interactive governance by designing or supporting collaborative policy arenas. The public embrace of interactive governance is driven by the expectation, whether naïve or not, that the participation of a range of private actors will mobilise additional resources, know how and/or political support. As such, the ultimate hope is that interactive policy making will increase (resource) efficiency and/or (goal) effectiveness of public policy making. Increased potentials for mutual learning, civic participation, political empowerment, social justice and democratic legitimacy are also frequently raised as possible benefits from extending policy making from a narrow circuit of politicians and civil servants acting within a more or less well-defined legal framework to a wider range of social and political actors whose interactions are monitored and influenced by different governing technologies and procedural designs. However, the public embrace of interactive governance does not mean that it is without critics. Some argue that interactive policy making leads to private interest government, which allows private interests to dominate public policy making (Streeck and Schmitter 1985), others that it supports the development of a managerial discourse that de-politicises public governance (Walters 2004), and yet others claim that it may undermine the primacy of politics by undercutting the influence of elected politicians (Klijn and Koppenjan 2000).

Whatever the reason for supporting or criticising interactive policy making, it seems clear it has not only spread to a large number of policy areas, but also to a different of politico-administrative levels or scales ranging from local institutions and municipalities, over regional counties and nation states, to supranational systems like the European Union (EU) and transnational arenas like the United Nations (UN) and World Trade Organisation (WTO) (Marcussen and Torfing 2007). In many countries, interactive policy making has for a long time been a key feature of public governance at the local level where public services and regulatory policies are produced and delivered through a relatively close interaction between public and private actors, which facilitates civic participation and adjustment to changing local needs and demands. More recently, the pressures on local governments 'to do more for less' have forced them to enhance and systematise the local efforts to mobilise the resources and energies of a range of private actors such as private providers, voluntary associations and local entrepreneurs. Regional and national authorities are confronted with much the same pressures to interact with private actors. Different political constituencies and socio-economic groups compete for resources and struggle to ensure that their particular needs and demands are met by public policies. The intensification of global economic competition and the abandonment of Keynesianism in favour of more strict monetary and fiscal policies have meant that most countries that are members of Organisation for Economic Co-operation and Development (OECD) during the last three decades have been subjected to strong pressures to adopt more efficient and legitimate forms of policy making and policy delivery. At the supranational level, the long tradition for lobbying through policy networks and interactive arenas in the EU has been supplemented by significantly new forms of policy making in the last decade or. Perhaps the Open Method of Coordination with its reliance on soft mechanisms of governance and the voluntary participation of member states, social partners and other private actors is the most important sign of this development. Finally, transnational institutions, such as the UN and the WTO, seem to develop into interactive policy arenas. While both institutions were originally established as international organisations based on co-operation between nation states, they are now in the process of developing into transnational networks as they are increasing the scope for interaction with independent expert groups and a whole range of non-governmental organisations (NGOs). Involvement of numerous private actors in the UN COP 15 climate conference in Copenhagen and the increasing role of NGOs in the dispute settlement mechanism in the WTO are clear indications of this significant trend.

In some countries and policy areas there are long-lasting traditions for involvement of private actors in interactive policy making. Accordingly, interactive policy making is not in itself a new phenomenon. What is new, however, is that interactive policy making is no longer considered a 'necessary evil' that should be avoided, if possible, because it breaks with Weberian and Wilsonian ideals of a strict separation between politics and the liberal-democratic ideals of a clear demarcation between public and private realms. Today, it is widely asserted that the growing amount of 'wicked problems' can only be tackled through an increasing reliance upon interactive policy making. This does not mean that we are witnessing a wholesale transformation from hierarchical forms of top-down steering associated with 'government' to interactive and networked forms of policy making associated with 'governance'. Law-based steering continues to be a fundamental element of liberal democracies and the lion's share of public services is still delivered through public bureaucracies. However, the traditional forms of government, and also the new forms of market-based governance advocated by the New Public

Management reforms, are increasingly supplemented with more or less formalised modes of interactive policy making that involve more or less intense dialogue between public and private actors and are supported and regulated by new governing technologies and different institutional designs.

The proliferation and transformation of interactive policy making can be explained, at least partly, with reference to processes of societal fragmentation and complexity, organisational developments in the public sector, and the advent of new ideas about how to govern and be governed. The societal factors behind the turn to interactive governance include the growing fragmentation of society, which is a result of the ongoing functional differentiation of systems and subsystems that generates a profound need for cross-cutting coordination and interaction, which is made difficult by the existence of different systemic codes for communication (Kooiman 1993). Society has also become more and more complex as an increasing number of policy problems appear to be 'wicked' in the sense that the problem definitions are blurred and finding a feasible solution requires access to different kinds of specialised knowledge, co-operation between a plurality of stakeholders with diverging interests and coordination across different sectors and levels (Koppenjan and Klijn 2004). The problems and challenges generated by fragmentation and complexity are becoming even bigger when we take into consideration the expansion of the horizontal and vertical space for strategic action that is associated with globalisation and localisation.

The driving forces inside the public administration are mainly associated with the spread of New Public Management reforms. The separation of the political 'steering' from the administrative 'rowing' and the resulting contracting out of service production to either quasi-autonomous public agencies or private providers has increased the internal fragmentation of the public sector and this makes it difficult to meet the growing demand for efficiency and effectiveness. The relatively autonomous contractors must be connected to each other in order to avoid service duplication, prevent a competitive 'race to the bottom', and enhance a trust-based exchange of new ideas and methods. The contractors should also be connected to the public purchasers in order to facilitate a constructive and effective performance management. Finally, both the public and private contractors should be accountable to their users, clients and customers. In all three cases, interactive governance can help to bring together the relevant actors. As such, interactive governance can be seen as a strategic response to fragmentation brought about by New Public Management (Rhodes 1997).

Finally, the ideational factors spurring the use of interactive policy making can be summarised under the heading 'regulated self-regulation' (Sørensen and Triantafillou 2009). The post-war expansion of the welfare state in most Western countries was supported by a strong belief in the regulatory capacity of the state. The behaviour of citizens and private firms was to be regulated through the issuing and enforcement of laws and regulations that provided detailed rules for the access to public benefits and services. This way of governing society placed a huge burden on the shoulders of the state, which explains the mounting critique of what the Trilateral Commission described as 'government overload'. The state could not keep up with the growing demands from citizens and firms. Under the mantra of 'less state, more market', the neoliberal solution was to encourage privatisation, contracting out and commercialisation of the remaining public sector. However, the irony seems to be that the creation and regulation of markets requires extensive regulation. The many new quasi-markets produce failures that governments were expected to rectify in order to ensure satisfactory provision of various benefits and services. 'More markets' then often seem to require 'more state'. Although the contracting out of public services through the creation of quasi-markets continues to play a crucial role in many countries, the ideas about how to govern society have taken a new turn. The key policy problem today seems to be not so much the presence of public monopolies and the solution is no longer the enhancement of market competition. Rather, the problem is the presence of substantial, strategic and institutional uncertainty and the solution is co-operation, coordination and collaboration (Koppenjan and Klijn 2004). There is uncertainty about the substance and nature of policy problems, about the interests, resources and strategies of the stakeholders, and about the impact of regulations produced at different levels or scales. Whereas New Public Management has aimed to reduce the growing uncertainty by disaggregating the public sector into small single-purpose agencies, the new ideas of how to govern society seek to manage uncertainty by creating spaces for self-regulation in which a plurality of actors interact within an overall regulatory framework defined by public authorities. On the one hand, societal actors are constructed as free, rational, resourceful and empowered agents capable of self-regulating a certain policy area. On the other hand, the self-regulating policy processes are regulated by a host of performance management technologies that ensure self-regulated actions are in line with the overall goals of the government (Dean 1999).

Needless to say, the analytical distinction between societal, organisational and ideational factors behind the turn to interactive policy making only serves heuristic purposes. In reality, all these factors combine in complex ways that inform the key decision-makers' interpretation of the reality of public governance as well as their strategies for making and amending public policy decisions.

There are a considerable number of studies of interactive policy making processes and their conditions of existence, but we need more empirical research on the different forms of policy interaction and in particular on how the outputs and outcomes of policy interaction are shaped by particular cultural and institutional contexts and different political actions.

Part I of this book aims to shed light on these important issues by presenting a number of empirical studies exploring the intricacies of interactive governance through networks at the local, regional, national and supranational level.

Metagovernance

Sometimes interactive modes of policy making emerge almost automatically as a reaction to the presence of interdependencies, or by default when other governance modes have been tried and failed. In those cases, interactive governance arenas are formed without much design. Yet today the public policy-makers seem to be increasingly eager to exploit the potentials of interactive policy making and to be increasingly ambitious when it comes to facilitating, developing or structuring policy interactions. Interactive policy making cannot be trusted to emerge spontaneously, but needs a convener to bring together the mutually-dependent policy actors around an important policy agenda. When the interactive arena is established and the relevant and affected policy actors are convened, then the next problem is that there is no guarantee that the actors will collaborate and contribute to the policy-making process in a constructive way. The actors engaged in interactive policy making may either fail to reach a policy decision due to the presence of collective action problems or irreconcilable conflicts or make a bad decision, which is ill-informed, incoherent and impossible to implement. Some kind of process management is needed in order to ensure the production of a joint and feasible solution. Finally, even when policy interaction results in well-informed, creative and reasonable policy proposals followed by a seamless implementation process, the problem may be that the course of the new policy strays too far from the government's policy line. In sum, we might conclude that interactive governance processes must not only be properly facilitated and managed, but must also be given a direction and aligned with overall policy objectives in order to realise their full potential as instruments for public governance.

The notion of *metagovernance* tries to capture the diverse political and administrative measures and interventions that aim to facilitate, manage and direct interactive policy processes without reverting to traditional forms of hierarchical rule based on control and command (Kickert, Klijn and Koppenjan 1997; Jessop 2002; Kooiman 2003, Meuleman 2008; Sørensen and Torfing 2009). The concept of metagovernance helps us to understand how traditional forms of government and new interactive modes of governance can be connected. It also helps us to rethink how the 'primacy of politics' can be maintained in areas where interactive policy making plays an important role. The bold claim is that a failure by governments to understand that metagovernance is a new and important assignment will result in them finding it increasingly difficult to achieve their policy goals. Metagovernance permits governments at different levels to create and develop interactive policy arenas while giving direction to the interactive policy process and holding the participating policy actors to account.

Metagovernance literally means 'the governance of governance' (Kooiman 2003). As such, in the generic sense of the term, metagovernance covers the repeated attempts of the European Council to reform the Treaty of the European Union, which provides the rules of the game for European policy making; the effort of federal states to regulate interstate cooperation and governance; and the endeavour of national governments to regulate the policy-making process in local municipalities. Hence, although the concept of metagovernance is new, the attempts of political authorities to govern particular processes of governance, be it processes of public regulation or the creation of competitive markets, are not. In fact the governing of governance processes is well described in the literature and captured by the idea of 'governance in the shadow of hierarchy (Scharpf 1994). However, in relation to interactive policy making through networks and partnerships, metagovernance has a slightly different meaning. Metagovernance here refers to the attempt to facilitate, regulate and frame decentred policy processes in which the social and political actors participate on a voluntary basis and in the anticipation of a considerable scope for self-regulation. Hence, we can in the context of this book redefine metagovernance as 'the governance of decentred and self-regulating governance processes'. This way of defining metagovernance poses a significant challenge to governments at all levels, especially those employing a top-down style based on sovereignty and imposition; they must now learn the art of governing interactive processes at a certain distance and through more or less indirect measures that aim to respect the relative autonomy of the interactive policy arena.

As hinted above, a frequently quoted motivation for exercising metagovernance is the attempt to reduce the risk of governance failure (Jessop 2002). There has been a lot of talk about the risk of market failure and government failure, but interactive governance also carries a similar risk, which is enhanced by the fact that interactive policy making often is only weakly institutionalised and, therefore, is a rather contingent and precarious process. Metagovernance may be applied to reduce the persistent risk of failure in interactive policy arenas. It may involve:

- the creation of incentives for the relevant stakeholders to participate in policy interaction;
- the definition of the overall purpose of policy interaction; an initial framing of the policy problem and the formulation of some broad policy goals;
- the construction of some basic rules of the game that facilitate collaboration and democratic deliberation;
- the reduction of transaction costs derived from interaction; the provision of resources to help realise policy proposals or to test new ideas on an experimental basis; and
- the establishment of procedures for monitoring progress, results and effects of interactive policy making.

Broadly speaking, we can distinguish between hands-off and hands-on metagovernance (Sørensen and Torfing 2009). Hands-off metagovernance can be exercised at a large distance from the interactive policy arena and without any direct interaction with the participating actors. It includes institutional design and structuring of the interactive policy processes, the provision of material and immaterial resources, and the political, legal and discursive framing of the interactive policy making. By designing a certain organisational framework, it becomes possible to shape the patterns of interaction and the channels of communication between the involved policy actors. By allocating resources according to more or less strict criteria, it is possible to create incentives for collaboration and to favour certain activities above others. Last but not least, by framing policy interactions in a certain way it becomes possible to set the overall agenda for the interactive policy arena.

Hands-on metagovernance is exercised in closer proximity to the actual policy interactions and involves direct interaction with the participating actors. It may take the form of process management or direct participation. Process management aims to reduce tensions and resolve conflicts, or to change the balance of power between the participating actors by empowering weak actors and/or restraining strong and potentially dominant actors. Direct participation aims to influence the policy agenda, the definition of policy problems and the political premises for finding a joint and feasible solution. Hands-on metagovernance aims to facilitate policy interactions that are conducive to the alignment of interests and the making of decisions that goes beyond the least common denominator while avoiding unwarranted cost-shifting.

Different theoretical approaches have different ideas about what metagovernors do, or should do, when metagoverning interactive policy making (Sørensen and Torfing 2007). *Interdependency theorists* (Rhodes 1997; Kickert, Klijn and Koppenjan 1997) recommend the use of hands-on network management, which can help to stabilise and improve the interaction processes in the face of diverging interests, conflicts and the lack of trust. *Governability theorists* (Mayntz 1993a, 1993b; Scharpf 1994) emphasise the need for hands-off metagovernance, which aims to structure the game-like interaction through institutional rules and incentives that foster cooperative strategies and create conditions for positive coordination in the face of collective action problems. *Normative integration theorists* (Powell and DiMaggio 1991; March and Olsen 1995) do not talk explicitly about metagovernance, but tend to see the development of the identities and capacities of the policy actors and the enhancement of the accountability and flexibility of interactive policy arenas as the key to successful policy making. Finally, *governmentality* theorists (Foucault 1991; Dean 1999), who do not use the term 'metagovernance', recommend either the combined use of 'technologies of agency', which aim to construct free, empowered and responsible policy actors, or 'technologies of performance', which aim to frame and monitor the interactive processes in order to ensure conformity with overall policy goals. The competing theoretical approaches provide different, but complementary, accounts of metagovernance that reflect their particular conception of interactive governance.

How metagovernance is exercised and precisely which metagovernance tool is used depends upon the specific context and upon the goals that the metagovernor(s) aims to achieve. Whatever the form of metagovernance, it is clear that not all policy actors can exercise metagovernance as it requires reflexive and operational capacity, and a general acceptance from the actors and arenas that are metagoverned. In many cases, public authorities are the primary metagovernors. As such, governments at different levels would appear to have both the capacity and legitimacy that is necessary for exercising metagovernance. In principle, other policy actors could also act as metagovernors, either because a government office has delegated the responsibility and power to a particular policy actor, or because a certain actor has acquired the status and experience that makes it capable of exercising metagovernance. Hence, there are examples of private firms being hired to metagovern a particular governance network. Similarly, trade unions or NGOs also provide examples of strong policy actors capable of metagoverning interactive policy arenas. Everything depends on the empirical circumstances, but as a general rule a would-be metagovernor must fulfil Christopher Hood's so-called 'NATO criteria', which specify the need for Nodality, Authority, Treasure and Organisation (Hood 1983) Hence, in order to metagovern an interactive policy arena, the would-be metagovernor must occupy a central position *vis-à-vis* the participating actors; have a sufficient, formal and/or informal authority; posses adequate financial resources; and have an organisation capable of monitoring, reflecting upon and intervening in the interactive policy processes. Thus, it comes down to a question of power conceived as a transformative capacity to make a difference. Sometimes there will be several actors who in varying degrees fulfil the NATO criteria, which may lead to rivalry and struggles about who should be the principal metagovernor of interactive policy making.

Rivalry between contending metagovernors could lead to metagovernance failure, but failure can also be a result of either too little or too much metagovernance, or the use of inadequate metagovernance tools. Because metagovernance can go wrong and fail to produce the intended effects, there is no guarantee that interactive governance processes will realise the potential of metagovernors. Therefore, the major task for public metagovernors is choosing between equally imperfect modes of governance.

Although there are already several studies of metagovernance (Whitehead 2003; Hovik and Vabo 2005; Bell and Park 2006; Sørensen 2006, Marcussen and Torfing 2007), the research on the problems and merits of metagovernance is still in its infancy. Accordingly, we need more empirical studies that systematically address the conditions under which, and the mechanisms by which, metagovernance produces particular results. Part II of this book takes up this challenge and endeavours to advance our understanding of metagovernance.

Democratic implications

Although there is considerable agreement that interactive policy making is gaining a foothold as an empirical phenomenon in liberal democracies, we still find heated debates about its political and normative implications. Among the critics of interactive policy making, some lament the loss of the public authority associated with representative government and the public ethos implicit to the Weberian ideals of an autonomous, impartial and rule-based public bureaucracy (Du Gay 2000). The increased participation and influence of private citizens and associations on the public services and regulations risk throwing out all the hard work of building up trustworthy and reliable governments based on *Rechtstaat* principles of equality before the law; instead, the possibility of various forms of clientelism and favouritism are opened up. Others critics claim that governance and interactive policy making are the institutional manifestation of neoliberal politics (De Angelis 2003; Marinetto 2003). In this rendition, interactive policy making and its appeal to dialogue and partnership is simply the sugar coating on the bitter pill of New Public Management reforms, cuts in public expenditures, and a generalised onslaught on the public services.

Among the supporters of interactive policy making, the argument is that these novel forms of politics hold the promise of raising the efficiency, effectiveness and even the democratic legitimacy of public policy and governance. By facilitating dialogue and collaboration between public authorities and the most affected citizens and organisations, we might increase the chances of adopting policies that reflect the needs and preferences of relevant constituencies rather than merely the ideological opinion of elected politicians and the technical and bureaucratic concerns of policy experts and public managers. We might also reduce resistance to implementation, not only because policies are more likely to accord with actual needs, but also because interactive policy making may latch on to and utilise the resources of relevant stakeholders in the implementation phase. Moreover, it is well documented that empowered participation in the formulation and implementation of policy enhances programme responsibility and helps to reach specific target groups.

Both camps have good arguments, but how is it possible that interactive policy making is evaluated so differently? Much of this disagreement has to do with the normative yardstick applied in the evaluation of interactive policy making. In particular, differing notions of democracy, which everybody seems to agree is a good thing, entail different assessments of the merits of interactive policy making.

Much of the criticism of interactive policy making is based on the ideals of liberal democracy, according to which a plurality of political elites compete for office and form majority coalitions responsible for making and amending public policies and are held to account for their deeds by the people they are representing. The political system is clearly separated from civil society, and the latter should not encroach on the former since that would undermine the democratic sovereignty of the elected politicians and the government. As interactive policy making explicitly seeks to facilitate some kind of co-governance based on dialogue and co-operation between public and private actors, the boundary between the political system and civil society will tend to become blurred. This explains why the champions of liberal democracy criticise interactive policy making. It also explains why people subscribing to the ideal of communicative reasoning propagated by Jürgen Habermas seem to have problems with interactive policy making. However, their concern is not the integrity of government, but rather the integrity of civil society. As such, it is argued that interactive governance exposes civil society to systemic logics of money and power and tends to undermine the core values of mutual recognition and power-free deliberation by subjecting political debate to narrow-minded and short-sighted strategic calculations and logics.

Another and closely-related source of criticism stems from the potential erosion of accountability. If a key feature of liberal democracy is the delegation of popular sovereignty to a representative government, it is crucial that people are able to hold the government accountable for its actions and inactions. Liberal democracies have developed a number of mechanisms ensuring accountability, ranging from regular parliamentary elections and judicial review to budgetary and fiscal control systems. Again, interactive policy making may seem detrimental to such mechanisms in as much as it depends on the collaboration of individuals and groups that usually are appointed rather than elected. Hence, we cannot vote the actors in networks and partnerships out of office. The responsibility for public policy making is shared between the public and private actors, but it is difficult to hold the private actors to account since most often they will not feel any commitment to the public ethos and insist on the legitimate right to pursue their own interests. Moreover, the collaborative interaction in networks and partnerships are often regulated by rules, procedures and funding schemes that are neither very transparent nor easily sanctioned. In short, proponents of liberal democracy have a strong case when they criticise interactive policy making through networks and partnerships for failing to meet the standard criteria of public accountability.

Some of the critique launched by the liberal democrats against interactive policy making may at least to some extent be accommodated by an adequate metagovernance. Whether through direct participation by elected politicians (hands-on) or through the allocation of resources or institutional design (hands-off), public metagovernors may provide interactive policy making with a certain degree of democratic legitimacy. At least, if the metagovernance of interactive policy making is firmly anchored in a democratically-elected government, the interactive policy arenas will tend to cohere with the key principles of liberal democracy. Even better, if the allocation of resources, the institutional design of the interactive policy arenas and the negotiated outputs and outcomes are open to public scrutiny, much of the liberal democratic critique may be fended off.

Notwithstanding the potentials of metagovernance, we should probably acknowledge that interactive policy making remains problematic when judged by liberal democrats. But the question is, should we uncritically accept liberal democracy rather than some other forms of democracy as our normative yardstick? While most of us would probably endorse much of the liberal democracy's normative framework, there is no reason why this should be considered as something beyond dispute or should not be supplemented with other views of democracy. Not only is the liberal version of democracy a rather recent invention, which was preceded by very different perceptions of democracy, its key tenets are increasingly challenged by different strands of political philosophy (Sørensen and Torfing 2005; Keane 2009).

The key tenets of liberal democracy have been criticised in the light of new societal developments. First, there is an assumption that democracy can be confined to a particular and sealed-off territory controlled by a sovereign government or state power. This entails a clear distinction between individuals acknowledged as state citizens and others who are excluded from such status, and thereby from participation in the territorially-defined democracy. However, the increasing number of policy problems and regulations that transgress territorial boundaries in the new global era questions the current ways of determining who should be able to

influence democratic decisions. Supranational and transnational organisations attempt to supersede the narrow confines of national democracies in their attempt
to address global and regional problems, but have so far not been able to establish
political and institutional procedures that ensure democratic decision-making and
accountability.

Secondly, the assumption that state and civil society can and should be carefully separated deserves rethinking. This is not only because many societal problems
may be handled more effectively by close co-operation between public and private
individuals and groups, but also because such institutionalised forms of interaction
may actually grant more people more influence on their everyday life. The anti-au-
thoritarian revolt in the 1960s and the general rise in the level of education means
that many people are no longer satisfied with having influence through the ballot
box and are capable of much more active participation in public decision-making.

Thirdly, direct participation of citizens and organisations in the governing of
societal problems has always sat somewhat uneasily with liberal democracy. Of
course, direct participation is neither foreign nor unacceptable to liberal democrats as the literature on democratic pluralism demonstrates. However, liberal democracy is first and foremost wedded to representative democracy, which is a
seen as the only way to only way to practice participatory democracy in modern
mass societies. The problem with more direct forms of participation is that they
tend to create a political bias by mobilising strong socio-economic groups with
particularistic concerns. Direct participation of stakeholders does not square well
with the universalising reference to 'the people as a whole', which can influence
political decisions only indirectly as voters. The solution provided by pluralism
is to insist that private and particularistic groups should compete over influence
and that the state should be the gatekeeper and arbiter determining when and how
private interest should be taken into consideration. However, if public and private
actors are mutually dependent on each other's knowledge, resources and support,
public authorities can at best have the status of *primus inter pares* in interactive
policy arenas. This and other critical concerns have been raised by what we could
call 'post-liberal democratic thought', which aims to 'problematise' and amend
theories of liberal democracy in order to take into account recent societal developments (Sørensen and Torfing 2005).

When judged on the basis of the normative standards endorsed by post-liberal
theories of democracy, interactive policy making may under certain conditions,
play a quite positive role for the democratic development of our societies. One
group of *aggregative democratic theories* may be defined by their attempt to further elaborate the aggregate dimension of liberal democracy that facilitates the
formation of collective solutions on the basis of competition between individual
actors. Eva Etzioni-Halevy (1993), for example, regards systematic competition
for influence between political elites as one of the defining traits of liberal democracy. Regular popular elections are hardly sufficient for avoiding power that
is monopolised by particular elites, let alone for ensuring the representation of
the interests of the entire demos. Accordingly, popular elections must be supplemented by other mechanisms that can enhance competition between several po-

litical elites. Interactive policy making, if properly regulated and open to public scrutiny, may be one way of ensuring such inter-elite competition (Etzioni-Halevy 1993: 193–194). Interactive policy making may even help to recruit new sub-elites that can challenge the established elites and, therefore, enhance elite competition. Paul Hirst's model of associative democracy may also be seen as an attempt to elaborate the aggregate dimension of democracy (Hirst 1994). His suggestion of the development of publicly-financed, but relatively autonomous local associations, charged with the task of providing public services, may not only function as a means of balancing the powers of the central state apparatus and linking state and civil society, but may also serve as a means of ensuring a certain degree of competition between local associations based on civic engagement and free user choice. Like Etzioni-Halevy, Hirst regards public transparency around the production of public services and the competition between the associations as a crucial precondition for the democratic quality. Both Etzioni-Halevy's elite-competition democracy and Hirst's associative democracy may resonate well with interactive policy making, provided it is metagoverned with a view to ensure competition and transparency between the various associations. However, interactive policy making is often launched to solve problems that the market cannot solve precisely because finding a solution requires sustained co-operation rather than competition. Accordingly, while properly metagoverned forms of interactive policy making may resonate with Etzioni-Halevy's and Hirst's models, there is also a tension.

Performance or output-based democratic theories seem more obvious companions with interactive policy making. Archon Fung and Erik Olin Wright's (2003) concept of 'empowered participatory governance' (EPC) emphasises the ability to solve policy problems in an effective manner. This implies the building of institutions with the capacity to adapt to concrete situations and problems, the participation of relevant stakeholders, and decision-making processes based on deliberation and mutual learning (Fung and Wright 2003: 16–20). Not only does this resonate well with interactive policy making, but Fung and Wright's insistence on a systematic coordination of the activities of such local EPC institutions also calls for some kind of metagovernance in order to avoid societal fragmentation and suboptimal solutions. In much the same vein, Iris Marion Young (2000) has suggested that democratic governance be evaluated according to its ability to produce just and equitable outcomes. Such outcomes are predicated on a broad participation of stakeholders, which under certain conditions will permit weaker groups to advance their demands and increase the chances for these demands to be taken into account by public authorities. Even those groups that are loud, passionate and use non-verbal means of expression, and thus do not live up to the standards of democratic deliberation, should be able to participate, provided they demonstrate agonistic respect towards other participants. Again, this resonates well with interactive policy making, though with the important qualification that this form of policy making must be subjected to procedural regulations to minimise the risk of the interactive arena being captured by local power elites. Again, properly-designed metagovernance may be a partial answer to such a risk.

Community-based democratic theory constitutes another branch of post-liberal political thought. Scholars Michael Sandel (1996) and March and Olsen (1995), for example, maintain that democracy cannot rely solely on procedures for aggregating individual wills into public policies. Democracy also depends on the development of democratic values, commitments and identities, which help to provide social and political integration. With increased societal fragmentation and globalisation, the nation-state becomes an ever more inadequate source of legitimacy. Instead, legitimacy must be based on a multiplicity of culturally-diverse communities, which in various ways are connected in the formulation of public issues and the provision of public value. By the same token, citizens with the will and capacity to navigate and negotiate between overlapping and often contradictory expectations become all the more important for the maintenance of democracy in the twenty-first century (Sandel 1996: 350). By bringing together discrete, but interdependent actors, interactive policy-making processes may help to counter the fragmentation and atomisation of society by constructing more or less unified communities that are compatible with a diversity of cultural values and sentiments. However, in order to ensure democratic forms of interactive governance, it is necessary to empower the social and political actors, develop a new set of democratic identities and create mechanisms for civilising conflicts (March and Olsen 1995).

Finally, *theories of agonistic democracy* may also show a greater appreciation of interactive policy making than that shown by more traditional liberal democracy. Based on an understanding of the political in terms of antagonistic conflict and aiming to reconcile social antagonism with plural democracy, Chantal Mouffe (2000, 2005) and William Connolly (1995) have both argued for a new form of democracy that seeks to transform antagonistic conflict between enemies into agonistic rivalry between adversaries. According to this view, many of the problems facing liberal democracies, and the theories supporting them, stem from vain attempts to eliminate and replace conflict with a post-political commitment to consensus obtained through reasoned deliberation. Not only is this impossible, it also runs the risk of excluding dissident opinions and voices that are deemed irrational, deviant or undesirable in other ways. An agonistic form of democracy should not try to eliminate conflicts, but instead facilitate and develop forums and mechanisms for translating such potentially violent and antagonistic conflicts into agonistic ones in which the opponents show respect for one another by adhering to some basic rules of engagement. On the one hand, such rules should allow for new and opposing interests and different subjectivities to confront one another and engage in a variety of critical exchanges. On the other hand, they should ensure that these conflicts respect basic moral and procedural rules that disallow physical oppression of minorities and the undermining of the democratic institutions ensuring agonistic forms of politics. Again, interactive policy making may contribute to translating antagonistic conflicts into agonistic ones by providing arenas for interaction and exchange between conflicting interests and subjectivities. In situations where problem solving between antagonistic, yet interdependent, actors, the latter may either be driven to formulate some common rules of the game through negotiation, or rely on an external metagovernor to define such procedural rules.

Interactive policy making seems, generally speaking, to be more in line with the normative standards proposed by the various strands of post-liberal democratic theory than with the ones propagated by liberal democratic theory. Yet this conclusion comes with some fundamental qualifications. First, the point is not that we should simply give up on the normative ideals informing liberal democracy. Not only is there no uncontested normative ground from which to do so but even the most radical post-liberal democratic theories explicitly or implicitly endorse much of the legacy of liberal democracy, such as the limitation to excessive state intervention, freedom of speech, fair and competitive elections, and a public administration that is, if not impartial then at least not captured by local political elites. Secondly, we cannot assume that just because interactive policy making resonates better with post-liberal democratic norms, they will automatically be in line with these norms. Interactive policy making may take a number of different forms and produce very different outputs that absolutely do not square with the normative stipulations of any of the aforementioned post-liberal theories. As such, there may be situations in which interactive policy making will lead to reduced political competition, inferior policy performance, the making of parochial policies favouring one particular community, or even the development of local policy-making rules that exclude other interests and subjectivities.

While the adoption of proper forms of metagovernance may mitigate some of these problems, there is no guarantee that this will happen since metagovernance is also prone to failure. In the first place, metagovernance may not be properly exercised due to lack of political will or the presence of political resistance and opposition. In the second place, our experiences with the conditions under which metagovernance is exercised and what forms it should take in different contexts are still limited and metagovernance may therefore have all kinds of unintended consequences. Accordingly, one of the main ambitions of this book is to address the variability of interactive policy making, the democratic implications it may have and the ways in which metagovernance can possibly tackle these issues.

Structure and content

This book presents recent research debates and empirical findings in the rapidly developing area of interactive policy making, metagovernance and democracy. Part I analyses interactive policy making and network governance at various levels and scales. Part II is concerned with metagovernance at both conceptual and different politico-administrative levels and thus looks at the manifold ways in which the interactions around policy-making processes are facilitated, managed and directed. Part III discusses the democratic implications of the changing patterns of policy making and the potential of interactive policy making to improve democratic performance.

In Part I, we find three studies of interactive policy making at the local, national and international levels. In Chapter 2, Jenny Lewis and Mark Considine examine the importance of network interactions at the frontline of the employment services in Australia and Great Britain in 1998 and in 2008. They analyse what makes network governance distinctive in relation to the delivery of frontline services and explore whether it can be seen as a significant mode of governance *vis-à-vis* market and procedural forms of governance. By adopting a methodological cal approach allowing them to study long-term changes, they are able show that over the years the most stable form of governance was the corporate-market type. The procedural and network types were less stable, and in particular, the network type varied substantially from context to context. This indicates that the network governance is a more fluid, less coherent and probably also less institutionalised type than the other more established types of governance. They also show that networking is used more by policy advisers when they are faced with new demands, as it is highest in contexts (countries and times) with the greatest system volatility. While advisers do engage in networks that might be useful to them in placing clients into work, this comes second to the importance of meeting the targets and knowing the rules.

In Chapter 3, Trine Fotel surveys the effectiveness of a governance network of Scandinavian regions. While the Nordic countries may display a number of similarities, her survey shows that the perceived effectiveness of the regional networks differs significantly amongst the various countries. Generally speaking, the Norwegian and the Danish governance networks received a score of high effectiveness, the Finnish a medium score and the Swedish governance networks received a low score. Some of these differences are related to the institutional context of the network actors, others reflect broader politico-historical differences by which the civil society of Denmark (and Norway until 1814) enjoyed a more autonomous status *vis-à-vis* the state compared to Sweden (and Finland until 1918/44).

Anders Esmark measures, in Chapter 4, the impact of the European Employment Strategy (EES) on national institutions and procedures in the area of employment policy. He focuses on three variables: the range of included interests, the role of included interests and their level of participation. He concludes that changes have indeed occurred on all dimensions, in particular with respect to the role of included interests and the level of participation. The direction and specific content of the observed changes include, on the one hand, trends that can be interpreted as approximation to EU norms leading to a certain level of convergence, in particular with respect to social dialogue and the role of social partners. On the other hand, some of the changes may be regarded as distinctly country-specific trends that depend on national traditions. In sum, this chapter suggests that the EES has had a significant, but differential impact, on national institutions and policy-making procedures in the area of employment.

Part II presents four studies on metagovernance. The first contribution is by Louis Meuleman in Chapter 5, who takes us through the theoretical potentials and limitations to the use of metagovernance with a view to examine the toolbox available to contemporary policy-makers. He argues that metagovernance of networks should be accompanied by another form of metagovernance, which takes a bird's eye view of network, hierarchical and market styles of governance. This form of metagovernance, which may be called 'second order metagovernance', enables policy-makers to change the combination of different governance style when circumstances seem to require this (e.g. when the policy-making process enters a distinctly different phase), and may ensure that new opportunities are fully exploited and emerging problems are solved by changing the overall governance mix. Public managers, who have chosen or are obliged to rely on interactive policy making, could expand their toolbox if they had second order metagovernance running in the background.

In Chapter 6, Keith Baker and Gerry Stoker examine the metagovernance of the UK nuclear industry. They show that the problems facing a revival of nuclear power in the UK are considerable and the state-centric view that a capable state can 'metagovern' effectively as long as it has access to key assets is questionable. They note that despite the government's claim to nodality, its ability to exercise authority, deploy treasure and organisational resources, its capacity for metagovernance is limited by political conflicts, international pressures, legal requirements, limited resources and organisational complexities. As the case may be considered a least-likely one (if metagovernance worked here, it could probably work in most other situations), the authors acknowledge that their findings cannot be immediately transferred to other policy fields. For a theory on metagovernance to develop, they conclude, that there is a need to refine its claims and develop a range of 'most difficult' tests comparable to the one offer here.

In Chapter 7, Joop Koppenjan, Mirjam Kars and Haiko van der Voort study how metagovernance as a strategy may reconcile representative democracy and a polity characterised by networked policy making. Based on a Dutch case of physical planning in an agricultural area, they show first that politicians are actually prepared and capable of engaging in the metagovernance of interactive network processes, and that this may be successful. Their case also shows that, given the limited resources of representatives, the expectations to the effects of their metagoverning activities should be modest. In particular, it seems unrealistic to expect political representatives to control the network process. Rather, the case shows how representatives align their steering attempts with those of the executive council, this way providing co-metagovernance. Nevertheless, by doing so, they may succeed in influencing the process, providing it with political steering and holding network actors accountable, thus effectively increasing the democratic legitimacy of the network process.

Finally in Part II, Peter Triantafillou examines, in Chapter 8, the interactions between performance measurement techniques on the one hand, and the goals and strategies of the Australian and Danish employment policies on the other. He argues that in order to properly understand interactive policy making we ought to analyse not only interactions between actors, but also interactions between policy goals and policy instruments because these may shape the room for manoeuvre experienced by individuals and organisations engaged in policy making and implementation. Based on this premise, he seeks to show that such performance measurement techniques seem to contribute to reinforce a work-first approach to the handling of unemployment in both Australia and Denmark. More precisely, the computer-based knowledge produces a particular visibility focusing on objective and quantifiable performance data. Moreover, while the performance measuring regimes in both countries were launched to focus more on outputs and outcomes, they actually seem to lead to an increased policy emphasis on process standards. Finally, the performance measurement regime favours the work-first approach because other employment policy approaches are almost inevitably rated as performing poorly.

In Part III, there are five studies of democracy and its relationship to interactive policy making and metagovernance. In Chapter 9, Jurian Edelenbos and Ingmar van Meerkerk examine the institutional evolution of local democracy on the basis of citizens' initiative in the municipality of Vlaardingen in the Netherlands. Their study testifies to the difficulty of putting participatory forms of democracy into practice within established institutions of representative democracy. In order to have a chance of success, proto-institutions of participatory democracy have to be connected with the established, representative political institutions. Three factors seem particularly important to establish a strong and effective connection between the participatory and representative institutions, namely trust, informal bridging networks and boundary spanning. These factors provide *institutional interaction*, which could be described as a co-evolving process wherein existing institutions slightly change or evolve by interacting agents, operating at the boundaries of these institutions. The boundary spanners connected the logics of the three different entities and played a crucial role in organising the embedding of new patterns of behaviour into existing institutional structures. They articulated new ways of organising within existing institutional procedures.

In Chapter 10, Simona Piattoni examines the problematic relationship between representative institutions and interactive forms of governance at the sub-national level. Drawing from material on experimentation with participatory forms of policy making conducted in Tuscany and Trentino, she concludes that participatory forms of democratic policy making are not immediately embraced unless they appear to be an answer to a widely-felt sense of isolation and precariousness on the part of regional and local governments. This, at least, is true in Italy, where the Napoleonic forms of state – which conventionally have entrusted to public administration both the decision-making and implementation of public policies – still bears the mark of its original imprint. Truly interactive forms of governance that not only invite the citizenry into the policy-making process, but also allow the very definition of problems to be tackled through public action, are few and far between. Yet, even in Italy, such forms are multiplying, in part because some services cannot be delivered without with the active collaboration of the citizens, and because escalating costs and the declining quality of public services are an inducement to off-load some of these services on to voluntary associations.

Erik-Hans Klijn discusses and develops, in Chapter 11, a number of criteria that may facilitate evaluation of the democratic value of interactive policy making and other forms of governance. Based on a precise review of some of the classical forms of liberal democratic theories, he deduces three broad criteria of legitimacy, namely accountability, voice and due deliberation. He inserts these 'classical' criteria into a model that acknowledges the crucial importance of the policy process in governance by distinguishing between policy input, throughput and output. Klijn applies this 'three times three' evaluative framework to a Dutch case of agricultural land management that involved the participation of a number of different public and private organisations and individuals. He concludes that the case scores relatively high on input and throughput legitimacy which, in turn, lead to high levels of output legitimacy. He also argues that this positive score was the result not of spontaneous civic action, but of active and quite carefully designed network management, i.e. metagovernance.

In Chapter 12, Nico van der Heiden and Paul Krummenacher explore innovative forms of citizen participation and deliberation in local Swiss politics. Based on a study of 48 citizen forums in urban municipal planning since the year 2000, they show that this type of deliberative policy making constitutes an advancement of democratic governance even in an extreme case like Switzerland with a long and firm tradition for direct democracy. Introducing elements of deliberation into a direct-democratic system thus adds a component instead of replacing one. This form of interactive governance has allowed Swiss citizens the possibility to participate in the early stages of the policy process. The chance to engage early in the policy process and to deliberate has been appreciated. At the same time, this increases the acceptance of the choices made by deliberating people by the ones whose interests have been dismissed in the process.

The possibilities for ensuring democratic participation and commitment through metagovernance are examined by Åsa Vifell in Chapter 13. Taking the point of departure in the attempt by the Swedish Government to increase organic food production, she examines how an association of stakeholders within the food industry and public agencies engaged in a joint project and developed an action plan. She shows that by deliberately supporting an inclusive framework, the government successfully facilitated the development of an interactive policy network that included both organisations with radical and with moderate views in the work. Notwithstanding this positive evaluation, time constraints attached to the policy delivery meant that deliberations, and the interests represented, made the actual scope of the resulting action plan narrower than allowed by the Government's mandate. In particular, the focus on consensus seems to crowd out the dealing with issues that – if they are solved – may have a much larger impact on the policy development.

Finally, in Chapter 14, Jacob Torfing and Peter Triantafillou briefly review the conclusions concerning interactive policy making, metagovernance and democracy. They reflect on where the research on interactive governance will be heading in the future and what it will take to further consolidate this new and expanding research area.

References

Bell, S. and Hindmoor, A. (2009) *Rethinking Governance: Bring the State Back In*, Cambridge: Cambridge University Press.

Bell, S. and Park, A. (2006) 'The Problematic Metagovernance of Networks: Water Reform in New South Wales', *Journal of Public Policy*, 26 (1): 63–83.

Benz, A. and Papadopoulos, Y. (2006) *Governance and Democracy*, London: Routledge.

Bohman, J. (2005) 'From Demos to Demoi: Democracy Across Borders', *Ratio Juris*, 18 (3): 293–314.

Catlaw, T. (2007) *Fabricating the People*, Tuscaloosa: The University of Alabama Press.

Connolly, W. E. (1995) *The Ethos of Pluralization*, Minneapolis: The University of Minneapolis Press.

De Angelis, M. (2003) 'Neoliberal Governance, reproduction and accumulation', *The Commoner*, 7: 1–28.

Dean, M. (1999) *Governmentality: Power and Rule in Modern Society*, London: Sage.

Du Gay, P. (2000) *In Praise of Bureaucracy*, London: Sage.

Etzioni-Halevy, E. (1993) *The Elite Connection: Problems and Potential of Western Democracy*, Cambridge: Polity Press.

Foucault, M. (1991) 'Governmentality', in G. Burchell, C. Gordon, and P. Miller (eds) *The Foucault Effect*, Hertfordshire: Harvester Wheatsheaf.

Fung, A. and Wright, E. -O. (2003) *Deepening Democracy*, London: Verso.

Hajer, M. and Wagenaar, H. (eds) (2003) *Deliberative Policy Analysis: Understanding in the Network Society*, Cambridge: Cambridge University Press.

Heffen, O. V., Kickert, W. J. M. and Thomassen, J. A. (eds) (2000) *Governance in Modern Society: Effects, Change and Formation of Government Institutions*, Dordrecht: Kluwer Academic Publishers.

Hirst, P. (1994) *Associative Democracy*, Cambridge: Polity Press.

Hood, C. (1983) *The Tools of Government*, Chatham: Chatham House.

Hovik, S. and Vabo, S. I. (2005) 'Norwegian local councils as democratic metagovernors?', *Scandinavian Political Studies*, 28(3): 257–75.

Jessop, B. (2002) *The Future of the Capitalist State*, Cambridge: Polity Press.

Kahler, M. (2009) *Network Politics: Agency, Power and Governance*, Ithaca: Cornell University Press.

Keane, J. (2010) *The Life and Death of Democracy*, London: Simon and Schuster.

Kickert, W. J. M., Klijn, E.-H. and Koppenjan, J. F. M. (eds) (1997) *Managing Complex Networks*, London: Sage.

Klijn, E.-H. and Koppenjan, J. F. M. (2000) 'Interactive decision making and representative democracy: institutional collisions and solutions', in O van Heffen, W. J. M. Kickert and J. J. A. Thomassen (eds) *Governance in Modern Society*, Dordrecht: Kluwer.

—— (2004) *Managing Uncertainties in Networks*, London: Routledge.

Klijn, E.-H. and Skelcher, C. (2007) 'Democracy and governance networks: compatible or not?', *Public Administration*, 85 (3): 587–608.

Kooiman, J. (ed.) (1993) *Modern Governance*, London: Sage.

— (2003) *Governing as Governance*, London: Sage.

Koppenjan, J. F. M. and Klijn, E. -H. (2004) *Managing Uncertainties in Networks*, London: Routledge.

March, J. G. and Olsen, J. P. (1995) *Democratic Governance*, New York: The Free Press.

Marcussen, M. and Torfing J. (eds) (2007) *Democratic Network Governance in Europe*, Basingstoke: Palgrave-Macmillan.

Marinetto, M. (2003) 'Governing beyond the centre: a critique of the Anglo-Governance School', *Political Studies*, 51(4): 592–608.

Marsh, D. (ed.) (1998) *Comparing Policy Networks*, Buckingham: Open University Press.

Matthews, F. (2011) 'Governance and state capacity', in D. Levi-Faur (ed.), *Oxford Handbook of Governance*, Oxford: Oxford University Press.

Mayntz, R. (1993a) 'Modernization and the logic of interorganizational networks', in J. Child, M. Crozier, and R. Mayntz (eds) *Societal Change Between Markets and Organization*, Aldershot: Avebury.

— (1993b) 'Governing failure and the problem of governability: Some comments on a theoretical paradigm', in J. Kooiman (ed.) *Modern Governance*, London: Sage.

Meuleman, L. (2008) *Public Management and the Metagovernance of Hierarchies, Networks and Markets*, Heidelberg: Physica Verlag.

Mouffe, C. (2000) *The Democratic Paradox*, London: Verso.

— (2005) *On the Political*, London: Routledge.

Powell, W. W. and DiMaggio, P. J. (1991) *The New Institutionalism in Organizational Analysis*, Chicago: University of Chicago Press.

Rhodes, R. A. W. (1997) *Understanding Governance*, Buckingham: Open University Press.

Sandel, M. J. (1996) *Democracy's Discontent – America in Search of a Public Philosophy*, Cambridge: Harvard University Press.

Scharpf, F. W. (1994) 'Games real actors could play: Positive and negative coordination in embedded negotiations', *Journal of Theoretical Politics*, 6 (1): 27–53.

Sørensen, E. (2006) 'Metagovernance: The changing role of politicians in processes of democratic governance', *The American Review of Public Administration*, 36 (1): 98–114.

Sørensen, E. and Triantafillou, P. (2009) *The Politics of Self-governance*, London: Ashgate.

Sørensen, E. and Torfing, J. (2005) 'Network governance and post-liberal democracy', *Administrative Theory and Praxis*, 27 (2): 197–237.

— (eds) (2007) *Theories of Democratic Network Governance*, Basingstoke: Palgrave-Macmillan.

— (2009) 'Making governance networks effective and democratic through metagovernance', *Public Administration*, 87 (2): 234–258.

Walters, W. (2005) 'Some critical notes on governance', *Studies in Political Economy*, 73 (3): 27–45.

Warren, M. E. (2002) 'What can democratic participation mean today?', *Political Theory*, 30 (5): 677–701.

Whitehead, M. (2003) 'In the shadow of hierarchy: meta-governance, policy reform and urban regeneration in the West Midlands', *Area*, 5 (1): 6–14.

Young, I. M. (2000) *Inclusion and Democracy*, Oxford: Oxford University Press.

PART I

INTERACTIVE POLICY MAKING
THROUGH GOVERNANCE NETWORKS

chapter two | network governance on the frontline

Jenny M. Lewis and Mark Considine

Introduction

Interactive policy making covers a variety of differently configured horizontal interactions between public and private actors engaged in the policy process. While much research interest in this topic is concentrated on the purposive design of various interactive arenas, some research on interactive policy making is inspired more by the policy networks literature. This is more interested in the spontaneous forms of coordination that have arisen in response to the splitting up of formerly unitary and strongly centralised public services, which occurred through the application of the New Public Management (NPM) principles (Rhodes 1997). Network governance, as it is defined and analysed in this chapter, sits firmly within this realm of concern. We concentrate on how staff on the frontline of service provision understand how they do their work in fragmented environments, and in particular, whether they try to 'join things up'. We also assess the relative importance of these network strategies on the frontline against other governance ideal types.

In opposition to the idea that nework forms of organisation sit somewhere between hierarchy and market on a continuum (Williamson 1975), with more regulated and ongoing transactions that reduce uncertainty and the costliness of investment in searches at one extreme, and straightforward, non-repetitive and low investment transactions at the other, Powell (1990) argued that networks are in fact distinct. Many firms engage in a form of collaboration, he claimed, which resembles neither arm's length contracting nor vertical integration, nor some hybrid of these two. Instead, there are network forms of organisation that are unique since they rest on relationships rather than prices or routines.

Since then, much has been written about the rise of networks as a new form of governing (see for example: Kooiman 1993; Rhodes 1997; Koppenjan and Klijn 2004), and many and varied classifications of different forms of governance have been put forward over the last two decades. Sørensen and Torfing (2007) distinguish between two generations of network governance research. The first generation was devoted to establishing that there was something novel about it, and spent time on explaining its formation, how it differs from other modes of governance, and how it contributes to effective governance. The second generation sees it as a given and the focus as being on explaining its formation, functioning and development, the sources of its failure and success, its regulation (metagovernance), and its implications for democracy. However, first-generation network governance research questions about its distinctiveness remain important. And while much has been claimed about networks as 'new governance', less has been settled by empirical accounts of network ideas, in terms of how coherent and widespread they are as a means of coordinating frontline service provision.

Key questions

This chapter poses the following questions:

- If network governance is distinctive, what is distinctive about it?
- What does an approach that approximates network governance look like on the frontline of service provision?
- Is network governance reflective of differences in national systems, and how does it change as systems change?
- Is it a dominant orientation in shaping how frontline staff see their work?

To answer these questions, data from a large survey of staff delivering services to the long-term unemployed in Australia and the United Kingdom, are used to examine different governance approaches on the frontline. The experiences of staff engaged in delivering these services, who must respond to the signals they receive about office priorities, which in turn reflect policy signals from national governments, are taken as indicators of the governance modes that shape the actions of these street-level bureaucrats. They signify the daily practices of staff, and represent how they understand the work they do. Applying different governance frames in this manner generates a clear picture of the reality of governance for staff at the coal face.

Governance and employment services

Over the last two decades, employment services in countries that are members of the Organisation for Economic Co-operation and Development (OECD) have been the subject of systemic reform by governments seeking greater economic efficiency and improved policy effectiveness. Successive waves of reform have transformed what were previously traditional public services into a range of complex activities held together by new governance arrangements. The result is a service delivery architecture based upon a mixture of public, private for-profit and non-profit agencies. Driving this complex set of institutions is a menu of incentives and regulatory devices to activate jobseekers and the frontline staff they deal with.

To manage this complexity New Public Management (NPM) techniques have been deployed including the use of quasi-market incentives, performance-based contracts and a focus on joined-up solutions. These aim to simultaneously motivate and integrate the very different interests that make up these systems. Employers are seen to need greater engagement by agencies seeking to place job seekers in an effort to overcome various barriers to employment. Jobseekers themselves are seen to require support, coaching and even discipline in order to move from welfare dependence to paid work. And the private and public agencies delivering these services are faced with conflicting signals and rewards that lead them to simultaneously attempt to maximise profits from their government contracts, act as a responsible state authority in dealing with vulnerable jobseekers, and use their relationships with people in other organisations to help jobseekers. These services exemplify many of the changes in public service patterns across the OECD in the last two decades (Aberbach and Christensen 2001; Aucoin 1995).

More specifically, employment services provide a particularly pertinent example of, and hence fruitful field of inquiry into, network governance. At the core of changes to these services is a new narrative concerning the nature of complex public services. In place of older bureaucratic nostrums, we see reformers embracing the idea that new forms of networking and the discretionary shaping of services by frontline staff will support flexible and tailor-made techniques to assist jobseekers to find work. At the same time, there are also increasing pressures on frontline staff to meet new goals and targets in placing jobseekers, while adhering to the rules of funding and following the directives coming from central government in the contracts their agencies hold to deliver these services.

In the model of practice required by these reforms, the frontline staff delivering services to the community on behalf of the state need to develop strategies to carry out their duties. In the case of employment services, this set of duties involves interviewing jobseekers and employers and then devising recommended service plans to meet their needs. A decade ago, in relation to employment services, we postulated that there were four identifiable governance modes (ideal types) with different characteristics (Considine and Lewis 1999). These were termed procedural, corporate, market and network modes of governance. Their key attributes are summarised in Table 2.1. A more detailed discussion of this for each of the types can be found in two earlier papers (Considine and Lewis 1999; 2003a).

Table 2.1: Governance types

	Source of Rationality	Form of Control	Primary Virtue	Service Delivery Focus
Procedural	Law	Rules	Reliability	Universal Treatments
Corporate	Management	Plans	Goal-driven	Target Groups
Market	Competition	Contracts	Cost-driven	Price
Network	Culture	Co-Production	Flexibility	Clients

These ideal types – like all ideal types – are simplifications of contrasting ideas that can and do overlap both conceptually and empirically. The two separate modes of corporate and market bureaucracy, for example, can be described as having quite separate sources of rationality, forms of control, primary virtues, and service-delivery foci, as outlined in Table 2.1. However, the NPM literature blends these together and the introduction of NPM into public services around the world resulted in hybrids of corporate and market ideas, with contracting out paired with more central planning. Likewise, the flexibility that is claimed as a primary virtue of networks in this four-way classification, can equally be claimed to be a virtue of markets. Hence, in examining these four ideal-types, it is worth bearing in mind that this is a conceptual device for interrogating the extent of their distinctiveness. Indeed, the four types collapse into three when the empirical evidence is analysed, as is described later in this chapter.

Of central theoretical interest here is the network form. This was the most speculative of the four types a decade ago, given the novelty of this form of organisation, compared with traditional procedural bureaucracy and NPM ideas (Considine and Lewis 2003a), the (not always helpful) positive gloss that often accompanies a discussion of networks, joined-up government and collaborative approaches to service delivery (Lewis 2010), and the lack of robust descriptions of how this actually functions as a form of management (Kickert, Klijn and Koppenjan 1997).

Employment services in Australia and the UK

Australia and the United Kingdom were chosen as cases because they are both members of the OECD; they had both substantially reformed their employment services in the late 1990s by engaging the non-profit or private sectors; and they both had national employment systems, rather than local or regional systems.

In the UK, reforms to the welfare state began in earnest in the late 1980s with some privatisation and the introduction of market-style competitive processes within the publically owned and delivered employment sector. These changes began under a conservative government, but the Blair Labour Government continued to re-invent the welfare state's method of providing job search assistance, drawing on the skills and expertise of the for-profit sector (Finn 2005). The UK employment sector's post-1997 reforms were also explicitly directed towards the development of partnerships across a broad range of service providers and agencies at the local and national levels, across government owned, private for-profit and private not-for-profit agencies, and with providers of a range of niche employment related services.

Jobcentre Plus (JCP) was created in April 2002, and became the key government agency tasked with delivering employment services in the UK. The Department for Work and Pensions was also created to manage employment services contracts and other funding arrangements, while various other 'social partners' contribute to the development, refinement and execution of employment policy. Private companies were invited to tender for the delivery of basic case-management employment services, in direct competition with JCP (Finn 2005). In some cases, private services worked in direct competition with JCP, and in other cases the private provider operated in partnership with the government-owned employment agency (Finn 2005). To complicate the picture further, a large number of the early contracts awarded as part of the government's 'Employment Zones' initiative went to Working Links, which is a private employment service provider owned jointly by the UK Government, an Australian not-for-profit agency, and two private for-profit companies.

The intellectual underpinnings of this sizable policy shift in the way employment services are delivered in the UK are varied. The restructuring of the employment sector may be understood as a tailored response to the twin challenges of growing longer-term unemployment and the social exclusion associated with it. These are both more prevalent among certain sections of the community and within specific geographical locations. This may account for the attractiveness of an employment assistance system which is decentralised; where government agencies work in partnership with local organisations to respond to particular types of disadvantage with greater flexibility in their delivery strategy; and which is also competitive and market driven. A decade ago, all UK frontline employment services staff were public servants. By 2008, the vast majority of frontline staff delivering employment assistance to Jobseekers Allowance (JSA) recipients were JCP employees, but a sizable proportion also worked for either a for-profit, or a not-for-profit employment agency.

Reform of the Australian employment sector commenced under the Keating Labor Government in the 1990s. In a 1994 White Paper, a new, competitive, client-focused employment system for Australia was defined for the first time. Under the new regime, the intention was to move away from processing large numbers of jobseekers through standard national programs, towards more accurate assessment of needs and more intensive plans to assist disadvantaged people (Keating 1994). This meant a shift away from the public delivery of employment services and a move towards harnessing the potential of the private sector and increasing competition (Keating 1994).

The first wave of reform occurred between 1994 and 1996. It involved such initiatives as the introduction of private employment service providers; individual case management for the long-term unemployed; the ability for jobseekers to choose their own employment agency and negotiate service contracts; the introduction of government funded training programs available to those who had been unemployed for over eighteen months; payment to private providers on a fee-for-success basis; and competition between providers based on the quality of their performance. Around one third of employment services moved from the public to the private sector (Considine 2005).

Further changes increased the private providers' market share from 30 to 50 per cent and substantially changed the way the sector was regulated. The provision of employment services was put out to tender in 1997, with the Department acting as sole purchaser. Centrelink was created as a new arm's length public agency tasked with the management of all social security payments as well as the provision of the public component of frontline employment services. By 2003, all jobseekers were referred to a private employment agency for customised assistance, and this was still the situation in 2008. A decade ago, Australian employment services were provided largely by three roughly equal groups – a public sector organisation with national coverage, a number of private for-profit and a larger group of not-for profit agencies. By the time of the 2008 survey, all frontline employment services staff in Australia worked for private or non-profit agencies.

Compared with the UK, Australia privatised some of its services earlier and then went on to do so completely. The focus has been more strongly related to quasi-market ideas about the need for competition between providers. Up until 2008, there was little discussion of partnerships or social exclusion by the incumbent Conservative Government. Attention was instead being directed towards the greater regulation of contracts, since the undesirable behaviour of some service providers in the treatment of jobseekers (e.g. cream skimming the easy-to-place clients and giving a low priority to those who were likely to be difficult to place) had come to light.

Analysing governance on the frontline

To examine whether the four ideal types outlined in Table 2.1 can be observed on the frontline, staff were surveyed about how they do their work in 1998 and 2008. For the purposes of this research, frontline staff are defined as: staff who work directly with jobseekers to help them become job-ready, or assist them to secure and/ or maintain employment. In the 1998 survey, participants completed the survey on paper and the response rate was 56 per cent in total (Considine 2001). In 2008, the survey was conducted online, and the overall response rate was 45 per cent.[1] The number of respondents for each year and country is provided in Table 2.2. The questionnaire used in both time periods comprised around 100 questions designed to solicit information about how frontline staff carry out the basic service delivery tasks required in assisting jobseekers find work.

Table 2.2: Number of survey responses in 1998 and 2008

	1998	2008	Total
Australia	625	1512	2137
UK	155	1196	1351
Total	780	2708	3488

The ten-year timeframe provides a valuable point of comparison as the UK and Australian employment sectors have both undergone aggressive reform over the last decade. In the original survey, the governance types were first tested against a sample of 345 Australian staff working in public, for-profit and not-for-profit agencies (Considine and Lewis 1999). The results were then confirmed using data from a survey of four countries (Australia, the UK, the Netherlands and New Zealand). The earlier analysis of the four governance modes was not conducted in

---

1.   Full results from the 2008 Australian survey are in Considine, Lewis, and O'Sullivan (2009a), and
      for the 2008 UK survey, Considine, Lewis, and O'Sullivan (2009b).

terms of differences between countries, since the focus was on examining whether identifiable modes of governance could be found. Differences are analysed in this chapter, since the focus here is on comparing between countries and over time, in order to answer questions about the robustness and stability of network governance, and its relative importance compared with other modes of governance. In the conclusion to our second paper on governance modes (Considine and Lewis 2003a), we called for more research to strengthen the network concept as an ideal type, in order to improve our understanding of this orientation, to explain how this links to actual networking behaviour, and to come to grips with whether this is an essential approach in determining frontline service provision.

Initially, the survey that was administered to frontline staff in Australia included 40 items that constituted the governance scales. The scale items used were devised from some initial exploratory work in focus groups and interviews with frontline staff in employment service delivery, which were turned into a series of statements and then pilot tested. They include items regarding the role of rules, discretion, supervision, technology, clients, outputs, discipline, goals, innovation and environmental relations (Considine and Lewis 1999). The original battery of 40 items was divided into four groups of ten statements that related to each of the governance types (procedural, corporate, market and network).

The exploratory factor analysis indicated that there were three rather than four types, with procedural and network types apparent, plus a hybrid of the corporate and market types.[2] The initial analysis also indicated that a number of scale items were contributing little to the three factors that arose from the factor analysis (procedural, corporate-market and network), or were reducing the reliability (based on Cronbach alpha coefficients) of the three scales that were subsequently created. A reduced set of 28 of these items was used in the remainder of the earlier study (Considine and Lewis 2003a), and in 2008. This reduction included removing four items that were intended to reflect core statements of the four hypothesised ideal types. Analysis of the responses to these items indicated that many staff agreed with all four orientations. A forced choice question was used instead in the later rounds of the previous study and in the 2008 study.

Since the initial study had found three coherent factors through an exploratory factor analysis and reliability analysis, and these three factors appeared again and achieved a reasonable 'goodness-of-fit' using confirmatory factor analysis on the full data set from the earlier study, we have focused on three factor solutions again here. However, in this instance, factor analysis was undertaken for the two countries separately, to examine system differences. Principal components analy-

2. Principal components analysis was used. The scree plot of the eigenvalues indicated that each of the three, four and five factor solutions were worth examining more closely. Using a combination of what had been hypothesised as the initial four ideal types, and the results from the initial factor analysis, the three factor solution made the most sense in relation to both the theory and the data. The three factor solution was then run using varimax (orthogonal) rotation. More information on factor analysis and the use of scree plots to determine the number of factors can be found in Tabachnik and Fidell (1996).

sis with varimax rotation was used to extract the factors, as per the earlier study. The factor loading from the three factor solutions for both countries in both time periods can be found in the Appendix to this chapter.

The three factors approximate those from the earlier study, with some variant of the corporate-market, network and procedural types appearing in each. A logical comparison in terms of assessing the stability of the three governance types from the earlier study, is to compare the level of correspondence of the results from each of the four factor analyses in 2008 with the factors obtained originally. This is shown in Table 2.3.

The corporate-market mode appears with the most consistency in each case. This had 10 items in the earlier study and the factors load on the same dimension for both countries with seven for Australia and 8 for the UK in 1998 matching the dimension, and 9 for both Australia and the UK in 2008. Only a small number of additional items (indicated after the + in the table) loaded onto this type, varying from zero to 2.

The procedural type is the next most stable, with either 4 or 5 of the original 7 items appearing on each, plus some new items added, especially for the UK in 1998 (4). Network governance has a smaller core set of items that remain stable, and more different items appear, especially in the UK case in 2008 (7). This analysis provides some evidence that a network orientation is more context (regime and time period) specific than the other two types. While the meaning of the procedural type also changes across cases, this is much more stable in 2008 than the network type.

Table 2.3: Correspondence between factors*

	Corporate-market	Network	Procedural
Original 1998	10	6	7
Australia 1998	7 + 1	4 + 3	4 + 3
UK 1998	8 + 2	4 + 3	5 + 4
Australia 2008	9 + 1	5 + 3	5 + 2
UK 2008	9 + 0	6 + 7	4 + 1

* – number of items that correspond with the original + number of additional items that load on a particular factor

This analysis suggests that system changes have strengthened the meaning of 'corporate-market' and (to a lesser extent) procedural governance in 2008. A less settled understanding of network governance is apparent in both countries, reflecting the effects of policy changes and changes to the range of organisations involved in delivering frontline employment services. Perhaps the network type is a transitional strategy for dealing with large institutional change? Its meaning moves around more than the other types which might relate to people searching for strategies to meet new work demands. Further analysis is required to understand what has happened with these three types, including a more detailed examination of four and five factor solutions, to see whether entirely new types can now be observed.[3] But in any case it is clear that, at least for the frontline advisers who participated in our surveys, network governance is by no means a settled or very distinct form of getting their work done.

Dominant mode of governance

In the initial survey of Australian staff, the governance scales included four items to reflect core statements of the different types. In analysing the responses to these scale items, it became clear that many staff agreed with all four orientations. To make an assessment of whether there was a dominant type, in later rounds of the survey, these four items were asked as a single question that forced a choice between the four types. We asked them to indicate which was the most important priority in their office: obeying the rules (procedural), meeting targets (corporate), competing with other service providers (market), or having a good set of contacts (network). This information was collected for 791 people, and included staff from each of the four countries. When forced to choose between the four ideal types, the majority of staff chose the corporate mode (70.3 per cent), followed by procedural (11.5 per cent), then market (10.7 per cent), and finally, network (7.5 per cent).

As was the case for the governance types, this was not analysed for individual countries in the earlier study, but is compared for the two countries and the two time periods here, in Tables 2.4 and 2.5. There are significant differences between the two countries in 1998, and again in 2008, and there are also significant differences for both Australia and the UK between the two time periods.[4]

Table 2.4 shows the comparison between Australia and the UK in 1998. The corporate type dominates in both countries, but was far more dominant in the UK (86.8 per cent) than in Australia (58.4 per cent) at this time. The greater market emphasis in the Australian case in 1998 shows through clearly, with 21.4 per cent of people saying that competing successfully is the most important priority in their office. Proceduralism is the highest priority for about 10 per cent in both countries, while networking is also around this level in Australia, but almost non-existent in the UK.

---

3.   Scree plots of the eigenvalues for these factor analyses indicate that three, four and five factor solutions are worth examining for 2008, as they were for the earlier study. Only the three factor solutions have been examined here, as the main interest is in determining stability in relation to the earlier results.

4.   All of the comparisons in these tables are statistically significant at $p<0.05$ (using a chi-squared test).

Table 2.4: Dominant mode of governance in the office 1998

	Percentage	
	Australia **(n = 382)**	**UK** **(n = 151)**
Knowing the rules and official procedures	9.1	11.3
Meeting the targets set by management	58.4	86.8
Competing successfully with other service providers	21.4	1.3
Having the best possible set of contacts outside the organisation	11.1	0.7

In 2008, the corporate type still dominated in both countries (47.7 per cent in Australia and 77.3 per cent in the UK). But the procedural type is much more important in Australia than in the UK, with 37.6 per cent nominating this as the most important office priority in Australia (see Table 2.5). The market type is still more popular in Australia than in the UK, but the network orientation in the UK at 6.1 per cent, is now higher than for Australia at 3.4 per cent.

Table 2.5: Dominant mode of governance in the office 2008

	Percentage	
	Australia **(n = 1098)**	**UK** **(n = 915)**
Knowing the rules and official procedures	37.6	11.4
Meeting the targets set by management	47.7	77.3
Competing successfully with other service providers	11.3	5.2
Having the best possible set of contacts outside the organisation	3.4	6.1

Comparing these same data across time rather than across countries, by comparing the first column of numbers in Tables 2.4 and 2.5, shows clearly the increase in the procedural orientation over the decade for Australia, and the subsequent decline in all of the other orientations. This is somewhat puzzling, given that the system has become more marketised over this time period and the shift to a fully private sector (for-profit and not-for-profit) provision of services. It probably reflects the increasing level of regulation and oversight that has been introduced over the decade. Indeed, the relatively low level of agreement with the market mode in all cases except Australia in 1998 is remarkable, given that these systems have been so heavily 'marketised'.

Comparing the second column of numbers in Tables 2.4 and 2.5 for the UK, highlights the shift towards more competitive and network orientations, most likely related to the increasing marketisation of services and the introduction of many new organisations delivering these services, compared with the single public service that was in operation a decade earlier.

However, in terms of addressing the questions of interest in this paper, the most outstanding result is the low subscription to the network orientation, when people are forced to make a choice between this and other priorities in doing their job. The highest percentage indicating a preference for a network orientation was 11.1 per cent, recorded for Australia in 1998. This is the only instance where it was scored higher than any of the other types, and it has since declined to just 3.4 per cent in Australia. While it has risen over the decade in the UK, it remains low at 6.1 per cent. While some people are choosing this as the most important priority in their office, it is clear that other orientations dominate their priorities. This network orientation might be reflective of the activity associated with substantial institutional change – hence the relatively high level in Australia in 1998 and in the UK in 2008, when the respective systems had recently undergone major reforms. Perhaps frontline staff engage in an increased search for new ways to manage changing conditions, which is followed by a decline in this once the new environment becomes more settled.

Table 2.6: Dominant mode of governance personally 2008

	Percentage	
	Australia (n = 1087)	**UK (n = 891)**
Knowing the rules and official procedures	45.2	28.4
Meeting the targets set by management	39.5	49.4
Competing successfully with other service providers	7.6	7.9
Having the best possible set of contacts outside the organisation	7.7	14.4

In 2008, we added a second version of this question, and asked about personal priorities as opposed to office priorities. The results from this can be seen in Table 2.6. It might be expected that the network orientation might be higher for these staff personally, even if it was not their office's dominant governance orientation. This was the case, with the percentage nominating the network orientation more than double, compared with the results in Table 2.5 (7.7 compared with 3.4 per cent in Australia, and 14.4 compared with 6.1 per cent in the UK). The corporate type still dominated in the UK, but this was overtaken by the procedural type in Australia, which had also risen for the UK. The market orientation was lower in

Australia but higher in the UK than the perceived office priorities.

These results seem to indicate a high level of personal resonance with sticking to the rules in the Australian case, and being guided by the targets in the UK case. Most importantly, there is some evidence of a stronger subscription to the network orientation *personally*. This fits with the notion that these actors are trying to make sense of the new work environment they inhabit, especially in the UK, by staying in touch with what others in the sector are doing, even if this is not such a priority for their office.

Conclusions

In this chapter, we have addressed the question of what makes network governance distinctive in relation to frontline service provision. We also examined how context-specific the idea of network governance is on the frontline and whether it can be seen as a strong governance orientation.

We found that the three different modes of governance identified in our previous work could also be observed to varying extents in different contexts and different time periods. The most stable of these was the corporate-market type, which had the highest level of correspondence with the original governance ideal types identified in 1999. The procedural and network types were less stable, and in particular, the network type varied substantially from context to context. This indicates that the network is a more fluid and less coherent orientation than the other more established types. Despite the fact that network governance has been a substantial field of research for two decades, it is harder to pin down in conceptual terms and also less clearly something that coheres in the minds of those working on the frontline of service delivery. It also appears that networking might represent a particular strategy for dealing with large system changes, rising in times of upheaval and then falling once these changes become established. This conclusion responds to the point raised earlier in this chapter about it being time for network governance research to move on from examinations of whether networks are an observable and distinct form. Our findings suggest that this is not the case – at least not for those dealing with the challenges of frontline service delivery in these new and differently structured environments with many organisations involved.

Even more interesting is the analysis of dominant modes. This clearly demonstrates shifts in what are seen as the highest priorities for those engaged in delivering these services, reflecting changes in the two systems. These shifts are not convincingly in the direction of networks and interactive ways of working. The low level of orientation towards a network priority in both countries and both periods of time speaks volumes about the package of signals being received in employment service organisations and also the signals being internally integrated as personal priorities, by staff on the frontline. While targets rule the list of priorities, there is also substantial evidence to suggest that procedures are important too, particularly for Australian staff.

This provides strong evidence that the environment in which these staff are working represent hybrid governing modes, which blend aspects of the ideal types

presented earlier in this chapter. The description of changes to employment services in Australia and the UK clearly demonstrate the mixture of priorities being
combined into recent policy directions – some of which are clearly based on relational ideas (partnerships) while others are clearly competition and rule based. The
heuristic value of using ideal types can be seen clearly here, where it is possible to
observe the impact of priorities in policy making that value control and targets but
also flexibility, attempting to combine various types of coordination. Perhaps the
dominant form of governing these services is now a corporate-procedural blend.

The analysis of dominant priorities seems to indicate that networking is used
more by staff when they are faced with new demands, as it is highest in contexts
(countries and times) with the greatest system volatility. It is also clear that interaction with contacts elsewhere is a substantially higher personal priority than it is
an office priority. This points to a subtle difference in how these staff experience
their work, with more emphasis placed on their networks as personal resources
which might be useful to them in placing clients into work, albeit well behind the
importance of meeting the targets and knowing the rules. Less emphasis is placed
on these contacts from an office point of view, where the focus seems to rest even
more strongly on target- and rule-driven modes of working.

This chapter suggests that network governance is far from being a settled or
clear-cut concept. Its meaning differs between countries and shifts over time.
Neither is it a very important orientation compared with other ways of working
for those engaged in highly interconnected service delivery worlds, although it is
more important personally and perhaps in times of major change. Perhaps we have
still to come to grips with a good ideal type of network governance, which can
be translated into an instrument for getting at how frontline staff understand their
work. It is also possible that network governance, because of its complex nature,
shifts continually and is much more context specific than other modes of governance. Further, it is apparent that 'pure' network governance, as it is defined in
this chapter, is likely to be rare. Policy making borrows and blends ideas, and the
result is a package that generally requires a hybrid of governance types. Finally,
examining networks and interaction as an important mode of governance, as it is
experienced on the frontline, remains a fruitful research topic.

Appendix

Governance scale items factor loadings for the three factor solution for:

- Australia 1998 and 2008; and
- UK 1998 and 2008.

Note: In each of these tables, the factor loadings are from a principal components analysis using varimax rotation on the three factor solution. Only the factor loadings with a magnitude of 0.30 or more are shown, for ease of interpretation.

Appendix: Australia 1998 and 2008 – factor loadings for three factor solutions

	1998 (24.5% of variance explained)			2008 (24.4% of variance explained)		
	Corp-mark	Net	Proc	Corp-mark	Net	Proc
1. I find that issuing Participation Reports (sanctions) can really damage your reputation with job seekers and others in the employment field						
2. The lines of authority are not clear in my work	.38		-.48			-.45
3. I do not like my competition (internal or external) to know how I go about getting my results	.40					
4. My job can be done by following a few basic rules						

	1998 (24.5% of variance explained)			2008 (24.4% of variance explained)		
	Corp-mark	Net	Proc	Corp-mark	Net	Proc
5. When it comes to day-to-day work I am free to decide for myself what I will do with each job seeker					.35	
6. My supervisor knows a lot about the work I do day-to-day			.66			.62
7. The really important rules in this job are the ones to do with obtaining assistance from other organisations	.50	.42			.54	
8. In my job, I am NOT influenced by numerical targets (including star rating)	-.45			-.55		
9. The main thing I have to do in this job is gain the trust of the job seeker		.51			.60	
10. Our organisation has targets for certain types of job seekers	.41			.45		
11. When I come across something not covered by the procedural guide, I refer it to my supervisor			.63			.54
12. The goal in this work is to find a middle ground between the needs of job seekers, employers, and the social security system					.52	
13. I use a lot of personal judgement to decide what is best for each job seeker		-.32			.46	

	1998 (24.5% of variance explained)			2008 (24.4% of variance explained)		
	Corp-mark	Net	Proc	Corp-mark	Net	Proc
14. Before reporting a job seeker for non-compliance, I would always consider which classification group they belonged to					.37	
15. I like to keep my own records and files on job seekers and programs		.36			.44	
16. Our computer system tells me what steps to take with job seekers and when to take them			.36			
17. When you get a good result with job seekers it's usually a team effort by yourself, trainer, other staff in your office, and the employer			.37			.49
18. To get job seekers to pay attention I often remind them that enforcing compliance is part of my job	.49			.35		.34
19. My job is determined by goals set elsewhere	.53			.44		
20. More and more the objective in this job is to maximise the organisation's financial outcomes	.49	-.49		.62		-.31
21. I think the objective in this job is to shift the maximum number of job seekers off benefits	.39	-.49		.49		
22. I use our information technology system to track priority job seekers			.38	.37		.31

	1998 (24.5% of variance explained)			2008 (24.4% of variance explained)		
	Corp-mark	Net	Proc	Corp-mark	Net	Proc
23. I do tend to take note of those actions with job seekers that will generate a payable outcome for the office		-.72		.58		
24. All my job seekers receive a similar service		.33				
25. I am often asked to suggest ways to improve things			.47			.51
26. I am aware that my organisation pays attention to the income I generate by placing job seekers				.53		
27. If an official from another employment organisation asked for help in using the computer, I would help them		.51			.35	
28. In my job, job seekers are organised into formal and informal priority groups	.38			.39		

Appendix: United Kingdom 1998 and 2008 – factor loadings for three factor solutions

	1998 (27.2% of variance explained)			2008 (26.8% of variance explained)		
	Corp-mark	Net	Proc	Corp-mark	Net	Proc
1. I find that issuing Participation Reports (sanctions) can really damage your reputation with job seekers and others in the employment field	.32				.40	
2. The lines of authority are not clear in my work	.49		-.38			-.65
3. I do not like my competition (internal or external) to know how I go about getting my results		-.33				-.44
4. My job can be done by following a few basic rules		.31	-.36			
5. When it comes to day-to-day work I am free to decide for myself what I will do with each job seeker		.46			.53	
6. My supervisor knows a lot about the work I do day-to-day	-.32		.55		.36	.46
7. The really important rules in this job are the ones to do with obtaining assistance from other organisations		.37			.48	
8. In my job, I am NOT influenced by numerical targets (including star rating)	-.34	.42				
9. The main thing I have to do in this job is gain the trust of the job seeker		.61			.47	
10. Our organisation has targets for certain types of job seekers	.38					

	1998 (27.2% of variance explained)			2008 (26.8% of variance explained)		
	Corp-mark	Net	Proc	Corp-mark	Net	Proc
11. When I come across something not covered by the procedural guide, I refer it to my supervisor			.46		.38	
12. The goal in this work is to find a middle ground between the needs of job seekers, employers, and the social security system			.33		.41	
13. I use a lot of personal judgement to decide what is best for each job seeker		.73			.40	
14. Before reporting a job seeker for non-compliance, I would always consider which classification group they belonged to	.43				.47	
15. I like to keep my own records and files on job seekers and programs		.45			.41	
16. Our computer system tells me what steps to take with job seekers and when to take them			.38			
17. When you get a good result with job seekers it's usually a team effort by yourself, trainer, other staff in your office, and the employer					.43	
18. To get job seekers to pay attention I often remind them that enforcing compliance is part of my job	.38					.34
19. My job is determined by goals set elsewhere	.65					

	1998 (27.2% of variance explained)			2008 (26.8% of variance explained)		
	Corp-mark	Net	Proc	Corp-mark	Net	Proc
20. More and more the objective in this job is to maximise the organisation's financial outcomes	.67					-.44
21. I think the objective in this job is to shift the maximum number of job seekers off benefits	.53				.53	
22. I use our information technology system to track priority job seekers			.39			
23. I do tend to take note of those actions with job seekers that will generate a payable outcome for the office	.34		.54		.40	
24. All my job seekers receive a similar service		.44				.42
25. I am often asked to suggest ways to improve things			.47		.49	.39
26. I am aware that my organisation pays attention to the income I generate by placing job seekers			.49		.56	
27. If an official from another employment organisation asked for help in using the computer, I would help them					.39	
28. In my job, job seekers are organised into formal and informal priority groups	.50					

References

Aberbach, J. D. and Christensen, T. (2001) 'Radical reform in New Zealand: crisis, windows of opportunity, and rational actors', *Public Administration*, 79(2): 403–422.

Aucoin, P. (1995) *The New Public Management: Canada in Comparative Perspective*, Montreal: Institute for research on Public Policy.

Considine, M (2001) *Enterprising States: the public management of welfare-to-work*, Cambridge: Cambridge University Press.

— (2005) 'The Reform that Never Ends: Quasi-markets and employment services in Australia', in E. Sol and M. Westervel (eds) *Contractualism in Employment Services: a new form of welfare state governance*, The Hague: Kluwer Law International.

— Considine, M. and Lewis, J. M. (1999) 'Governance at ground level: The frontline bureaucrat in the age of markets and networks', *Public Administration Review*, 59(6): 467–480.

— (2003a) 'Bureaucracy, network or enterprise? Comparing models of governance in Australia, Britain, the Netherlands, and New Zealand', *Public Administration Review* 63(2): 131–140.

— (2003b) 'Networks and interactivity: making sense of front-line governance in the United Kingdom, the Netherlands and Australia', *Journal of European Public Policy* 10(1): 25–58.

Considine, M., Lewis, J. M., and O'Sullivan, S. (2009a) 'Activating States: transforming the delivery of "welfare to work" services in Australia, the UK and the Netherlands'. Australian report back to Industry Partners. Available online at http://www.public-policy.unimelb.edu.au/research/Activating_States_Aust_Report_2008.pdf. Accessed 21/7/09.

— (2009b) 'Activating States: transforming the delivery of "welfare to work" services in Australia, the UK and the Netherlands'. UK report back to Industry Partners. Online. Available http://www.public-policy.unimelb.edu.au/research/Activating_States_Industry_Report_2009.pdf (accessed 21 July 2009).

Finn, D. (2005) 'The Role of Contracts and the Private Sector in Delivering Britain's "Employment First" Welfare State', in E. Sol and M. Westerveld (eds) *Contractualism in Employment Services: a new forms of welfare state governance*, The Hague: Kluwer Law International.

Keating, P. J. (1994) *Working Nation: policies and programs* (Government of Australia White Paper), Canberra, Australia: Australian Government Publishing Service.

Kickert, W., Klijn, E. H. and Koppenjan, J. (eds) (1997) *Managing Complex Networks: Strategies for the Public Sector*, London: Sage.

Koppenjan, J. and Klijn, E. H. (2004) *Managing Uncertainties in Networks. A Network Approach to Problem Solving and Decision Making*, London: Routledge.

Kooiman, J. (ed.) (1993) *Modern Governance: New Government-Society*

Interactions, London: Sage.

Lewis, J. M. (2010) *Connecting and Cooperating: Social Capital and Public Policy*, Sydney: UNSW Press.

Powell, W. W. (1990) 'Neither market nor hierarchy: Network forms of organization', *Research in Organizational Behavior*, 12: 295–336.

Rhodes, R. A. W. (1997) *Understanding Governance: Policy Networks, Governance, Reflexivity and Accountability*, Buckingham: Open University Press.

Sørensen, E. and Torfing, J. (eds) (2008) *Theories of Democratic Network Governance*, Basingstoke UK: Palgrave.

Tabachnick, B. G. and Fidell, L. S. (1996) *Using Multivariate Statistics*, 3rd edn., New York: HarperCollins.

Williamson, O. E. (1975) *Markets and hierarchies: Analysis and Antitrust Implications*, New York: Free Press.

chapter three | perceptions of effectiveness in governance networks – a comparative analysis

Trine Fotel

Introduction

The effectiveness of governance networks is often taken for granted. A large international body of literature illustrates that, compared to traditional hierarchical government or market-based service delivery, governance networks often provide more innovative solutions to complex public policy problems (Kickert, Klijn and Koppenjan 1999; Sørensen and Torfing 2009; Rhodes 2000: 355). However, we have a minimum amount of knowledge concerning how to *measure* the effectiveness of network-based policies. Keith Provan and Brinton Milward's research on the effectiveness of service implementation networks is a unique exception, although the authors also point out that it is 'premature to conclude that networks are effective mechanisms for addressing complex policy problems, despite their promise' (2001: 145). If governance networks are supposed to be a viable strategy for the public sector, then we need to examine ways of measuring their effectiveness.

This chapter explores the perceptions and attitudes of effectiveness amongst Nordic regional governance network participants. A three-dimensional model addressing network effectiveness is developed and the relations between effectiveness and general policy context are discussed. The analysis builds on a large comparative survey conducted amongst regional development networks in Denmark, Finland, Norway and Sweden in 2007. These countries have all undertaken regional government reforms within the last decades and public debates have often pointed towards the added value of governance networks to regional performance and innovation, a fact that is also reflected in the international regional policy literature (Amin 1999; Keating *et al.* 2003; Sagan and Halkier 2005; Statskontoret 2007; Hall and Montin 2007; Bache and Olsson 2001). Despite this focus on economic performance, we lack extensive explorations of regional governance network effectiveness.

The results presented in this chapter counter the long-standing belief that the Nordic countries are relatively similar welfare states. Regional governance actors perceive the effectiveness of their networks differently. The perceptional differences can be explained by several contextual and institutional dynamics. These include the institutional background of the network actors and the ways that metagovernance forms a contextual regulation of the networks. Furthermore, different historical and political trajectories in the east-Nordic and the east-west countries respectively, influence the effectiveness of the networks. The outlined model, as well as the actual results, contribute to international research on governance networks and add to a fuller understanding of regional public policy dynamics in the north.

The three-dimensional model of effectiveness

Effectiveness is a 'critical concept', which 'cannot simply be ignored' (Milward and Kenis 2007). However, measurements of public service delivery have mainly focused on traditional government modes of hierarchies and markets. The understanding of effectiveness of hierarchical government is often based on government's ability to be cost-effective by reaching predefined goals through mechanisms of control and command. In comparison, market-based regulation is presumed effective when it produces an optimal Pareto-equilibrium, where costs and benefits are allocated in order to ensure that 'the marginal utility equals the marginal costs for all actors' (Sørensen and Torfing 2009: 240; Bogason 2006).

Neither of these two common ways of measuring effectiveness is applicable to governance networks (Jessop 2002: 236; Sørensen and Torfing 2009). As a wide array of public and private actors from across sectors and levels of government participate in interactive governance networks, the solutions agreed upon will not usually satisfy the marginal utilities or the marginal costs of all the actors. Furthermore, the definition of goals and policy instruments is not predefined, but dynamic. Solutions to difficult policy problems, which transgress traditional policy spheres, appear in the course of interaction amongst the network participants (Weber and Khademian 2008). The networks are embedded in non-market coordination and negotiated rationalities, which facilitate cooperation and the ability to reach common goals (Scharpf 1994). Measuring the effectiveness of governance networks presupposes an acknowledgement of circumstances and contextual character.

However, there seems to be a positive bias in the contemporary literature on governance networks. Most studies praise all the merits of networks, especially in terms of their innovative and dynamic policy solutions. Furthermore, governance networks are seen as being more effective than hierarchies and markets per se, but as Bob Jessop notes (2002: 236 *et seq.*), we should keep our minds open to the possibility of governance failure, although failed networks often disappear and are obviously not easy to scrutinise. The argument made here is that in order to identify a potential risk of governance failure, we must first identify a set of criteria and measurable variables addressing the relative success or failure of networks. This enables us to evaluate the character of governance networks in a comparative framework and understand the 'virtuous and vicious circles' (Peters 2007) found in contemporary governance.

Based on the contemporary international literature on governance networks, the effectiveness of networks is mainly ascribed to their flexible and inclusive *dynamics*, their critical potential for agonistic *politics*, and their ability to reach innovative *results*. An assessment of network effectiveness should apply variables within each of these criteria. The criteria are suitable for addressing the functioning of individual networks. Relations between the network and broader society can be included by a supplementary analysis of metagovernance, defined as the regulation of self-regulating networks (see Chapter 1). The content of the three assessment criteria and metagovernance as a tool to enhance, or restrict, network effectiveness, are elaborated on below.

The criteria of effective *dynamics* are based on the ability of the network to establish trustful exchanges and active engagement between a widely dispersed set of public and private actors and to create favorable conditions for future co-operation through cognitive, strategic and institutional learning (Koppenjan and Klijn 2004: 125–9). It is pertinent to address whether the right actors are included. An inclusion of too many or the 'wrong' actors could hinder the effectiveness inherent in a common institutional framework and the ability to develop common goals and aims. Furthermore, it is important that the network is able to change the composition of the network in order to be more efficient in addressing current policy problems.

Effective dynamics in turn create the foundations for effective *politics*. Effective political contestations are most likely to produce innovative policy decisions that move beyond the lowest common denominator. The participants of a network must be able to cope with persistent conflicts and power struggles. Ideally, the network must 'create a regulative, normative and cognitive framework that facilitates problem-oriented negotiations' (Sørensen and Torfing 2007: 98). Such a political process may be fostered by an atmosphere of agonistic pluralism, with mutual respect for diverging interests (Mouffe 1995). In order to explore these dimensions, the analysis below addresses, amongst other things, how network participants experience their ability to set their own agenda and whether their network is marked by consensus or practicalities.

Finally effective networks must be able to produce *results*, such as public policy strategies, interventions and a flexible implementation of joint decisions (Börzel and Panke 2007: 157). The fact that networks consist of public and private partners is a *sine qua non* for the networks innovative ability to identify and define relevant policy problems and determine their interrelations and causes (Sørensen and Torfing 2007: 98). However, preferences, goals and policy aims are not defined *a priori* but produced in the course of interaction between network participants. An analysis of effectiveness must include the perceptional fact that:

> Policy making can be seen as effective when it has led to a policy result which the players of the game consider satisfactory in the light of the goals they have prioritised at the moment when they determine the policy result.

(Kickert *et al.* 1999: 14)

In order to fully understand the character of these three criteria of effectiveness, it is important also to include variables targeting the external contextual regulation of networks. Metagovernance can influence the effectiveness of governance in various ways. Most often politicians regulate self-regulating networks by defining their discursive, legal or financial conditions and politicians either participate directly in the networks or govern them at a distance (Sørensen 2006). An analysis of the relations between metagovernance and network-based effectiveness should include a focus on both the formal institutional regulation and the informal discursive regulation of networks (Sørensen and Torfing 2009). The Nordic regional governance networks are all embedded in multilevel governance arrangements which metagovern the networks. Even though Norway is not a member of the European Union (EU), the EU structural funds policy as well as national policies, all influence the dynamics, politics and result producing capacities of the Nordic regional networks.

The variables chosen to address the effectiveness of Nordic network governance all take the plural and wicked character of regional development policies into account. Rather than focusing on how networks are perceived as effective in communities of organisations, as in the implementation research by Milward and Provan (2001), the perceptions of network actors themselves are taken as a proxy of the effective functioning of the networks.

Nordic regional governance networks

The institutional contexts in Denmark, Finland, Norway and Sweden are to a large extent similar and the comparative analysis was undertaken with a 'most similar' design (Windhoff-Héritier 1993). All countries have a three-tier system and they share the same history of the Scandinavian Welfare state (Esping Andersen 1990). Furthermore there seems to be a 'common Scandinavian model' when it comes to meso-level government (Hansen 1993: 313). In all countries, state policies form a flexible 'shadow of hierarchy' (Scharpf 1994; Fotel and Hanssen 2009) and the regions (and local municipalities) are considered to implement, fill in and complement nationally defined and financed public welfare and service policies related to, for example, health, education and infrastructure (Halkier *et al.* 2008; Baldersheim *et al.* 2001; Sharpe 1993). The two main differences are that Norway is not a member of the European Union, and that while Norway, Sweden and Denmark have directly elected bodies on the regional level, in Finland the municipalities select their representatives for regional bodies (only the Kainuu-region has directly-elected bodies, which is an experiment).

While the regional level (sub-national/meso) has been strengthened elsewhere in Europe (Sharpe 1993), it is highly contested in Nordic countries. The Nordic regions are political-administrative units at sub-national level, and they are not necessarily defined by a long common history, identity or marked by a politically engaged citizenry. Recent research suggests that a business-inspired discourse tends to de-politicise Nordic regional development (Hall and Montin, 2007: 9), a fact that may reduce their effectiveness. Furthermore, the Nordic regions are dependent upon central government resources, several of the recent reforms have reduced their tasks, they lack legitimacy and their existence is often publicly debated (Mydske, Granlund and Disch 2006). These characteristics may reduce the effectiveness of regional networks; however, the issue has been surprisingly underexplored.

A comparative survey

A team of researchers from Norway, Finland, Sweden and Denmark carefully selected the networks included in the survey. The networks are all important bodies
responsible for formulating plans or programs for regional development and for
distributing a considerable amount of public and private funds. The programs,
plans and policies are first and foremost joint efforts to promote economic competitiveness through the coordination of a relatively fragmented governmental
structure. The Nordic tradition of including civil society actors in political decision-making (corporatism and pluralism) is reflected in the networks which all
include actors from the private and third sectors (Table 3.1).

The questionnaire was first written in English, and then translated to the respective Nordic languages. The average response rate was 34 percent. A non-response
analysis confirms the reliability of the data and illustrates that the respondents are
fairly representative for the total sample (see Appendix 1). However, despite the
general representativeness of the data, respondents may be inclined to be either
overly negative or overly positive of the governance network in question. This
inclination need not cause a comparative problem. As the survey addressed the

Table 3.1: Total universe of participants in the networks. Percent (actual numbers)
(Total N=1910)

	Denmark	Sweden*	Norway	Finland
State	0% (1)	10%	22% (63)	32% (145)
Regional politicians	45% (207)	4%	15% (42)	12% (55)
Regional administration	9% (40)	13%	15% (42)	–
Local level (total)	30% (137)	26%	15% (42)	21% (94)
Research and education		10%	8% (24)	4% (20)
Private and third sector	}16% (77)	25%	25% (74)	31% (140)
Other		10%		
Total Universe = 1910	100% (461)	100 (531 = 75% of total N = 708)	100% (287)	100% (454)
Response rate	36	38	28	30
Time of carrying out the survey	December 2007–January 2008	December 2007–January 2008	July–September 2007	August–November 2007

*   Due to problems having the actual frequencies of the total universe of the Swedish
     networks, the frequencies (in percent) are based on the Nutek survey of 2006, with a
     response rate of 75% (Airaksinen, 2009).

effectiveness of the respondent's own network-based efforts in regional policy, it can be assumed that there is a general inclination to positive self-evaluation in all of the countries. Still, future research could interestingly survey the attitudes of both network participants and external respondents in order to explicitly compare internal and external evaluations of regional network effectiveness.

In general, attitudinal surveys run the risk of 'individualistic fallacy' because individual perceptions do not necessarily represent a collective unit such as governance network (Peters 1998: 44). In order to cope with the fact that a variety of potential parameters influence the perceptions of the Nordic governance actors, the data analysis is sensitive to contextual dimensions. National research representatives carefully carried out the survey and addressed the contextual and institutional character of the specific regional governance arrangements in each of the countries. Based on this methodological sensitiveness, it appears that the attitudes of respondents generally reflect current policy discussions appearing in each of the countries, reported for instance in policy reports, the media and so forth. Hence, it can be assumed that the attitudes reported in the survey data reflect a representative understanding of the general regional policy dynamics.

The Finnish and Norwegian data contains a slight underrepresentation of the respondents representing politicians (both regional and local) and the Norwegian data further contains a slight over-representation of respondents from the state (most of them representing the 'regional state', i.e. the regional entities of state institutions, like the County Governor). In the Finnish dataset, there is an additional minor overrepresentation of research institutions, as well as the private and the third sectors. While all networks are composed of a plurality of public and private actors, the Danish networks have the highest number of politicians and almost no state-actors, while the Finnish networks include a high number of participants from the state and the private sectors (Table 3.1).

The analysis explores and compares network effectiveness with variables addressing both dynamics, politics and results *in* the networks and variables addressing the *external*, contextual regulation of the networks (see Appendix 2). The attitudes of respondents are related to both the individual country and to the institutional affiliation of the network participants. Results are discussed and explained with reference to both current policy contexts, the institutional characteristics of each governance network and the way the networks are metagoverned.

Special attention is paid to the ways that national cultures and political trajectories may influence the attitudes of network participants. Knudsen and Rothstein (1994) identify an interesting east-west divide amongst the Nordic countries, which is also confirmed by Jacobsson *et al.* (2004) and Sandberg and Ståhlberg (2000). Denmark (including Norway until 1814) has, on the one hand, a tradition of strong central minister control of individual policy areas which create strong, yet flexible, links between state and civil society. On the other hand, the political culture is also marked by a heritage of liberal individualism and self-reliant opposition to the state, which in part relates to the strong historical autonomy of the Danish peasantry. The Swedish trajectory (including Finland until 1809) is marked by a strong state-based 'paternalistic corporatism', which includes strong cabinets and autonomous central agencies independent of political bodies (Knudsen and Rothstein 1994: 218). This creates both fragmentation in public policies as well as a strict top-down definition of responsibilities and authorities on each level of the public sector, including the regional level (Sandberg and Ståhlberg 2000: 35).

Aspects of these national trajectories are reflected in the institutional dynamics of regional governance. The Nordic regional development networks have recently been discussed (Fotel and Hanssen 2009) and a short characteristic of institutional differences and similarities is provided below.

The *Finnish* respondents are participants in the Regional Management Committees (RMCs) in the nineteen Finnish regions. The Board of Regional Council appoints members to the RMC. The RMCs represent a highly regulated form of network working in the field of regional development. They are responsible for the coordinating and financing of the Regional Strategic Programs and they contribute to preparing the annual Implementation Plans. The composition, tasks and decision-making principles of the RMCs are highly related to their responsibility for executing EU programs. The RMC is made up of representatives from three equally important groups: the municipalities, state authorities and private and third sector representatives. The sample includes local and regional level politicians and administrators, administrators of regional state agencies, universities and third sector and private organisations.

The *Swedish* survey targeted participants in the regional public-private partnerships formulating Regional Growth Plans (RGPs) in each of the nineteen Swedish regions. The partnerships include all the dispersed actors that work with questions concerning sustainable growth. Hence, the sample includes private actors, representatives from the non-profit sectors and politicians and administrators at the local and regional levels and administrators in regional state agencies. The responsibility to develop and implement the Growth Programs lies within the entire partnership, but the partnership has no formal mandate to make decisions. Instead, each actor decides about different measures independently. This means that regional authorities have loyalties both within their sector (sometimes through a supervisory central authority) and *vis-à-vis* the other members in the partnership. County Administrative Boards, representing the state at the regional level, have by tradition been responsible for regional development activities, including programs of this kind. However, processes of regionalisation have spurred the formation of two political self-governing regions and a few regions with municipal co-operation bodies. These regions have inherited the responsibility for the Growth Program from the County Administrative Board.

In *Norway*, the survey addressed actors involved in the Regional Development Programs (RDPs) in the eighteen Norwegian regions. These programs are negotiated agreements and several actors are included in the process of formulating the annual program, as well as in financing and implementing the program. The RDPs include projects that are implemented and co-financed by a wider range of actors (such as entrepreneurial actors, universities, etc.). The Ministry of Local Government and Regional Development has given clear instructions about whom to invite into the programs and in practice the involvement is mandatory. Even though representation is regulated, the counties have the opportunity to include other actors as well. In some of the counties, politicians are included as participants in the networks; in others, they only 'ratify' the programs in the formal decision-making process in the county council or the county executive committee. Representatives from the county administration are always represented. With the exception of some of the networks having mayors from municipalities as participants, the networks are not linked to decision-making processes at the local level. However, municipalities can be central in implementing the projects in the RDPs.

The *Danish* respondents were participating in five important regional settings: The Regional Council, the Regional Forums for Growth, Health Coordination Networks and Municipal Contact Councils. Participants in these organisations as well as related administrators all interact in order to formulate regional development plans and policies. The tasks of the Regional Councils are defined in Law 65: 'Law on regions and on the dismantling of counties, the Capital's Development Council and the Capital's Hospital Community of June 9th 2005'. Regional Forums for Growth have been established by law in each of the regions to strengthen the industrial and commercial development across municipal boarders. The main tasks and the composition of the Regional Forums for Growth are defined in Law 602, 'The promotion of trade and industry'. Each forum is to consist of about twenty members, appointed by the respective Regional Councils. The Health Coordination Network involves representatives from the region, the municipalities in the region as well as professionals from the health sector. Its overall aim is to strengthen coordination and cooperation when dealing with public health. The role of municipalities in the area of regional policy has grown and local politicians participate in the Municipal Contact Councils (MCCs) in order to coordinate general policies affecting the individual municipalities in each region. The MCCs do not have the mandate to make formal decisions, but their recommendations are to be followed up by discussions in the Regional Council and the Municipal Councils.

This brief presentation of institutional characteristics at the regional level provides a contextual insight into each of the countries. The attitudinal data are rich and multifaceted; however, due to space limitations, the analysis below extracts only the most important comparative elements in order to characterise differences and similarities amongst the Nordic regions.

Perceptions of effectiveness

Individual variables measure how network participants in Denmark, Finland, Norway and Sweden, perceive the dynamics, the politics and the results of their networks (see Appendix 2). A series of correlation and factor analyses confirms the three assessment-criteria and all the data presented are highly significant, at the two-tailed $p = .000$ level. The analysis presents traditional frequencies and relates these to the individual country and the institutional affiliation of the network participants.

Effective network dynamics

The Nordic governance actors have several similar perceptions of the dynamics of their network and they are in general, satisfied with the plural composition of their regional network. Between 60 and 80 per cent state that if their networks should succeed in promoting regional development, then representatives of the main organisation of employers and wage earners, and representative research institutions and universities, must participate. The network participants report unanimously that they want to include the private sector and represent the interests of the private sector. However, more than two-thirds of the Finnish and Swedish participants experience that the private sector is not really interested in their network. Just one third of the respondents in Denmark and half of the respondents in Norway experience problems relating to the private sector.

The Nordic networks appear relatively flexible and about half of all the participants state that they are able to include participants from the outside their networks. However, the Swedish governance actors experience a comparatively higher degree of flexibility. The Danish, and especially the Finnish networks, are comparatively fixed in their composition. The Finnish networks are furthermore not able to define their own common goals and aims. Fifty-nine per cent report that the network has defined its own common goals and aims only 'to a little extent or not at all'. This contrasts with the network characteristics in all of the other Nordic countries.

A comparative evaluation of all the variables on network dynamics suggests that the Finnish networks receive a *low* score and the Norwegian a *high* score. The Norwegian networks are flexible when it comes to including new participants and they are able to define their own policy agendas. The Swedish and Danish networks are placed in between with a medium score in relation to effective dynamics. This verdict is based, amongst other things, on the fact that the Swedish networks have problems relating to the private sector and the Danish networks are relatively fixed in their composition.

Effective network politics

Data illustrates that the Nordic network participants have different attitudes towards the political atmosphere in their networks. About half of both public and private network participants in Denmark, Norway and Sweden agree that their network has the ability to set its own policy agenda. However, only one third of the Finnish actors state that their network has the ability to set its own agenda. Furthermore, 71 per cent of the Finnish respondents state that 'networks of this kind are primarily *practical instruments* for a specific purpose and should not be influenced by political considerations' and 58 per cent perceive their network to be marked by consensus. This characteristic reflects a *medium* degree of politics, ascribed to the fact that the Finnish regional management committees are highly regulated and appointed bodies having no direct political elections.

The Swedish networks are given a *low* score on the effectiveness of network politics. Half of the participants perceive that the work of the network is too focused on obtaining the consensus of all involved and the respondents are both private and public actors. Furthermore, half of the participants, including an equal share of public and private actors, experience that the members of the network have a too restricted mandate for effective decision-making. Only one fifth of the Norwegian and Danish network participants agree with that statement. Furthermore, nearly half of the Swedish participants find that the politics and the decision-making in the network do not reflect entrepreneurial interests.

The Danish and the Norwegian networks both score a comparatively *high* effectiveness. Very few of the network participants in both countries find that the networks have a restricted mandate and the interests of the business sector especially are reflected in the Danish network decisions. Only 12 per cent of the Danish participants and 39 per cent of the Norwegian agree with the statement that networks are practical instruments that should not be influenced by political considerations. While this indicates a very high level of political engagement, comparatively speaking, in the Danish networks a contradictory finding is that over half of the Danish networks actors and only one third of the Norwegian perceive the network to be too focused on obtaining the consensus of all involved.

Despite the minor differences reported above, it is plausible to suggest that the data reflects traces of an east-west divide in political cultures and administrative structure. The Danish and the Norwegian networks both have a high level of political contestation, while the Swedish and the Finnish have a medium-low level. This finding resembles the heritage of liberal political opposition in Denmark and the heritage of a more state-regulated and less oppositional political tradition in Sweden (Knudsen and Rothstein 1994).

Effective network results

A general puzzle in governance network research is how networks balance the need for an equal, agonistic dialogue amongst multiple participants and the need for a general management of the network – perhaps by the chairman? Networks can be managed using various toolkits (Kickert and Koppenjan 1999) and the general statement amongst the Nordic network participants is that their networks would be more effective in reaching objectives if they were controlled and guided by less top-heavy methods of management. This characterises the Finnish networks in particular, but also to a certain degree the Danish and the Swedish networks. Only 29 per cent of the Norwegian participants agree with the statement that indicates that they are either relatively satisfied with their ability to reach objectives and/or that they are managed using more horizontal methods.

The Nordic networks develop regional development policies, strategies and guidelines, and these results are related to a wide range of policy sectors and governmental levels. The networks are not implementing or delivering frontline services, but the data illustrates country-wide differences in the degree to which participants feel that they have control over the ways their policies are operationalised and carried out. While 58–61 per cent of the participants in Denmark and

Norwegian networks experience that they are generally able to influence the manner in which individual projects are carried out, only 27–30 per cent of Swedish and Finnish network participants have the same experience. Furthermore, the Swedish and Finnish network participants are the ones reporting the least control of the operational level.

The same tendency is reflected in the question of whether the network has an impact on regional development. The Danish and Norwegian actors are less likely to agree that their networks do *not* have an impact than their Swedish and Finnish counterparts. These country-wide differences reflect an east-west divide in the perceptions of network policy impact. The Danish heritage of political opposition leaves more scope for network policies, while the Swedish heritage of a greater state control creates a 'shadow of hierarchy', which produces less confidence in terms of network impact. The majority of the Norwegian respondents are state actors and the respondents in the three other countries are distributed fairly equally amongst both public and private actors and levels of government. The negative perception of network impact amongst Norwegian state actors might reflect a previously identified rivalry amongst multilevel actors in the Norwegian regional development policies (Mydske *et al.* 2006). In conclusion, the effectiveness of network results is *high* in Norway and Denmark and *low* in Finland and Sweden. Furthermore, the data suggests that a high degree of network politics is most likely to produce a high degree of perceived network results.

Contextual variables and effectiveness

The model outlined above suggests the effectiveness of contemporary governance to be assessed by addressing dimensions of network dynamics, network politics and network results. Based on the above analysis, the following verdict concerning the Nordic regional governance networks can be reached:

Table 3.2: Individual assessment and total score of effectiveness in Nordic regional governance networks

	Dynamics	Politics	Results	Total score
High effectiveness	NO	DK, NO	DK, NO	DK, NO
Medium effectiveness	DK, FI	FI		FI
Low effectiveness	SV	SV	FI, SV	SV

All the networks solve important tasks in their countries, but the comparative analysis did reveal three general challenges related to the effectiveness of politics and results in especially the east-Nordic networks, the character of external regulation and the relations to the private sector.

Traces of the east-west divide have been identified especially in relation to the character of network politics and network results. Here, the Danish and Norwegian networks scored relatively high and Swedish and Finnish networks scored relatively low. This reflects the previously identified historic tradition of a more liberal autonomous political atmosphere in Denmark (and Norway until 1814) and a more paternalistic state in Sweden (and Finland until 1809).

An important remaining question concerns the relations between network effectiveness and the contextual regulation of the networks, in particular how the networks are metagoverned and influenced by current policy contexts. In general, the data shows that 47 per cent of all the participants want political representatives to be more involved with the work of the networks. This reflects a wish amongst the network actors to improve the regional democratic deficits, also described in recent research reports (Mydske *et al.* 2006). The perspective is common amongst both public and private actors in Norway and Sweden, however this is stated primarily by the Danish regional politicians themselves. While the reform of Danish local government in 2007 left very little authority to regional governments, data reflects that the regional politicians want to have a more central role. Interestingly, it is mainly the Finnish participants from the private sector who want to see greater involvement on behalf of the politicians. Current debates in Finland are concerned with the need to introduce direct elections to the regional management committees (Hall *et al.* 2009: 519). Direct elections may reduce the shadow of a 'paternalistic state' and dissolve the east-west divide in terms of political cultures as a valid explanation of differences amongst the Nordic countries.

Metagovernance and a certain 'shadow of hierarchy' is said to be decisive for network governance effectiveness (Sharpf 1994: 40; Sørensen and Torfing 2009). Several metagovernance tools are suitable for influencing the effective performance and democratic potentials of local networks. Metagovernors are able to design, frame and manage networks to varying degrees (Sørensen and Torfing 2009: 248). However, as data suggests, the Nordic network participants also feel troubled by external regulations.

Danish network participants experience the strongest national government restrictions amongst the Nordic countries and the majority of Danish participants say that the capacity of their network is dependent on a framework decided by national politicians. This finding is slightly contradictory to previous celebrations of autonomous Danish local networks (Bogason, 1996) and to the east-west characteristics, but the finding may be contextually influenced by the top-down implementation of the 2007 local government reform. The reform created frustrations on behalf of the politicians as they found their scope of action heavily circumscribed (Christiansen and Klitgaard 2008; Blom-Hansen *et al.* 2008).

Nearly half of the Swedish participants also experience strong restrictions from the national state and they are the only Nordic actors who say that their networks are significantly restricted by EU regulations. The statements are primarily made by Swedish private actors, probably signalling their opposition both to the strong state-led partnership model in Sweden (Östhol and Svensson 2002: 241) and to the enrollment of the Swedish regionalisation in the functional European development policies (Mydske *et al.* 2006: 42; Karlsson *et al.* 2009: 30).

Norwegian public and private partners both experience that regional politicians set the capacity of their networks, but the participating state actors, in particular, have a minimal trust in network policy impact. These findings reflect the previous identification of a certain rivalry between state and regional actors in Norwegian regional development policies (Mydske *et al.* 2006: 34).

The findings confirm that metagovernance by regional, national or European politicians regulate regional governance networks in various ways. It is plausible to suggest that fewer restrictions and regulations coming from national politicians in Norway, Denmark and Sweden would produce an even higher effectiveness of regional governance in those countries. The Swedish respondents are troubled by EU regulations, a fact which may be bettered by future initiatives from regional and national Swedish metagovernors. Finland is the only country in which participants are not significantly troubled by any external regulation. The finding is surprising, but may be subscribed to the fact that the *comme il faut* (acting in accordance with convention) of the participants in the Finnish regional management committees is to be highly regulated both in their composition and their tasks (Kettunen *et al.* 2007: 5; Neubauer 2007: 74).

Finally, metagovernance may be a tool with which the relations between the regional networks and the private sector can be improved. As regional development is often enrolled in discourses of innovations and economic competitiveness (Bache and Olsson 2001; Hall and Montin 2007), it is surprising that almost all regional governance actors report it as being very problematic to include the private sector in their politics and policies. The Danish networks are relatively better at including the private sector, which reflects historic traditions of local public-private partnerships (Östhol and Svensson 2002: 242). Metagovernance may be a tool with which national and regional politicians would be able to improve relations to the private sector. This can be done, for instance, by either legal incentives or softer regulations of the regulative, normative and cognitive framework that guide the regional governance dynamics. An improved inclusion of the private sector would most likely produce a knock-on effect concerning the general effectiveness of regional development policies.

Tangible effectiveness

While the international literature on network governance presupposes an *a priori* effectiveness of network based policies, few attempts to actually measure effectiveness have been made. The complexity of public governance networks entails that traditional models of cost-effectiveness or Pareto-optimal allocations of costs and benefits cannot be applied. Instead, this chapter suggested a three-dimensional, generally applicable model with the three assessment criteria reflecting effective dynamics, effective politics and effective results. Including variables addressing the contextual regulation of governance networks provide a full picture of their effective capacity.

While the Nordic countries belong to the same Nordic state tradition and provide 'an almost complete "most-similar-systems" research design' (Blom-Hansen 2000: 178), the current analysis illustrates, however, several differences in the perceptions of network effectiveness amongst the Nordic countries. Most notably, traces of the east-west divide have been identified in relation to the character of network politics and network results. Danish and Norwegian networks scored relatively high and Swedish and Finnish networks scored relatively low on the assessment criteria of politics and results. These results confirm the previously identified historic tradition of a more liberal autonomous political atmosphere in Denmark (and Norway until 1814) and a more paternalistic state in Sweden (and Finland until 1809).

Furthermore, the careful contextual analysis of variables targeting the complex, plural and multilevel character of regional governance in the north illustrates that the institutional regulation of the networks differs. Due to their formal institutional regulation and the ways that metagovernance influence their policy context, not all of the networks have the possibility of being equally autonomous, self-regulated and effective performers. The analysis of the dynamics, politics and results related to regional governance, however, also illustrates that metagovernance may be a tool that can amplify and strengthen its effectiveness.

The current analysis of Nordic regional governance networks contributes to filling in the identified lacuna of comparative research amongst the Nordic countries (Blom-Hansen 2000: 178). While much has been said about effectiveness in the international governance network literature, little has actually been done in terms of measuring this concept. The model and the results outlined in this chapter suggest that the effectiveness of comparative regional governance is multi-faceted and highly relevant to further investigations.

Appendix

1. Non-response analysis[1]

Appendix: Tables with non-response analysis of the countries

Denmark	Sample	Answered	Not answered	Representation in the Nordic survey	Response rate
Administrator (local and regional)	40	18	22	11%	45%
Municipal politicians	137	116	228	70%	34%
Regional politicians	207				
Private or other actors	77	31	46	19%	40%
Total	461	165	296	100%	

---

1. A similar non-response analysis appears in Fotel and Hanssen 2009.

Norway	Sample	Average representation in the networks studied	Answered	Representation in the Nordic survey	Response rate by group
Municipalities	42	15%	10	12%	24%
County government administrators	42	15%	12	15%	29%
County government politicians	42	15%	6	7%	14%
Regional state agencies	63	22%	25	31%	40%
Universities and research organisations	24	10%	5	6%	21%
Organisations of employers and employees (LO/ NHO)	28	8%	16	20%	57%
Other interest organisations	42	15%	6	8%	14%
The Norwegian Association of Local and Regional Authorities (KS)	4	1%	1	1%	25%
Total	287	101%	81	100%	

Sweden	Nutek survey 2006	Nordic Survey 2007	Difference
Local Government	20,8	20,1	-0,7
County Administrative Board	12,4	11,2	-1,2
Local Government Cooperative Body	8,6	5,9	-2,7
Business Organisation	8,6	10,0	1,4
University	7,0	9,7	2,7
County Labor Market Board	5,8	5,2	-,06
Interest Organisation	4,9	4,1	-0,8
Trade Union	4,7	4,8	-0,1
County Council	4,4	5,6	1,2
Municipal Association	4,4	2,6	-1,8
ALMI	4,2	3,3	-1,1
Private Company	2,8	5,2	2,4
Regional Self Government Body	1,6	3,0	1,4
Other Organisation	9,8	9,3	-0,5
Total	100	100	

Finland	Sample	Average representation in the network studied	Answered	Representation in the Nordic survey	Response rate by group
State agency	145	33%	49	36%	33%
Regional council	55		17		
Municipalities	94	33%	15	23%	21%
University and research organisation	20		3		
Private company	60	33%	5	41%	36%
Association	80		49		
Total	454	99%	138	100%	

2. Survey variables addressing different dimensions of network effectiveness

Dynamics

- The main organisations of employers and wage earners in the regions must take part if the networks are to succeed in promoting regional development.
- Networks of this kind must involve research institutions and universities if they are to succeed in promoting regional development.
- The problem with networks of this kind is that the private sector is not really interested in them.
- The network has the ability to include new participants from outside.
- The network has own common goals and aims which it has defined itself.

Politics

- The network has the ability to set its own policy agenda.
- Networks of this kind are primarily practical instruments for a specific purpose and should not be influenced by political considerations.
- The work of the network is too much focused on obtaining the consensus of all involved.
- The members of the network have a too restricted mandate for efficient decision-making.
- Decision-making in the network does not really reflect regional business interests very well.

Results

- The objectives of the network could be obtained in a more efficient manner by less top-heavy methods of management.
- The regional network has little control over what happens at the operational level.
- The regional network is usually able to influence the manner in which individual projects are carried out.
- The network does not have a great impact on regional development.
- The objectives of the network could be obtained in a more efficient manner with fewer participants.

Policy context

- Political representatives should be more involved with the work of the network.
- The network works under strong national restrictions.

- The network works under strong European restrictions.
- The capacity of the network is dependent on a framework decided by national politicians.
- The capacity of the network is dependent on a framework decided by politicians at the regional level.

References

Airaksinen, J. (2009) *Survey Report: Nordic survey on Regional Network Governance.* Working paper, Series 2009:2, Center for Democratic Network Governance, Roskilde: Roskilde University.

Amin, A. (1999) 'An Institutionalist Perspective on Regional Economic Development', *International Journal of Urban and Regional Research*, 23: 365–78.

Bache, I. and Olsson. J. (2001) 'Legitimacy through partnerships? EU policy diffusion in Britain and Sweden', *Scandinavian Political Studies*, 24: 215–37.

Baldersheim, H. S., Sandberg, K., Ståhlberg and Øgard. M. (2001) *Norden i regionernas Europa*, Nord 2001: 18 Copenhagen: Nordic Council.

Blom-Hansen, J. (2000) 'Still corporatism in Scandinavia? A survey of recent empirical findings', Review article, *Scandinavian Political Studies*, 23 (2): 157–81.

Bogason, P. (1996) *New Modes of Local Organizing: Local Government Fragmentation in Scandinavia*, New York: Nova Science Publishers Inc.

— (2006) 'Networks and Bargaining in Policy Analysis', in G. Peters and J. Pierre (eds) *Handbook of Public Policy*, London: Sage Publications.

Börzel, T. A. and Panke, D. (2007) 'Network governance: effective and legitimate?', in E. Sørensen and J. Torfing (eds) *Theories of Democratic Network Governance*, Basingstoke: Palgrave-Macmillan, 153–168.

Christiansen, P. and Klitgaard, M. (2008) *Den utænkelige reform. Strukturreformens tilblivelse 2002-2005*, Odense: University Press of Southern Denmark.

Esping-Andersen, G. (1990) *The Three Worlds of Welfare Capitalism*, Cambridge: Polity Press.

Fotel, T. and Hanssen, G. S. (2009) 'Meta-Governance of Regional Governance Networks in Nordic Countries', *Local Government Studies, New Network Modes of Nordic Local Governance*, 35 (5): 557–76.

Halkier, H., Bukve, O. and de Souza, P. (eds) (2008) *Towards New Nordic Regions: Politics, Administration and Regional Development*, Aalborg: Aalborg Universitetsforlag.

Hall, P. and Montin, S. (2007) *Governance networks and democracy at regional and local level in Sweden*, Working paper 2007:9, Center for Democratic Network Governance, Roskilde: Roskilde University.

Hall, P. *et al.* (2009) 'Is there a Nordic approach to questions of democracy in studies of network governance?', *Local Government Studies, New Network Modes of Nordic Local Governance*, 35 (5): 515–38.

Hansen, T. (1993) 'Appendix: Meso Government in Denmark and Sweden', in L. Sharpe (ed.) *The Rise of Meso Government in Europe*, London: Sage Publications.

Jacobsson, B., Lægreid, B. and Pedersen, O. K. (2004) *Europeanization and Transnational States: Comparing Nordic Central Governments*, London: Routledge.

Jessop, B. (2003) *The Future of the Capitalist State*, Cambridge: Polity Press.

Karlsson, A., Lindström, B. and Van Well, L. (2009) 'Mot den tredje generationens regionpolitik', *Nordregio Report 2009*, 1, Stockholm.

Keating, M., Loughlin, J. and Deschouwer, K. (2003) *Culture, Institutions, and Economic Development: A Study of Eight European Regions*, Cheltenham: Edward Elgar.

Kickert, W. J. M. and Koppenjan, J. F. M. (1999) Public Management and Network Management: An overview', in J. M. Walter, J. M. Kickert, E-H. Klijn and J. F. M. Koppenjan (eds) *Managing Complex Networks: Strategies for the Public Sector*, London: Sage Publications.

Koppenjan, J. F. M. and Klijn, E. -H. (2006) *Managing Uncertainties in Networks: A network approach to problem solving and decision making*, London: Routledge.

Kettunen, P., Haveri, A., Nyholm, I., Pehk, T. and Anttiroiko, A-V. (2007) *Network Governance at Regional and Local Level in Finland*, Working paper 2007:7, Centre for Democratic Network Governance, Roskilde: Roskilde University.

Knudsen, T. and Rothstein, B. (1994) 'State building in Scandinavia', *Comparative Politics*, 26 (2): 203–220.

Peters, G. (1998) *Comparative Politics*, New York: Palgrave.

—   (2007) 'Virtuous and vicious circles in democratic network governance', in E. Sørensen and J. Torfing (eds) *Theories of Democratic Network Governance*, Basingstoke: Palgrave Macmillan.

Provan, K. and Kenis, P. (2007) 'Modes of network governance: Structure, management, and effectiveness', *Journal of Public Administration Research and Theory*, August (2): 1–24.

Provan, K. and Milward, B. (1995) 'A preliminary theory of interorganizational network effectiveness: A comparative study of four community mental health systems', *Administrative Science Quarterly*, 40 (1): 1–33.

—   (2001) 'Do networks really work? A framework for evaluating public-sector organizational networks', *Public Administration Review*, 61 (4): 414–23.

Mouffe, C. (2005) *On the Political*, Abingdon: Routledge.

Mydske, P. K., Granlund T. O. and Disch, P. D. (2006) 'Den politiske regionen – før og nå', in P. K. Mydske (ed.) *Skandinaviske regioner – plass for politikk?*, Bergen: Fagbokforlaget.

Neubauer, J. *et al.* (2007) *Regional Development in the Nordic Counties*, Stockholm: Nordregio.

Rhodes, R. A. W. (2000) 'The governance narrative: Key findings and lessons from the ESRC's

—   Whitehall programme', *Public Administration*, 78 (2): 345–63.

Sagan, I. and Halkier, H. (eds) (2005) *Regionalism Contested: Institution, Society and Governance*, Aldershot: Ashgate.

Sandberg, S. and Ståhlberg, K. (2000) *Nordisk regionalförvaltning i förändring*, Åbo: Åbo Akademis tryckeri.

Scharpf, F. W. (1994) 'Games real actors could play: Positive and negative coordination in embedded negotiations', *Journal of Theoretical Politics*, 6 (1): 27–53.

Sharpe, L. (ed.) (1993) *The Rise of Meso Government in Europe*, Sage Modern Politics Series, London: Sage Publications.

Östhol, A. and Svensson, B. (2002) 'Conclusions on Regional Partnership and Institutional Change in the Nordic Area', in A. Ôsthol and B. Svensson (eds) *Partnership Responses – Regional Governance in the Nordic states*, Stockholm: Nordregio Report 2002: 6.

Statskontoret, (2007) *Joining-up for Regional Development. How Governments Deal with a Wicked Problem, Overlapping Policies and Fragmented Responsibilities*, Statskontoret 2007:2, Stockholm: Statskontoret.

Sørensen, E. (2006) 'Metagovernance: The changing roles of politicians in processes of democratic governance', *American Review of Public Administration*, 36 (1): 98–114.

Sørensen, E. and Torfing, J. (2007) 'Theoretical Approaches to Governance Network Failure', in E. Sørensen and J. Torfing (eds), *Theories of Democratic Network Governance*, Basingtoke: Palgrave Macmillan.

— (2009) 'Making governance networks effective and democratic through metagovernance', *Public Administration*, 87 (2): 234–58.

Weber, E. P. and Khademian, A. M. (2008) 'Wicked problems, knowledge challenges, and collaborative capacity builders in network settings', *Public Administration Review*, 68 (2): 334–349.

Windhoff-Héritier, A. (1993) 'Policy Network Analysis: A Tool for Comparative Political Research in Comparative Politics', in Hans Keman (ed.) *New Directions in Theory and Method*, Amsterdam: VU University Press.

chapter | europeanisation of employment
four | polity – changing partnership
| inclusion in denmark, great
| britain and france

Anders Esmark

Europeanisation against the odds

Building on the framework of Europeanisation research (Cowles *et al.* 2001; Héritier *et al.* 2001; Featherstone and Radaelli 2003; Graziano and Vink 2008), this chapter presents a study of the Europeanisation of national employment polity in Denmark, Great Britain and France, placing particular emphasis on the inclusion of private interest organisations in the formulation and implementation of national employment policy. The key question is whether the existence of a common European Employment Strategy (EES) within the European Union (EU) pursued through the regulatory framework of the Open Method of Coordination (OMC) has been able to change national employment polity with respect to partnership inclusion.

The main conclusion of the study is that important Europeanisation effects can be observed in terms of the extent to which labor market organisations perceive the EES and OMC as an important policy arena and in terms of governmental approaches to partnership inclusion. The direction and specific content the observed changes include trends that can be interpreted as approximation to EU norms leading to a certain level of convergence, in particular with respect to social dialogue and the role of social partners, as well as trends that are distinctly country-specific and dependent on national traditions, suggesting a differential impact on national institutions and procedures.

The pervasiveness of europeanisation

The extent of changes in partnership inclusion found in the conducted study gives reason to reconsider the ability of EU norms to change national policy. Europeanisation studies tend to focus mainly on the ability of the EU to generate national policy change, including studies of the EES and the OMC, which have focused on the overall potential for policy learning (De La Porte and Pochet 2002; Mosher and Trubek 2003; Nedergaard 2006; Kerber and Eckhardt 2007; Mabett 2007; Hartlapp 2009) and the effects on overall welfare policy and labour market reforms (Zeitlin, Pochet and Magnusson 2005; Büchs 2007; Heidenreich and Zeitlin 2009) or specific policy areas such as social inclusion (Atkinson, Marlier and Nolan, 2004; Dieckhoff and Gallie 2007; Marlier *et al.* 2007), pension policy (Vanhercke

2009), childcare (Weishaupt 2009) and gender equality (Braams 2007; Liebert 2008). Correspondingly, most studies implicitly exclude the impact of the EES on national polity or deal with such impact only as an indirect effect of policy change.

In order to measure the impact of EES on national employment partnerships, the study relies on a widely-used distinction between three levels of change inspired by (neo-)institutional theory:

1. A low degree of domestic change called 'absorption', suggesting that member states find ways to incorporate changes into existing structures.
2. Modest to significant changes labelled 'accommodation', which imply modification of existing policies and institutions, as well as the addition of new policies and institutions, leaving the essential features of the national political system untouched.
3. Paradigmatic change, or transformation, i.e. wholesale changes of the constitutive institutions, procedures, strategies and beliefs of the political system in question (Börzel and Risse 2000 2003).

In the case of partnership inclusion, the overall typology can be specified along the following dimensions:

1. The range of included interests, which pertains to the number and type of non-state organisations granted the status of partners and included in the formulation and/or implementation of national employment policy.
2. The role of included interests: in contrast to the number and type of specific organisations included, this dimension involves changes in the role of included interests in the field of employment, such as approximation to the role of social partner.
3. The level of participation, which pertains to the extent and institutional forms of integrating partners in public policy making. In this dimension, changes can be seen as shifts upwards or downwards 'the ladder of participation' (Arnstein 1969; Fung and Wright 2001; Fung 2006), ranging from information procedures limited to keeping partners briefed about actions and decisions by state actors to consultation and hearings and further to deliberation, through which partners gain the possibility of influencing political strategies and decisions more thoroughly through open debate, and finally to delegation, where partners obtain a level of autonomous responsibility for the development and/or implementation of policy through various forms of corporation with state actors such as corporatist procedures and governance networks.

Moreover, changes can be identified on the side of labour markets organisations and other societal interests as well as on the side of government and state actors. In the first case, the issue is to what extent EES and the OMC is interpreted by labour markets organisations and other societal interests as a relevant policy framework, i.e. the extent to which the EES and OMC are seen as a important additions to existing frameworks of interaction with state and government actors, either reinforcing existing channels of influence or providing additional opportunities otherwise not present. In the second case, the question is to what extent state and government actors perceive and use the OMC and the EES as an opportunity to change existing mechanisms of inclusion of interaction with labour markets organisations and other societal interest groups.

Empirically, the analysis of changes in both of these dimensions relies on a combination of document analysis of key governmental documents, primarily the so-called National Action Plans (NAPs) and the National Reform Programmes (NRPs). Being government reports, the NAPs and NRPs are, of course, subject to the same level of strategic purpose, limitations and potential omissions as other governmental sources. In particular, the nature of the subject makes such documents liable to overemphasise the inclusion and impact of external partners in order to suggest compliance with EU norms. However, the documents are used primarily for fact-finding in terms of included interests and specific inputs from labour markets organisations, which lessens concerns about bias or deliberate omissions to a considerable degree. In general, both NAPs and NRPs provide rather factual overviews of the range and role of the included interests as well as the method of inclusion that fall well within the standards of credibility usually attested to governmental sources in the three included countries.

The analysis is based on interviews with representatives from the key labour and management organisations in the three included countries, providing a control to the use of government reports and better insight into the perspective of labour market organisations. By agreement with the interviewees, these are represented by institutional position only. Whereas NAPs and NRPs may tend to overemphasise inclusion of partners, sources from the partner side can be seen to have vested interests in downplaying inclusion in order to state claims for strengthened inclusion. Such bias has been countered by giving priority to factual questions about specific processes and forums of interaction as well as cross-checking with government sources. In order to provide an external check, however, the analysis also relies on three independent national expert reports commissioned for the study. The experts were asked to give their written assessments of the key issues of the study such as the importance attested to the EES guidelines and the NAP, and NRP processes, the inclusion and role of partners, key developments and decisive factors, etc. The experts were from a mix of scientific and governmental backgrounds, selected by their contributions to existing reports on employment policy in the three countries. The experts were granted anonymity in the presentation of the results in order to minimise the influence of personal concerns on the assessments given.

Procedural and substantive norms of the EES

To determine the level and substance of the direct and indirect pressure on national policy to adapt, I briefly survey the procedural and substantive norms of the European Employment Strategy (EES). 'Procedural norms' can be defined as: the basic rules of the decision-making framework put in place to aid the realisation of the strategic goals and targets of the EES. Procedural norms pertain directly to policy, including the identification of included actors, their roles and competences, sequencing of their interaction, time-frames, expected inputs, etc. 'Substantive norms' can be defined as: constitutive ideas and perceptions about the fundamental policy problems, solutions, goals, values and objectives of a policy domain, thus constituting a source of indirect pressure on national policy.

Procedural norms

The basic set of procedural norms related to the EES is that of the Open Method of Coordination (OMC). The OMC was introduced as the foundation for the EES by articles 128 and 129 of the Amsterdam Treaty and elaborated by the Luxembourg meeting in 1997 and the Lisbon summit in 2000, inspired by existing procedure for coordination of the macro-economic policies of the member states. The core of the OMC is coordination of national policy based on guidelines, performance indicators, benchmarks and identification of best practice. Between 1998 and 2004, the OMC required member states to submit National Action Plans (NAPs) to the European Commission each year, outlining the development of national employment policy in relation to the guidelines and indicators of the EES, based on which the Commission submits recommendations. Following a major overhaul of the EES in 2005, the NAPs were substituted by three-year National Reform Programs (NRPs) covering a more extensive policy portfolio than the NAPs, which were concerned specifically with employment policy. Currently, member states are operating within the 2008–10 NRP, following the 2005–08 NRP.

The procedural details and raison d'être of the OMC have been discussed extensively elsewhere. In terms of adaptational pressure, the core of the OMC is that it requires member states to perform self-evaluation of national policy within the targets and benchmarks defined by the EES. Insofar as the OMC can be interpreted as a procedure for self-evaluation, it is in fact relatively indifferent to the inclusion of non-governmental partners. The subjects of the OMC are the national governments. The EES is, however, also supported by two other procedural arrangements: social dialogue and broad stakeholder inclusion.

Social dialogue has been wedded to the EES since the Amsterdam Treaty, which states that the Commission shall 'consult with management and labour' in 'fulfilling its mandate' of monitoring national employment policy (art. 130). Social dialogue has a much longer history in the EU than the OMC, beginning with informal joint declarations by ETUC and UNICE (now BusinessEurope) in the 1980s and subsequent acknowledgement of their role in the social protocol annexed to the Maastricht Treaty. The Amsterdam Treaty further institutionalised the role of the so-called social partners and formalised tripartite consultation (art. 138) and a procedure for reaching binding agreements at the EU level in the area of social policy (art. 139). Mirroring such provisions for social dialogue at the EU level, the procedural norms of the EES called for increased interaction between government and social partners at the national level since its inception (Council Resolution OJ C30). Building on this basic premise, the procedural norms put forward by the EU have increasingly emphasised the importance of pursuing social dialogue not only at the EU level, but also at the national and the local levels of governance (European Commission 2007a).

Finally, the EES involves a set of procedural norms for *broad stakeholder inclusion*. Stakeholder inclusion derives neither from the OMC nor from social dialogue, but most significantly from the highly influential white paper on European Governance from 2001 (COM (2001) 428). In contrast to social dialogue, the stakeholder approach involves 'representatives of civil society' in general (Council Decision 2001/63/EC) and 'all actors' that might contribute to the overall goals of the EES' (European Commission 2007a). In contrast to the role of the social partners, the role of stakeholders is not based on labour market relations and established prerogatives within specific policy areas, but rather dependent on the specific policy problems and intended solutions, making stakeholder inclusion more variable as well as potentially more inclusive than social dialogue.

Substantive norms

Operating within the framework introduced by the Amsterdam Treaty, and from the year 2000 by the Lisbon summit, to make the EU the most competitive world economy, the substantive norms of the EES have been organised in terms of general and specific guidelines and a growing number of indicators and benchmarks. The guidelines have been modified and reshuffled since first adopted (Council Resolution OJ C30), but the only major reform occurred in 2005. Following the widespread recognition that the goals of the Lisbon strategy were not being met, the EES was overhauled and integrated with the Broad Economic Policy Guidelines (BEPGs) to form the 'Integrated Guidelines for Growth and Jobs' (European Commission 2005). Currently, the EES consists of guidelines 17–24 of the integrated guidelines (European Commission 2007b).

In contrast to studies of policy change, the focus here is not so much on the content of the EES guidelines and their impact on national policy as on the indirect effects on national policy. In this respect, two aspects are important. First, the EES, in particular since the 2005 reform including the employment guidelines in the general set of BEPGs, has a different policy configuration than in the national setting. As such, the BEPGs generate a need for coordination between employment policy and other policy fields that may or may not be strongly integrated in the national setting. Moreover, the policy configuration at the EU involves a certain hierarchy of policies that may also have effects on the responsible institutions at the national level. The 2005 reform embedded the EES in a macro-economic paradigm focused on competitiveness and innovation. This development has been under way since the Lisbon Treaty, but the 2005 reform shifted the balance decisively towards macro-economic policy, essentially making the EES part of macro-economic policy, although formally still consisting of guidelines presented side by side with BEPGs.

Denmark – cracks in the tradition of labour market corporatism

Denmark is widely regarded as an exemplar of labour market corporatism, granting substantial autonomy to labour and management in the area of wage formation and including both parties in all significant decisions on employment policy through permanent or ad hoc tripartite bodies. On the side of labour, the peak organisation is the Danish Confederation of Trade Unions (LO), whereas the side of management is centred on the Confederation of Danish Employers (DA). The strong tradition of labour market corporatism makes it an important feature of the Danish case that the 'normal condition' already provides labour market organisations with much more extensive influence than suggested by the procedural norms underpinning the Open Method of Coordination (OMC).

Although structurally similar, social dialogue can be said to grant the social partners a less decisive role than established labour market relations in Denmark. In other words, the European Employment Strategy adds up to less than what Danish labour market organisations already have. Consequently, both labour and management have remained cautious about social dialogue and the terminology of social partners based on the stance that social dialogue provides much more rudimentary consultation procedures than the fully-developed bipartite and tripartite negotiation of the Danish model.

Although the European Employment Strategy (EES) is not seen to provide new or better channels of influence, it is none the less recognised as a relevant policy framework included in the ongoing policy development of the labour market organisations and the existing mechanisms of bipartite and tripartite negotiation. Although both labour and management remain adamant that labour market policy is first and foremost determined by national arenas and national strategies, the EES is recognised as a policy framework actively included in such arenas and strategies (Interview 1: 31–40, Interview 2: 1289–93). More specifically, management and labour recognise EES guidelines as a reference point for broader policy debates and policy development as well as a subject for reaching specific and binding agreements through the existing mechanisms of the Danish model (Danish Government, 2007, 2008).

This development is not particular to Denmark as labour and management as in most member states are at some level engaged in the national initiatives relevant to the EES (De la Porte and Pochet 2005). In the Danish case, involvement in implementation of the EES has, however, been extensive. EES guidelines have become an integrated part of the policy framework of bipartite and tripartite interactions and have even made it into the heart of the Danish model insofar as the implications of the yearly binding settlements are now systematically analysed in terms of EES implications (Danish Government 2007, 2008). Through this development, labour and management have also expanded their policy profiles to accommodate the policy configuration of the EES, in particular with respect to the integration of social policy and employment policy.

As is well known from the general debate on corporatism, the privileged position of certain organisations often means that other less resourceful groups find it difficult to gain access to relevant policy arenas. Danish labour market corporatism is no exception in this respect, meaning that the representative monopoly of the labour organisations are far from always seen as beneficial from the perspective of other groups attempting to state alternative claims to representation. For the latter, the procedural norms of wider stakeholder inclusion and especially the different policy configuration on the EU level can be seen as providing an opportunity structure for gaining access and breaking the representative monopoly of the labour market organisations. Although the EES has clearly not generated a paradigmatic break with Danish labour market corporatism, it is worth noting that it has led to certain cracks in the representative monopoly of the labour market organisations.

The most immediate expression of this tendency is the establishment of a commission (*kontaktudvalget*) charged with the overall coordination of all policy initiatives pertaining to the EES guidelines and later the BEPGs in 2001. This commission is in itself an institutional innovation and additional to the existing institutional arrangement underpinning Danish EU policy, established as a direct response to the OMC based on the premise that the particular nature of the OMC requires a broad coordinating forum not provided by existing institutions. Given the central position of the Commission, membership can be interpreted as the most sign of inclusion in the range of interests deemed relevant to the OMC (Danish Government 2010). As such, the fact the membership is extended not only to labour markets organisations, but also to organisations such as Greenpeace, the Organisation of Danish Youth and the Danish Council of Disabled People, provides an important widening of interests to be included beyond the representative monopoly of labour market organisations.

Among this wider array of institutions the Danish Council of Disabled People seems to have been most successful in also providing specific policy inputs to the National Reform Programmes (Danish Government 2005, 2008). Perhaps not so surprisingly, the widening of included interests has met with some resistance from the labour market organisations. In general, both labour and management see themselves as holding a legitimate representative monopoly and emphasise that any inclusion of additional interest should only be seen as ad hoc inclusion of highly particular interests not to be confused with the established prerogatives of the Danish model (Interview 1: 489–94, Interview 2: 237–40). However, it remains clear that the particular policy configuration of the EES combined with the norms of broader stakeholder inclusion has led to a widening of included interests in spite of the stance taken by the labour market organisation.

A key issue in this respect is the extent to which the widening of included interest is part of a more fundamental development towards a weakening of management and labour. As mentioned, the 2005 reform at the EU enveloped EES in the BEPGs, effectively subjecting employment policy to the overall macro-economic framework. Responding to the overall macro-economic focus of the integrated guidelines, control of the National Reform Programmes (NRPs) was placed in the Ministry of Finance, providing the Ministry with a long sought-after role in Danish EU policy at the cost of the Ministry of Employment as well as the Ministry of Foreign Affairs, the traditional coordinator of Danish EU policy (Interview 3: 510–11). However, the Ministry of Finance has no tradition of social dialogue or any other form of stakeholder involvement, perceiving such mechanisms as completely unnecessary for proper macro-economic policy development (Interview 4: 770–2).

Although labour and management retain existing levels of inclusion with the Ministry of Employment, the fact that the Ministry of Finance takes on the role of controller in relation to the BEPGs and the NRPs has lead to a diminished role for the labour market organisations. This concern, or rather conclusion, is expressed most directly by labour (Interview 2: 23–5), whereas management seems rather to insist that other avenues of influence provide sufficient opportunities to counter the loss of inclusion generated by the approach to policy development pursued by the Ministry of Finance (Interview 1: 619–23).

In sum, the EES and OMC may not have yielded a full-scale paradigmatic break with the much heralded Danish model, but the widening and weakening of interest inclusion none the less suggests changes in procedures and institutional balances concomitant with the notion of accommodation. On the one hand, the initial absorption of EES and OMC into existing bipartite and tripartite arrangements has been supplemented by the addition of new institutions, such as '*kontaktudvalget*', which are designed to include a wider set of interests. On the other hand, the 2005 reform provided the Ministry of Finance with the opportunity to take on the role as controller and exercise this role based on a highly adversarial stance towards involvement of other actors. As such, the widening of included interests by no means suggest that other social interests are also included on the level traditionally afforded the labour market organisations, but rather that the overall framework of inclusion tends to reduce the level of participation, relying more on limited consultations and hearings than stable networks of interaction.

Great Britain – social partners among stakeholders

It seems uncontroversial to claim that the British case is an example of a relatively pluralistic and pragmatic approach to policy development and implementation, at least when compared to the strong tradition of labour market corporatism in the Danish case. Other vital components of the British case are the tradition for co-operation with the voluntary sector and local service delivery based on network arrangements. Finally, government opposition to the very idea of labour market organisations as legitimate actors as displayed by Thatcherism, focusing on the side of labour, is also without parallel in the Danish and French cases.

Briefly put, the normal condition is clearly one of less institutionalised interaction as suggested by the notion of social partners and the norms of social dialogue in the British case. Neither the British Trades Union Congress (TUC) nor the Confederation of British Industry (CBI) has embraced EU norms or placed strong emphasis on the Open Method of Coordination (OMC) as an avenue to strengthen inclusion and influence. Although the TUC has definitely taken the more positive stance, belief in EU norms as a method to gain leverage is lukewarm at best (Interview 5: 70–2). The CBI, for its part, has taken a decidedly antagonistic stance towards bipartite negotiation, even though the European Employment Strategy (EES) is acknowledged as an important policy arena (Interview 6: 116–31). Despite these positions, reflecting both an adversarial labour market tradition and British euro-scepticism, both the TUC and CBI have some level of accommodation to the principles of social partnerships.

Although fully-fledged social dialogue has not been introduced as a wholesale mode of policy making, the TUC and CBI have moved closer to the role of social partners and this has been recognised as such by the key Governmental actors. In this sense, the EES has in fact caused the TUC and CBI to emerge as something approximating social partners, although without the concerted structures of social dialogue (British Expert Report 2008: 2). The emergence of the TUC and CBI as social partners constitutes a significant process of accommodation to the procedural norms underpinning the EES taking place within the overall rejection of social dialogue, which on the surface seems to suggest a case of outright rejection of EU-level norms in favour of established national traditions.

The TUC and CBI each acknowledges that the EES has to some extent introduced the role of social partner to British employment policy and been conducive to the establishment of institutionalised, although rather rudimentary, forums of tripartite consultation (Interview 5: 167–8, Interview 6: 171–5). In contrast to the adversarial tradition, both parties acknowledge the commitment to the focus on common ground and joint positions in relation to the EES, although bipartite negotiation is still considered largely irrelevant by the CBI (Interview 6: 423). Assessments of the developments also differ, however. Whereas the CBI still distances itself clearly from the terminology of social partnerships and social dialogue, it seems clear that the TUC would like to move closer to consolidated social dialogue (Interview 5: 167–8).

Turning to the governmental approach, a constitutive feature of the British reaction to the European Employment Strategy has been the commitment to the principles of wide stakeholder inclusion. Since the inception of the EES, its linking with national policy has been based on the 'involvement of a wide partnership' as the key aspect of the 'UK model' (Department for Work and Pensions 2003: 47). From 2005, the UK model is coined specifically in the terms of stakeholder input (HM Government 2005) and stakeholder involvement is framed with an increased emphasis on 'transparency' (HM Government 2006, 2008). As such, the UK model for partnership inclusion corresponds more or less directly to the procedural norms of wide stakeholder inclusion at the EU level. Given the initial conditions in the British case, such correspondence suggests modest change to existing institutions and procedures of employment policy. As such, the commitment to the stakeholder approach can in large part be seen as a continuation of the pluralistic ad hoc approach to partnerships engrained in the British tradition prior to the development of the EES.

None the less, the approximation to the role of social partners is also reflected in the government approach to stakeholder inclusion, which goes beyond a purely symbolic reframing of existing structures and procedures (British Expert Report

2008: 3). Within the stakeholder paradigm, labour and management are in principle just stakeholders among other stakeholders – in marked contrast to the privileged position bestowed upon them by tri- and bipartite labour market corporatism. In principle, this approach to labour and management organisations has been confirmed by the adversarial stance towards social dialogue consistently taken by the British government and CBI. From the onset, the British response to the EES has been defined by a clear rejection of social dialogue and the willing acceptance of the stakeholder approach. As stated squarely in one of the National Action Plans (NAPs): '…the UK does not work through institutionalised social dialogue arrangements' (Department for Work and Pensions 2003: 47).

Following the introduction of the EES, the TUC and CBI were acknowledged as social partners in the terminology of the EU and invited by the British Government, specifically the Department for Work and Pensions (DWP) to contribute the process of relating overall policy and specific projects and initiatives at the operational level to the EES (Department for Work and Pensions 1998: 3). Following this invitation, they have been systematically included in the yearly surveys of national policy and the development of various policy solutions considered relevant to the EES. They have also engaged in joint task forces and produced joint agreements in response to the employment guidelines (Department for Work and Pensions 2003, 2004, Interview 5: 201–2, Interview 6: 149–57). As such, accommodation to the EES has included development of tripartite consultations, which departs from British tradition and the overall commitment to the stakeholder paradigm identifying labour and management as just stakeholders among other stakeholders.

Although not very well developed to begin with, the rudimentary tripartite arrangements seem, however, to have been compartmentalised to some extent by macro-economic discourse and the transference of overall strategic control from the DWP to the Treasury, not unlike in the Danish case. The realignment of policy within the National Reform Programmes (NRPs) has meant increased coordination between government agencies including the Department for Work and Pensions and the Department for Trade and Industry (renamed the Department for Business, Innovation and Skills), but allowing for a degree of compartmentalisation of employment policy within the integrated framework under the supervision and overall control of the Treasury. One particular consequence of this arrangement is that the role of the TUC and CBI has been consistently downplayed by the NRPs compared to the NAPs. Whereas the overall rejection of social dialogue was accompanied by the development of operational tripartite and bipartite arrangements between 1998 and 2004, the importance of such arrangements and the role of the social partners have subsequently been diminished within the economic regime maintained by the Treasury. Although potentially reversing the direction of earlier changes, this development constitutes a clear Europeanisation effect.

Part of the commitment to the stakeholder paradigm of inclusion has been the consistent use of information and consultation as the preferred mode of interaction. The clear distinction between stakeholder involvement and social dialogue largely corresponds to a demarcation between information and consultation on the one hand, and more demanding and less desirable forms of interaction on the other, such as sustained deliberation and delegation. Prior to 2005, consultations were employed mostly as an instrument of resource sharing and mutual interests, emphasising the importance of the know-how and capacities of the various stakeholders in relation to the goals and guidelines of the EES. During this period, some consultations seem to have approximated a more sustained dialogue, in particular with respect to the tripartite consultations between government, labour and management. After 2005, the function of consultations has increasingly been reframed as a question of providing 'transparency' and giving stakeholders the possibility of 'scrutinising' governmental programmes and initiatives (HM Government 2007, 2008).

As in the Danish case, the British response to the EES and the OMC falls well short of paradigmatic change. One aspect of the British case is undoubtedly the continuous reliance on broad stakeholder inclusion, suggesting minimal absorption based on a smooth fit between EU norms about wide stakeholder inclusion and existing practice. None the less, the emerging institutional arrangements of joint tripartite interaction and approximation to the role of social partners on the side of labour and management suggests institutional changes that can reasonably be interpreted as accommodation. The British response to the EES has involved the development of more inclusive and stable procedures of consultation, in some cases approximating the level of sustained dialogue. Even considering the official resistance towards the procedural norms of social dialogue, the emerging tripartite arrangements do signify an upwards motion on the ladder of participation generated by the EES, which again seems to have been somewhat hampered by compartmentalisation of employment policy within macro-economic policy from 2005 onwards.

France – approaching social dialogue

The institutions and procedures of the French labour market are different from those of Denmark and Great Britain in a number of ways. The French tradition of strong state prerogatives and intervention ('dirigisme') differs substantially from the relatively balanced social-liberal traditions of state intervention in Denmark and the largely liberal approach of Great Britain, as does the rather politicised environment of employment policy. Additionally, French labour market organisations have a rather adversarial tradition and the French labour market has historically been much more fragmented along functional and territorial lines than the Danish and British labour markets.

Initially, the inclusion of social partners in the coordination of national policy was more or less ignored in favour of the strong state tradition (French Expert Report 2005: 4). Inclusion of social partners was limited to short consultations, working primarily as a way to keep the social partners informed on government initiatives (Ministeré de l'Emploi 1998, 2003). The image of limited direct influence of the social partners is reinforced by the consistent complaint of the Mouvement des Entreprises de France (MEDEF) – which is the largest and most influential employers' organisation representing companies within all sectors – over the Government's unwillingness to let the social partners participate more directly in the coordination of national policy (Interview 7: 312–14). Similar complaints were voiced by two of the most important unions: Confédération Générale du Travail (CGT) and Confédération Française Démocratique du Travail (CFDT), suggesting a limited governmental interest in inclusion of labour and management beyond areas considered part of their 'competence' such as vocational training (Interview 8: 46–52). It also seems clear, however, that initial limitation of inclusion of partners in European Employment Strategy (EES) discussions was not just the result of governmental preferences, but certainly also a substantial level of euro scepticism among the most important labour and management organisations (French Expert Report 2005: 3).

In spite of the lukewarm stance of key actors, the initial French response to the EES also included the creation of a new committee in 1998 designed specifically to involve labour and management in coordination policy related to the EES: Comité du dialogue social pour les questions européennes et internationales (CDSEI). Reflecting the relatively fragmented nature of the French labour market, the committee includes representatives from five of the most important organisations on the side of labour and on the employer's side, as well as representatives from the farm unions and the liberal professions (Ministeré de l'Emploi 1998). The list of organisations included in CDSEI is essentially also the list of organisations considered relevant stakeholders in the French case throughout the entire period of observation. The creation of the CDSEI can be considered as the direct institutionalisation of the principles of social dialogue furthered by the EES and, to some extent, a deliberate governmental strategy to bring French labour and management closer to the role of social partners, accepting some level of responsibility for the EES (Kerschen 2009).

Following initial debates on the working procedures of the CDSEI and the stance of the various organisations, the ensuing years have seen more contributions from the social partners, the explicit inclusion of such contributions since 2000 and the consolidation of a 'more participative method' (including partners more substantially in the National Action Plan process), establishing issue-specific working groups in the CDSEI, incorporating partner views systematically even on the level of overall strategy (Ministeré de l'Emploi, 2001) and finally adopting a 'new strategy' for dialogue 'without relying solely on the national government' (Ministeré de l'Emploi 2003: 51, French Expert Report 2005: 5). As part of the renewed method, 'partnership groups' designed to monitor the implementation and evaluate the results of several major themes relating to the link between national employment policy and the EES have become an integral part of the CDSEI.

In addition to the NAP-related procedures, the social partners have jointly expressed their wish to consolidate social dialogue in France, resulting in a general commitment of the French Government to consult with labour and management in 2004 and the so-called 'Chertier report' in 2006, suggesting a return to collective bargaining for reforms related to work relations, quoting existing procedures at the European level as the key source of inspiration. The most decisive step towards social dialogue was taken in 2007 with the adoption of a new law on modernisation of social dialogue, introducing a preliminary chapter on social dialogue in the labour code. The 2007 law has established a formal framework for 'dialogue and consultation; partly inspired by those applicable at the European level' (French Government Report 2007: 34, Kerschen 2009). Both labour and management have contributed actively to this reinforcement of social dialogue and have taken on responsibilities for mutual consultation within an increasing number of sub-areas in the field of employment policy, although contributions are still based on taking individual rather than joint positions (Interview 7: 234–8, Interview 8: 117-24).

In contrast to Denmark and Great Britain, the 2005 revision of the Lisbon strategy seems to have had limited impact in France. Whereas the 2005 reform shifted the logic of development and the position of key actors significantly in the both the Danish and the British cases, the most basic logic of French developments is the gradual approximation to the norms of social dialogue throughout the entire period of observation. In contrast to Danish and British NRPs, the French NRPs consistently highlight the role of social dialogue and the role of social partners as the institutional foundation for reaching stated goals, although streamlining with the BEPG's and compartmentalisation within macro-economic discourse is apparent on the level of policy (French Republic, 2007, 2009). As such, the 2005 reform at the EU-level has not halted the gradual approximation of social dialogue in the French case.

Given the initial condition of the French case, the observed impact of EU norms has less to do with a substantial widening of included interests than with a certain movement towards social dialogue and the role of social partners. Social dialogue is far from overcoming the adversarial and fragmented labour market, and thus far from generating paradigmatic change. However, the French case is also notable for the consistent expression of procedural EU norms about social dialogue as a source of inspiration for national arrangements, which has elsewhere also been recognised as having '...opened a new space for negotiation for the social partners in France' (Kerschen 2009: 5). Although still embryonic, the budding mechanisms of social dialogue remain limited to consultation and the individual positioning of labour and management, suggesting a level of change somewhere between absorption and accommodation.

Conclusion

The chapter has traced the effects of the European Employment Strategy (EES) on partnership inclusion in three highly different national settings (Denmark, the Great Britain and France). In all three cases, the institutional effects of the Open Method of Coordination and EES suggest changes on the level of accommodation rather than paradigmatic change. The lack of paradigmatic change is hardly surprising, given that such change involves wholesale transformation of constitutive features of the member states. Rather, the analysis points to the fact that even lower levels of change can indeed be rather significant to the national setting. However, impact of the EES is not symmetrical across variables or cases. In terms of variables, impact on the range of included interests is modest, whereas the impact on the role of included interests is significant, in particular with respect to the approximation to norms of social dialogue as defined by the EES. Impact on the level of participation and the institutional forms of inclusion is less pronounced, but still significant. With respect to variation between the three cases, the level and substance of changes have proven highly dependent on the national traditions of the initial condition: the three processes of Europeanisation are substantially different, and the direction of changes varies considerably. This finding confirms the thesis of a differential impact of EU norms. However, the substantial impact of the norms pertaining to social dialogue and the role of social partners also shows that processes of convergence should not be ruled out by Europeanisation studies.

References

Arnstein, S. R. (1969) 'A ladder of citizen participation', *Journal of the American Planning Association*, 35 (4): 216–24.

Atkinson, T., Marlier, E. and Nolan, B. (2004) 'Indicators and targets for social inclusion in the European Union', *Journal of Common Market Studies*, 42 (1): 47–75.

Borras, S. and Jacobsson, K. (2004) 'The Open Method of Coordination and New Governance Patterns in the EU', *Journal of European Public Policy*, 11 (2); 185–208.

Büchs, M. (2007) *New Governance in European Social Policy. The European Employment Strategy in the United Kingdom and Germany*, London: Routledge.

British Expert Report 2005 (Anonymous Report Commissioned for the Study).

Börzel, T. (1999) 'Towards convergence in Europe? Institutional adaptation to Europeanization in Germany and Spain', *Journal of Common Market Studies*, 39(4): 573–96.

Börzel, T. and Risse, T. (2000) 'When Europe hits home: Europeanization and domestic change', *European Integration Online Papers*, 4 (15).

Council Decision 2008/618/EC of 15 July 2008 *on guidelines for the employment policies of the Member States.*

Council Resolution of 15 December 1997 *on the 1998 Employment Guidelines*, OJ C 30.

Cowles, M. G., Caporaso, J. and Risse, T. (eds) (2001) *Transforming Europe: Europeanization and domestic change*, Ithica: Cornell University Press.

Danish Government, *Denmark's National Reform Programme. Contribution to the EU's Growth and Employment Strategy (The Lisbon Strategy)*, 2005, 2007 (progress report), 2008.

De la Porte, C. and Pochet, P., (eds) (2002) *Building Social Europe through the Open Method of Coordination*, Brussels: Peter Lang.

— (2005) 'Participation in the Open Method of Coordination. The Cases of Employment and Social Inclusion', in J. Zeitlin, P. Pochet and L. Magnusson (eds) *The Open Method of Coordination in Action: The European Employment and Social Inclusion Strategies*, Brussels: Peter Lang.

Department for Work and Pensions, *United Kingdom, Employment Action Plan 1998, 2003, 2004.*

Dieckhoff, M. and Gallie, D. (2007) 'The renewed Lisbon Strategy and social exclusion policy', *Industrial Relations Journal*, 38 (6): 480–502.

European Commission (2001) *European Governance – a white paper*, Com (2001) 428.

— (2005) Communication to the Spring European Council, *Working Together for Growth and Jobs. Integrated Guidelines for Growth and Jobs (2005–08).*

— (2007a) *Ten Years of the European Employment Strategy.*

—   (2007b) Communication to the Spring European Council, *Integrated Guidelines for Growth and Jobs (2008–10)*, COM (2007) 803.

French Expert Report 2005 (Anonymous Report Commissioned for the Study).

French Republic, *National Reform Programme for Economic and Social Growth, 2005, 2007* (progress report).

Fung, A. (2006) 'Varieties of participation in complex governance', *Public Administration Review*, Dec. 2006, Special Issue: 66–75.

Graziono, P. and Vink, M. P. (eds) (2008) *Europeanization –New Research Agendas*, Basingstoke: Palgrave Macmillan.

Hartlapp, M. (2009) 'Learning about policy learning. Reflections on the European Employment Strategy', *European Integration Papers Online*, special issue 1, 13, art. 17.

Heidenreich, M. and Zeitlin, J. (eds) (2009) *Changing European Employment and Welfare Regimes: the Influence of the Open Method of Coordination on National Labour Market and Social Welfare Reforms*, London: Routledge.

Héritier, A. *et al.* (2001) *Differential Europe: the European Union Impact on National Policymaking*, Lanham: Rowman and Littlefield Publishers.

HM Government, *Lisbon Strategy for Growth and Jobs. UK National Reform Programme, 2005, 2008, 2009*.

Hodson, D. (2004): 'Macroeconomic co-ordination in the euro areas: the scope and limits of the open method', *Journal of European Public Policy*, 11 (2): 231–49.

Hodson, D. and Maher, I. (2001) 'The Open Method as a New Mode of Governance', *Journal of Common Market Studies*, 39 (4): 719–46.

Interview 1: DA (The Confederation of Danish Employers), 2008.

Interview 2: LO (The Confederation of Danish Trade Unions), 2008.

Interview 3: Danish Ministry of Foreign Affairs, 2009.

Interview 4: Danish Ministry of Finance, 2009.

Interview 5: TUC (British Trades Union Congress), 2005.

Interview 6: CBI (Confederation of British Industry), 2005.

Interview 7: MEDEF (Mouvement des Entreprises de France), 2006.

Interview 8: CGT (Confédération Générale du Travail), 2006.

Interview 9: CFDT (Confédération Française Démocratique du Travail), 2006.

Kerber, W. and Eckhardt, M. (2007) 'Policy learning in Europe: the open method of coordination and laboratory federalism', *Journal of European Public Policy*, 14 (2): 227–47.

Kerschen, N. (2009) 'Europeanization as an Opportunity to Change the French Welfare State?', Paper presented at the ESPAnet conference, Urbino, September 2009.

Kröger, S. (2009) 'The Effectiveness of soft governance in the field of European Anti-poverty policy: operationalisation and empirical evidence', *Journal of Comparative Policy Analysis*, 11 (2): 197–211.

Liebert, U. (2008) 'Europeanization and the "Needle's Eye": The transformation of employment policy in Germany', *Review of Policy Research*, 20 (3): 479–92.

López-Santana, M. (2009) 'Having a Say and Acting: Assessing the effectiveness of the European Employment Strategy as an intra-governmental coordinative instrument', *European Integration Papers Online*, special issue 1, 13, art. 15.

Mabett, D. (2007) 'Learning by numbers? The use of indicators in the coordination of social inclusion policies in Europe', *Journal of European Public Policy*, 14 (1): 78–95.

Mailand, M. (2005) 'The Involvement of Social Partners in Active Labour Market Policy – do the Patterns fit Expectations from Regimes Theories?', in F. Bredgaard and F. Larsen (eds) *Employment Policy from Different Angles*, Danish Center for Studies in Workinglife.

— (2009) 'North, South, East, West: the implementation of the European Employment Strategy in Denmark, the UK, Spain, and Poland', in M. Heidenreich and J. Zeitlin (eds) *The Micro-Politics of the Open Method of Coordination: NGOs and the Social Inclusion Process in Sweden*, Madison: University of Wisconsin.

Marlier, E., Atkinson, A. B., Cantillon, B. and Nolan, B. (2007) *The EU and Social Inclusion. Facing the Challenges*, Bristol: Policy Press.

Ministère de l'Emploi (1998) *National Employment Action Plan 1998, 2003, 2004.*

Ministry of Employment (2002) *NAP 2002. The Government: Denmark's national action plan for employment 2002, 2003, 2004.*

Ministry of Labour and Economic Affairs, Denmark, *National Action Plan for Employment 1998, 1999, 2000, 2001.*

Mosher, J. S. and Trubek, D. M. (2003) 'Alternative approaches to governance in the EU: EU social policy and the European Employment Strategy', *Journal of Common Market Studies*, 41 (1): 63–88.

Nedergaard, P. (2006) 'Policy learning in the European Union: The case of the European Employment Strategy', *Policy Studies*, 27 (4): 311–23.

Niechoj, T. (2009) 'Does supranational coordination erode its national basis? The case of European labour market policy and German industrial relations', *European Integration online Papers*.

Radaelli, C. M. (2004) 'Europeanisation: Solution or Problem?', in *European Integration online Papers*, 8, 16.

Sabel, C. F. and Zeitlin, J. (2008) 'Learning from difference: The new architecture of experimentalist governance in the European Union', *European Law Journal*, 14 (3): 271–327.

Vanhercke, B. (2009) 'Against the odds. The Open Method of Coordination as a selective amplifier for reforming Belgian pension policies, *European Integration Papers Online*, special issue 1, 13, art. 16.

Zeitlin, J., Pochet, P. and Magnusson, L. (eds) (2005) *The Open Method of Coordination in Action: The European Employment and Social Inclusion Strategies*, Brussels: Peter Lang.

PART II

METAGOVERNANCE

chapter five | metagoverning governance styles – broadening the public manager's action perspective

Louis Meuleman

Co-existence of hierarchical, network and market governance

Before the 'discovery' of policy networks and the mechanisms of different types of network governance, social coordination was considered to take place in two distinct forms: hierarchies and markets.[1] Market coordination was the second ideal type described after Weber's bureaucratic ideal type had become the prototype for a classical hierarchy. Networks were for a long time considered a hybrid form of these ideal types. We find the fiercest defenders of the idea of a hierarchy-market dichotomy among economists. Ruys *et al.* (2007) argue that 'market contracting' (market governance) is the 'original state of affairs', and call the opposite 'vertical integration' (hierarchical governance), while all governance styles between these extremes are called 'hybrid relationships'. However, economists were also among the first to argue that networks form a separate type of social coordination (e.g. Powell 1991, Thompson 2003).

Already in 1986, Thorelli stated that the network form is a distinct form of societal coordination, and not 'just' a hybrid form that combines hierarchy and markets. Meanwhile, there is a huge public administration literature based on the idea that network governance, after hierarchical and market governance, has become the third ideal type. Network governance as an alternative to hierarchical or market governance is not only accepted in public management, but is also widely applied in knowledge-intensive businesses (Roobeek 2007) and in private enterprises in general (e.g. Assens and Baroncelli 2004, Larson 1992). The network concept has become so popular that sometimes a new dichotomy emerges, namely 'hierarchy versus networks', while market governance is neglected (Koffijberg 2005, Kalders *et al.* 2004).

Others reserve the term 'governance' for what they call the 'new modes of governance' (i.e. market and network[2]) – which is a contradiction in terms: hierarchy

---

1. Thompson (2003: 37) makes a useful distinction between 'coordination' (alignment of the elements in a system) and 'governance' (the regulation of their alignment). He places them on a continuum: coordination simply brings together elements in an ordered pattern, and governance does this by direction and design. Hierarchies, networks and markets can be used as coordination mechanisms and as governance structures as well.

2. E.g. European Commission (2002: 7): Report from the Commission on European Governance. Rhodes is ambivalent too: he defines 'hierarchy' as one of the governance structures besides

must then also be a governance style, namely the 'old' mode of governance. Peters bridges this contradiction by bringing network and market governance approaches under the umbrella of 'informal governance', besides the 'formal governance' of hierarchies (Peters 2005: 1). Notwithstanding the overwhelming empirical evidence that the trichotomy of hierarchy-network-market has more analytical power than the hierarchy-market dichotomy or the hierarchy-network dichotomy, there is still a dispute among scholars about whether this trichotomy makes sense. This dispute is emotional and value-laden; not surprisingly, because different world views or belief systems collide in this debate (Meuleman 2010).

Hierarchy, or 'bureaucratic management' in a Weberian sense, continues to exist in a complicated mixture with market and network thinking, and sometimes disguised as network or market governance. The 'dinosaur scenario', which emphasises that hierarchy is undesirable and not viable, and that a shift toward market or network governance is inevitable, is an insufficient explanation for contemporary public-sector governance: 'Bureaucratic organization and the success criteria in which it is embedded are still with us' (Olsen 2006: 17–18).

It is therefore useful to distinguish three basic styles of governance: hierarchical, network and market governance, which differ in at least thirty-five ways and appear in combinations, and may or may not function well (Meuleman 2008: 45–50). Nevertheless, much of the academic literature on governance of the last decade seems to concentrate on forms of network governance like interactive governance, deliberative governance, adaptive governance, et cetera. There is a 'conceptual crowd' within the governance spectrum around network governance. There are good reasons for this focus – our societies are confronted with vaguely defined, complex and thus essentially 'wicked' problems, for which such an approach seems to be appropriate.

On the other hand, the academic focus on network governance may also be criticised. If the entire world was a complex issue, this would imply nothing is a complex issue (Thompson 2004: 413). From the viewpoint of a public manager, a great deal of his or her daily work consists of routine issues and, to a lesser extent, crisis and conflict management. For such issues, respectively market governance and hierarchical governance are in many cases the most successful approach. Moreover, it has been shown that the governance approach applied in a specific situation does not depend only upon how the problem at hand is framed. Sometimes, a complex and wicked issue requires a hierarchical approach when network governance does not work (Meuleman 2008: 145). In addition, public policy processes often show several phases or rounds that require different governance styles (Lowndes and Skelcher 1998). Finally, network governance has characteristic failures that can be addressed by using elements of hierarchical and market governance. This implies that all three styles of governance should be included in governance research and in governance practice.

---

market and network (Rhodes 1997: 47, *Understanding Governance*) and elsewhere in the same book defines 'governance' in a network connotation, as an alternative to markets and hierarchies (Rhodes 1997: 53).

Problems of governance style combinations

Governance style combinations sometimes fail. Three problems seem to be linked to such failure:

1. governance styles have typical failures;
2. governance styles may undermine each other;
3. governance styles tend to be used as panaceas because of their attractive internal logic.

Typical failures of governance styles

Although some consider network forms of governance as panaceas, which can be illustrated by the widespread use of the term 'governance' as synonymous to 'network governance', it is disputable if this approach can be successfully used in every situation. Like all styles of governance, network governance has its typical weak points (Meyer and Baltes 2004: 42). Networks are unstable constructions that tend to either disintegrate, or convert into a formal organisation. They are not very efficient compared to markets and hierarchies. The advantage (compared to hierarchies) that networks are open can also be a threat. Being closed can enable security, which again is a condition for trust, a key dimension of network governance. Sørensen (2006) argues that network governance marginalises politicians and thereby weakens democracy: it 'stretches' democracy and raises issues regarding equity, accountability and democratic legitimacy. Depending on how democracy is defined, this may be problematic. Klijn and Koppenjan (2000a: 376–377) distinguish an instrumental vision (democracy is an efficient way of decision-making) and a substantive perspective (democracy is a societal ideal, a value in itself). Proponents of participatory or direct democracy usually take the latter view.

A final weakness of network governance worth mentioning here is inherent to networks. Networks are not 'democratic': there are always people who possess a much higher number of links with other people than most do, and these 'hubs' guarantee high-speed communication. However, if such hubs are removed, networks may break down into isolated pieces (Barabási 2003). Moreover, hubs establish a kind of hierarchy in a network and actors who find themselves in such a key position have an advantage over other players (Thompson 2004: 413). This makes the selection of participants in network governance processes problematic. In addition, there are no commonly accepted procedures for selection, and the risk is that privileged actors join in technocratic decision-making, which may result in a decrease of citizens' participation compared to the classical representative forms of democratic decision-making (Von Blumenthal (2005: 1165).

Hierarchical governance can also be characterised by typical failures. For example, the following premises of hierarchical governance are not useful when a complex, disputed and dynamic problem is tabled (Herbst 1976: 23–8):

– A task can nearly always be decomposed into smaller and smaller independent parts;

- An organisation has a simple inflexible structure which can be visualised in an organigram (or chart) with lines of responsibility;
- Organisations are of a uniform type;
- Organisational units have a single, exclusive boundary.

Market governance is characterised by the use of techniques which have flourished in the private sector. However, some of these techniques and mechanisms have turned out to be inappropriate for use in the public sector. For example, a high degree of flexibility and discretion may conflict sharply with the rigidities created by complicated civil service laws and regulations (Ingraham 1996: 262–263). Market governance principles are responsible for at least three structural problems (discovered in an international survey on New Public Management (NPM) in local governments; Naschold *et al.* 1997):

1. quality management often degenerates to a simple instrument of legitimising the administration;
2. ideologically driven privatisation programs end up in short-term, non-durable solutions;
3. outcome-orientation often falls back to the traditional hierarchical steering concept.

Another problem is that market governance advocates suggest that the private sector is by definition superior to the public sector. This has contributed to a low morale in public administration (Savoie (2000: 8–9). Furthermore, market thinking may threaten democratic processes, just as network governance does (Perry 2007). Finally, considering citizens as customers restricts the task of governments to providing services and products; citizens are also subjects, voters and nationals, in which roles they expect more than only service provision (Ringeling 2001: 34).

The governance styles also have their typical 'perversities'. Hierarchy can lead to abuse of power, network governance to abuse of trust (manipulation) and market governance to abuse of money (for example corruption).

Undermining characteristics of hierarchical, network and market governance

The second problem noted is that combinations of hierarchy, market and network may produce a variety of conflicts. Rhodes considers networks, markets and (hierarchical) bureaucracy as rivalling ways of allocating resources and co-ordinating policy and its implementation (Rhodes 2000: 345). Meyer and Baltes (2004: 46) argue that the main source of 'network failures' is the 'dualistic pressures from both market and hierarchy' on the network coordination principle. A major reason why the conflict potential is high is that the three styles express different types of relations with other parties: dependency (hierarchy), interdependency (network) or independency/autonomy (market) (Kickert 2003: 127). A hierarchical 'command and control' style of leadership will seldom lead to a consensus (network style) – even if this was the only feasible outcome of a policy process, which government is not able to 'steer' with legal instruments. Decentralisation or out-sourcing (a typical market governance strategy) makes actors more autonomous. They become frustrated when detailed control mechanisms are introduced (or re-introduced), i.e. hierarchical governance. The coexistence of 'new modes of gov-ernance' with compulsory regulation, or hierarchy, is problematic (Héritier 2003; Eberlein and Kerwer 2004: 121).

Other examples of possible conflicts between three pairs of governance styles are given below. Most examples are taken from 'external' governance-mixture conflicts: they emerge in the relationship between administration and societal actors.[3] However, they are usually 'mirrored' inside public sector organisations. Sometimes attempts to a network approach are undermined by hierarchical gov-ernance inside one and the same public sector organisation (Meuleman 2003).

From the perspective of the classical hierarchical governance style, network governance is problematic because 'governments, such as the church, will find networks messy and carp at the mess' (Bevir *et al.* 2003: 206). Internal competi-tion with the traditional hierarchical governance style is one of the reasons that the introduction of network governance sometimes fails. This competition has led to obstruction from other public sector organisations or other parts of the same or-ganisation, and to unreliable behaviour (not keeping promises, sudden withdrawal of negotiation mandate) (Meuleman 2003: 39–41; 203). Network governance has also met some resistance caused by distrust and irritation, such as when network governance is a disguise for gaining (or regaining) control and (hierarchical) steer-ing information (Bauer 2002: 778–9). Klijn and Koppenjan (2000b: 155) con-cluded that experiments with network governance in the Netherlands often remain marginal and half-hearted, because a government hesitates when abandoning ex-isting routines and giving up unilateral power.

When hierarchical ('vertical') and network ('horizontal') steering are applied at the same time by one public administration organisation, paradoxical situa-tions appear, in which this organisation ends up in a 'split'. Kalders *et al.* (2004: 339–343) investigated nine cases in the Dutch public sector and found five typical tensions between hierarchical and network governance:

1. *The 'double hat' problem:* the administration combines hierarchical and net-work governance in a way that is counter-productive. Voluntary agreements[4] are frustrated by strict accountability procedures for the same policy issue.

2. *The 'steering split':* an actor wants to comply with norms and expectations that come from hierarchical and network relations simultaneously.

3. *The 'accountability curve':* a decentralised government is held accountable for the performance of its partner organisations with which it does not have hierarchical relations.

---

3. Most governance literature focuses on the external component of governance.

4. Kalders *et al.* consider voluntary agreements a network governance instrument, but it seems to be more related to market governance: such agreements are forms of performance contracts.

4. *'Horizontal disguise':* a network instrument, such as a covenant, is used in a hierarchical way, when the central government unilaterally decides on the rules of the game.

5. *The 'vertical reflex':* (a) bottom-up, if decentralised governments ask central government for more direction, or (b) top-down, if central government forces decentralised governments to start network co-operation with its partners, within a very strict framework.

Network-style 'interactive decision-making' can lead to major tensions and conflicts with hierarchy when elected politicians, who have the formal authority to take final decisions, reverse a consensual outcome of an 'interactive' process (Kickert 2003: 126). Edelenbos and Teisman (2004) developed governance mechanisms that link hierarchical and network principles in a productive way. However, like Kalders *et al.* they did not include an analysis of the third force, the market governance paradigm with drivers like price (cost-effectiveness) and autonomy. To take an example: one of their mechanisms is improving the management of expectations about the degree of influence stakeholders will have on formal decision-making. The problem here may be that hierarchy (rules, formal decision power) may be predictable and reliable, but market thinking is not – a government agency with an autonomous position will be considered still part of government by the public, but does not have to follow hierarchical instructions anymore. In other words, management of expectations is feasible in the relationship between hierarchy and networks, but not when market thinking is also involved.

Market governance has the potential to conflict with network governance on the way decisions are made. Competition in a market setting asks for quick decisions of independent actors, who strive to optimise their own interests. Decision-making may take a lot of time in a network setting. Moreover, the type of decision, a consensus, may not be the optimal outcome for actors' competitiveness. The interdependency of actors in a network governance setting may conflict with the autonomy a market approach demands. Network governance relies on trust; hierarchical and market attitudes can damage the trust between network partners.

Governance styles as panaceas: the cultural dimension

The third problem is that each of the three basic governance styles, hierarchical, network and market governance has its own internal logic. If we define a culture as 'the values, attitudes, beliefs, orientations, and underlying assumptions prevalent among people in a society' (Huntington 2000: xv) and consider cultures also as a dynamic pattern of assumptions in a given group (Schein 1987: 9), the three styles *are* cultures or 'ways of life' (cultural theory, see Thomson, Ellis and Wildavsky 1990). They are lenses through which one can only see part of reality. The central value of hierarchical governance is authority; therefore, authoritative and legitimate results are sought. The central values of network governance are empathy and trust, and therefore the results are preferably based on consensus. Market governance is based on competition and price, which makes it logical that the best results are the most competitive and cheapest products.

This internal logic seems so attractive that many public managers and politicians adopted one of the styles as their belief system or doctrine. To them it presents a truth that has to be accepted without proof. Cases of environmental policy making in the United Kingdom, the Netherlands and Germany show that the governance style closest to the national culture was the first style to be tried as the dominant style (Meuleman 2010). Only when this did not work, were the other styles considered and a situational mixture emerged.

Metagovernance as the governance of governance

Governance style conflicts outside and inside public sector organisations exist and may produce serious performance problems. How, and to what extent, can these conflicts be prevented and mitigated and how can synergy be stimulated inside these organisations? Jessop (1997) suggested that it might help to go one step beyond, one step above the governance concept. He coined the term 'metagovernance' as a concept 'above and beyond' governance. From the emerging literature on the governance of governance, or metagovernance, two forms of metagovernance can be distinguished, depending on how governance is defined:

1. Metagovernance as supporting a chosen governance style by use of elements of the two other styles, and/or by protecting it against undermining influences of the other two styles. This could be called *first-order metagovernance*.

2. Metagovernance as combining and managing combinations of the three styles, without an a priori preference for one style. This could be called *second-order metagovernance*.

An often-used version of first-order metagovernance defines metagovernance as 'the governing of networks' (Sørensen and Torfing 2007). It aims at improving the results of the interactive network style of governance and at mitigating its typical failures. It may introduce hierarchical elements such as entrance or exit rules and legally-binding measures to secure consensual results. In addition, such market governance principles as efficiency, empowerment and entrepreneurship may be introduced in order to overcome the typical network pitfall of never-ending talks.

Others, such as Kelly (2006), define metagovernance as an attempt to regain state control over new forms of governance. They observe that hierarchical governance emerges in a new form to coordinate network and market styles of governance. Similarly, a metagovernance of market governance could be defined.

First-order metagovernance: hierarchical and market styles supporting network governance

A case study on policy changes in the Dutch Housing Ministry concluded that hierarchical and network types of strategies are often 'situationally' combined (Koffijberg 2005: 363). The initiative for a network approach often begins with a hierarchical decision. Another example comes from an analysis of partnerships between police departments and community development corporations. It was noticed that networking strategies were used to establish the hierarchical structures within which action takes place thereafter (Thacher 2004: 123).

Synergies have also been found between market and network governance. The introduction of market techniques has resulted in a fragmented institutional infrastructure of the public sector; networks put it back together again (Davis and Rhodes 2000: 21). Poppo *et al* (2002) showed empirically that managers in inter-organisational relationships may use contracts (market) and 'relational governance' (network) as complements: the results are, for example, better customised contracts.

Two examples are given below of how network governance may be used in productive combination with the other styles. They are based on case studies used to investigate the feasibility of metagovernance (Meuleman 2008).

Example 1: Network governance and the German Soil Protection Act

The first case study investigated the last phase of the preparation, and first phase of the implementation of the federal Soil Protection Act of 1999, in the period between 1996 and 2001. Germany is a country with a deeply-rooted hierarchical culture dating back to the Prussian state. In Prussia, a government developed by coercion and subjection (Raadschelders and Rutgers 1996: 76) and the centralised Prussian administration, which dates from around 1650, became the role model for the German state formed in 1871, and still in essence characterises the current German administration (Mayntz 1997: 23–25).

Network governance occurred in the form of the meetings that the Soil Working Group held with stakeholder groups, although close relationships only developed with a few groups. The Environment Ministry (BMU) representatives participated in a soil protection working group of the German industry federation (BDI) (Smeddinck and Tils 2002: 132). Because mutual trust, a basic characteristic of network governance, had developed, it was possible for BMU to discuss draft texts of the Soil Protection Act with BDI without too much risk of 'leaks'. The goal was to reach acceptance among the industry. The interviewees regarded this relationship as a success: in the end, the chair of the BDI advised the prime minister to support the Act. Also, the relationship with the farmers' association had elements of a network approach (building trust), but here the negotiating style was more like bargaining (market governance) than reaching consensus (network governance).

After the Soil Protection Act 1999 had come into force, network governance became more important. The German Environment Agency (UBA) used its relatively independent position to initiate a series of non-hierarchical governance actions, besides its primary task to contribute to new legislation with scientific knowledge. The UBA had already built a scientific and technical expert community around annual conferences since the early 1990s and now took the initiative to establish two professional associations with their own magazines: one on contaminated soils (around 1,000 members in 2006) and one on preventive soil protection (around 550 members in 2006). The process design was different in the phase of preparation of the Soil Protection Act (more hierarchical with elements of networking), compared with the phase of implementation and the raising of awareness for prevention (mainly networking with elements of market governance).

Example 2: Network governance and the Dutch Soil Policy Letter

The Dutch state is based on a consensus model of democracy. Lijphart (1999: 31) distinguishes this from the Anglo-Saxon Westminster or the 'majoritorian model', in which power is concentrated in the hands of the majority. In a consensus democracy, power is shared in broad coalition cabinets and a majority will always try not to exclude minorities. The Netherlands has a strong underlying corporatist-consensual model of deliberation with interest groups and pragmatic compromise (Kickert 2003: 127).

The Netherlands had already issued a Soil Protection Act in 1987. From 1995, an evaluation commenced, which was primarily a network governance process. However, this process did not lead to common conclusions. Pressure rose to stop the 'endless' internal discussions and reach a common standpoint within the ministry as soon as possible. The two responsible directors in the ministry decided to switch from the network style that had failed, to a *hierarchical* internal decision-making style and a 'command and control' leadership style, in order to produce what became the 2003 Policy Letter. A tight time schedule was agreed, which resulted in a 'closed shop' approach where there was no time for communication with external parties (except for two other involved ministries). The 'game' was altered from a slow and costly joint problem-solving game, in which value creation was the interaction mode, to a unilateral decision-type of game, which is faster and has minimal transaction costs (Scharpf 1997: 172). This is an example of metagovernance as the conscious application of one governance style (hierarchy) to produce policy measures characterised by another style (market governance).

In a way, the ministry used the distrust that had developed after the failure of the pre-project to create an internal policy breakthrough (Meuleman 2008):

> It was difficult to find a balance: on the one hand, VROM had to take the lead, and on the other hand, everybody had to be involved. At the same time, the net production time for the Soil Policy Letter was only three months. In addition, we also had to do some 'damage control': the relations with the decentred governments had been disturbed.

This hierarchical approach was feasible because the decentred (i.e. local) government partners of the 2000 project all blamed the Ministry for the failure and requested that the Ministry solve the problems internally first. Local government, businesses and NGOs received a draft text for comments towards the very end, leaving only a few weeks in which to react.

In the implementation phase of the Soil Policy Letter, a network co-operation was restored with local government and the two other involved ministries. Davis and Rhodes (2000: 21) describe the phenomenon whereby networks can put the fragmentation caused by market governance back together. This also seems to apply to the restoration of trust after a hierarchical approach has destroyed it.

Inherent problems of metagovernance

The application in research and in practice of metagovernance – defined as the governance of networks (a form of first-order metagovernance) – may lead to a number of problems as set out below.

Network bias: not all problems should be tackled by using network governance

Each of the basic styles of governance is inadequate for tackling certain types of societal problems, and better equipped for other problem types. Hierarchical governance may destroy trust in a complex, unstructured, 'wicked' problem setting, but is often the best approach for crisis management. There seems to be no better approach to routine issues than market governance, but the opportunistic focus on efficiency may lead to questions of legitimacy and a disregard of social values. Network governance is too time-consuming for emergencies and too inefficient for routine issues, but probably the best approach for tackling 'wicked', complex, and/or unstructured problems. Therefore, there are good reasons to focus on network governance when a complex policy issue emerges or is the object of analysis.

Problem reframing

Because all societal problems are socially constructed and this construction is contingent and, by definition, temporal, complex problems may suddenly be reframed into urgent questions, such as when there is finally a political window of opportunity. When this happens, the main governance style usually switches from network to hierarchical governance. There are many examples of this in environmental policy, e.g. acid rain in the 1980s, eutrophication by agricultural waste in the 1990s and climate change in the 2000s.

Loss of effectiveness when a new policy phase begins

A new phase or round in the policy process may require a different governance approach (Lowndes and Skelcher 1998). The ability to switch from one style to another depends on the ability to apply all three styles and their hybrids. Analysing only political behaviour by means of the network concept may grasp an important part of the picture, but not the whole story. Many politicians think in terms of hierarchy, talk in terms of network and act by using market governance mechanisms. It does not seem enough to embed aspects of hierarchical and market governance in the network paradigm (by calling hierarchical structures power networks, for example): all three governance styles are sophisticated, complete and useful logical systems.

Complexity bias

The constructed nature of 'wicked' problems may lead to overlooking rational solutions for sub-problems that can be solved by applying hierarchical measures or market mechanisms, when network governance is applied dogmatically.

Poor use of knowledge

Failure to comprehend the affinity of different epistemological roads with different governance styles may lead to sub-optimal decisions regarding the production and use of knowledge. Scientifically-sound knowledge may not be accepted in a network governance setting when the producers of this knowledge are not trusted.

Communication problems

In which language should the communication take place between project managers of network governance projects and principals (or other key actors) who are believers of hierarchical or market governance?

Second-order metagovernance: combining hierarchies, networks and markets

The above leads to the assumption that it may be effective to accompany metagovernance of networks by another form of metagovernance, which would take a bird's eye view of network, hierarchical and market styles of governance. This second-order metagovernance has been applied by experienced public managers, under certain conditions. They use three strategies (Meuleman 2008):

1. *Combining styles* – this strategy not only prevents conflicts, but also creates synergy. Hierarchy brings structure and market governance enriches a network with efficiency and entrepreneurship. Network governance may secure just enough empathy in the New Public Management approach (which is a combination of the two rational ideal type hierarchies and market).

2. *Switching between styles when the situation requires* – a policy project may start with a network approach and then introduce hierarchy by establishing rules while the next phase may be dominated by market mechanisms such as efficiency-driven autonomous activities of the involved stakeholders. A hierarchical phase may be necessary to secure the results, after which a new

network phase may start.

3. *Maintenance of situationally successful governance style mixtures* – this is a second-order strategy that complements the combining and switching strategies. For example, when conflicts are prevented by isolation – separating a team's approach from being undermined by characteristics of the other styles – or empowerment: giving the team a sufficient high degree of discretion. Maintenance requires awareness of the weaknesses of the three ideal types. During a crisis, for example, the almost unlimited discretion may lead to abuse.

The multi-perspective view that is characteristic of this form of metagovernance may increase the ability of public managers to communicate with actors who find other governance styles than interactive governance more appropriate in a specific situation. Public managers who have chosen or are commissioned to apply interactive governance would increase their action perspective if they had second-order metagovernance at least running in the background. It would make the range of possibilities of public managers much richer compared to when they are 'stuck' with only network governance: 'If you only have a hammer, you tend to see every problem as a nail.'[5]

Mutatis mutandis this also applies to scholars who analyse political decision-making or implementation wearing only the network governance glasses: taking (also) a second-order metagovernance perspective may lead to a richer understanding of 'extra-paradigmatical' mechanisms and processes.

---

5. Quote attributed to Abraham Maslov (1907–1970). Citation retrieved from http://www.brainyquote.com on 28

References

Assens, C. and Baroncelli, A. (2004) 'Marché, Réseau, Hiérarchie : à la recherche de l'organisation idéale', *Direction et Gestion, La Revue des Sciences de Gestion*, 207, 43–55.

Barabási, A-L. (2003) *Linked: How everything is connected to everything else and what it means for business, science and everyday life*, London: Penguin Books Ltd.

Bauer, M. W. (2002) 'The EU "Partnership Principle": still a sustainable governance device across multiple administrative arenas?', *Public Administration*, 80 (4): 769–89.

Bevir, M. and Rhodes, R. A. W. (2001) 'A decentered theory of governance: Rational choice, institutionalism, and interpretation', Working Paper 2001-10, Institute for Governmental Studies, Berkely: University of California.

Bogason, P. and Musso, J. A. (2006) 'The democratic prospects of network governance', *American Review of Public Administration*, 36 (1): 3–18.

Davis, G. and Rhodes, R. A. W. (2000) 'From hierarchy to contracts and back again: Reforming the Australian public service', Paper for the Political Studies Association-UK 50th Annual Conference, London, 10–13 April 2000.

Edelenbos, J. and Teisman, G. (2004) 'Interactief beleid en besluitvorming', *Openbaar Bestuur*, November 2004: 12–15.

European Commission (2002) *Report from the Commission on European Governance*. COM(2002)705 final, Brussels.

Herbst, P. G. (1976) *Alternatives to Hierarchies*, Leiden: Martinus Nijhoff.

Héritier, A. (2003) 'New Modes of Governance in Europe', Seminar, European University Institute, Florence, 2003.

Huntington, S. P. (2000) 'Cultures Count', in L. E. Harrison and S. P. Huntington (eds) *Culture Matters: How values shape human progress*, New York: Basic Books.

Ingraham, P. W. (1996) 'The reform agenda for national civil service systems: external stress and internal strains', in Bekke H. A. *et al.*, *Civil Service Systems in Comparative Perspective*, Bloominton, Ind.: Indiana University Press.

Jessop, B. (1997) 'Capitalism and its future: remarks on regulation, government and governance', *Review of International Political Economy*, 4, 561–81.

Kalders, P., van Erp, J. and Peters, K. (2004)' Overheid in spagaat. Over spanningen tussen verticale en horizontale sturing', *Bestuurskunde*, 13 (8): 338–46.

Kickert, W. J. M. (2003): Beneath consensual corporatism: Traditions of governance in the Netherlands, *Public Administration*, 81 (1): 119–40.

Klijn, E.H. and Koppenjan, J. F. M (2000a) 'Politicians and interactive decision making: Spoilsports or playmakers', *Public Administration*, 78 (2): 365–87.

—   (2000b) 'Public management and policy networks: Foundations of a network approach to governance', *Public Management*, 2 (2): 135–58.

Koffijberg, J. (2005) *Getijden van beleid: omslagpunten in de volkshuisvesting*, Dissertation, Delft: OTB.

Larson, A. (1992) 'Network dyads in entrepreneurial settings: a study of the governance of exchange relationships', *Administrative Science Quarterly*, March 1992, 37, 76–104.

Lowndes, V. and Skelcher, C. (1998) 'The dynamics of multi-organisational partnerships: an analysis of changing modes of governance', *Public Administration*, 76, 313–33.

Lijphart, A. (1999) *Patterns of Democracy: Government Forms and Performance in Thirty-Six Countries*, New Haven: Yale University Press.

Mayntz, R. (1997) *Soziologie der öffentlichen Verwaltung. 4. Durchgesehene Auflage*, Heidelberg: C. F. Müller Verlag.

Meuleman, L. (2003) *The Pegasus Principle: Reinventing a credible public sector*, Utrecht: Lemma.

— (2010) 'The cultural dimension of metagovernance: Why governance doctrines may fail', *Public Organization Review*, 10 (1): 49–70.

Meyer, W. and Baltes, K. (2004) 'Network failures – How realistic is durable cooperation in global governance?', in K. Jacob, M. Binder and A. Wieczorek (eds) *Governance for Industrial Transformation. Proceedings of the 2003 Berlin Conference on the Human Dimensions of Global Environmental Change*, Environmental Policy Research Centre: Berlin.

Naschold, F., Oppen, F. M. and Wegener, A. (1997) 'International trends of local government modernisation. An assessment for the mid-1990s', paper prepared for the Annual Meeting of the International Public Management Network (IPMN) in Potsdam, Germany, June 26–27 1997.

Olsen, J. P. (2006) 'Maybe It Is Time to Rediscover Bureaucracy', *Journal of Public Administration Research and Theory*, 16 (1): 1–24.

Perry, J. L. (2007) 'Democracy and the new public service', *The American Review of Public Administration*, 36 (1): 3–16.

Peters, B. G. (2005) 'Forms of informal governance: Searching for efficiency and democracy', paper presented at the NOPSA conference, Reykjavik, Iceland, 11–13 August 2005.

Poppo, L, Zeng Zhou, K. and Zenger, T., *The Economic and Social Embeddedness of Relational Governance: An Emirical Study Exploring Origins and Effectiveness*, Academy of Management Best Conference paper, 2003.

Powell, W. W. (1991) 'Neither market nor hierarchy: network forms of organisation', in G. Thompson *et al.*(eds) *Markets, Hierarchies and Networks*, adapted from *Research in Organizational Behaviour*, 12 (1990).

Raadschelders, J. C. N. and Rutgers, M. R. (1996) 'The evolution of civil service systems', in Bekke, H. A. *et al.*, *Civil Service Systems in Comparative Perspective*, Bloominton, Ind.: Indiana University Press.

Rhodes, R. A. W. (1997) *Understanding Governance*, Maidenhead: Open University Press.

— (2000) 'The Governance Narrative: Key Findings and Lessons from the

ESRC'S Whitehall Programme', *Public Administration*, 78 (2): 245–63.

Ringeling, A. B. (2001) 'Rare klanten hoor, die klanten van de overhead', in H. Van Duivenboden en M. Lips (eds) *Klantgericht werken in de publieke sector*, Utrecht: Lemma.

Roobeek, A. J. M. (2007) *The Networking Landscape. Navigation for the route to networking organisations*, The Hague: Academic Service.

Ruys, P. H. M., Bruil, J. and Dix, H (2007) 'Modes of governance in the Dutch social housing sector', *Annals of Public and Cooperative Economics*, 78 (3): 381–413.

Savoie, D. J. (2000) *Governance in the Twenty-First Century: Introducing the Topic*, Montral and Kingston: Canadian Centre for Management Development.

Scharpf, F. W. (1997) *Games Real Actors Play: Actor-Centered Institutionalism in Policy Research*, Boulder, Co.: Westview Press.

Schein, E. (1987) *Organizational Culture and Leadership*, San Francisco: Jossey-Bass.

Smeddinck, U. and Tils, R. (2002) Normgenese und Handlungslogiken in der Ministerialverwaltung. Die Entstehung des Bundes-Bodenschutzgesetzes: eine politik- und rechtswissenschaftliche Analyse, Baden-Baden: Nomos Verlag.

Sørensen, E. (2006) 'Meta-governance: The changing roles of politicians in processes of democratic governance', *American Review of Public Administration*, 36 (1): 98–114.

Sørensen, E. and Torfing, J. (eds) (2007) *Theories of Democratic Network Governance*, Basingstoke: Palgrave Macmillan.

Thacher, D. (2004) 'Interorganizational partnerships as inchoate hierarchies. A case study of the Community Security Initiative', *Administration and Society*, 36 (1): 91–127.

Thompson, G. F. (2003) *Between hierarchies and markets: The Logic and Limits of Network Forms of Organization,* Oxford: Oxford University Press.

—— (2004) 'Is all the world a complex network?', *Economy and Society*, 33 (3): 411–24.

Thompson, M., Ellis, R. and Wildavsky, A (1990) *Cultural Theory*, Boulder, CO: Westview Press.

Thorelli, H. B. (1986) 'Networks: Between Markets and Hierarchies', *Strategic Management Journal*, 7 (1): 37–51.

Von Blumenthal, J. (2005) ‚Governance – eine kritische Zwissenbilanz‘, *Zeitschrift für Politikwissenschaft*, 15 (4): 1149–1180.

chapter six | metagovernance and the uk nuclear industry – a limiting case

Keith Baker and Gerry Stoker

Introduction

The subject of governance has become the focus of much academic debate (Rhodes 1997; Stoker 1998; Sørensen and Torfing 2008; Chhotray and Stoker 2009). This interest in governance owes much to the realisation that organisations in both the public and private sectors increasingly operate within complex interdependent networks in which decision-making is decentred (Kickert, Klijn and Koppenjan 1997; Koppenjan and Klijn 2004). In the early work on governance much was made of the idea of 'governance without government' (Rhodes 1997), but subsequent debate has been quick to recognise the potential for an effective role for the state in governance (Pierre and Peters 2000). States achieve their goals through what has become known as the practice of metagovernance (Sørensen and Torfing, 2009). From a state-centric perspective, the state is viewed as the primary metagovernor and the only actor equal to the task. The argument is that the state has become more powerful as it has developed a capacity to work with and through non-state actors (Bell and Hindmoor 2009).

We propose to develop and specify this emerging theory of metagovernance through adapting a framework that examines the tools available to the state. We then plan to test the theory of metagovernance using a single case study of the prospects for the United Kingdom to 'metagovern' its way to a revival of nuclear power in Britain. We are proposing that this case constitutes a 'least likely' (most difficult) test for effective metagovernance to emerge (George and Bennett 2005; Gerring 2007: 118).

Much of the existing work on metagovernance (Sørensen 2006; Bell and Park 2006) tends to make claims about the capability of the state to metagovern using evidence from cases where the state has had a chance to learn new tactics and techniques and where its resources tend to dwarf those around it. Neither of these conditions applies in the case of nuclear policy, given that the United Kingdom has not had a substantial nuclear industry since the late 1970s and has privatised its electricity supply industry. The case of the renaissance of the UK's nuclear industry lends itself to what Jack Levy refers to as the 'Sinatra inference: if it can make it here, it can make it anywhere' (quoted in Gerring 2007: 119). The odds appear stacked against metagovernance. The United Kingdom is a medium-sized government with a tradition of Anglo-American capitalism and liberal industrial policy, there is a considerable degree of public scepticism about the plans to revive nuclear power, the scale and novelty of the outcome demanded appears daunting and the structure of existing energy provision arrangements add to the complexities involved. If we can nevertheless conclude that the prospects for a nuclear renaissance are high then we could infer that a state-centric view of metagovernance is a strong theory applicable to all conditions. If on the other hand we show serious doubts about the UK's capacity to metagovern effectively in this area, we can indicate a need for further theoretical refinement and thereby show a way that theory could be developed in the complex world of governance studies.

Approaching metagovernance

Bell and Hindmoor (2009: 190) argue that embedded states, those intertwined in complex governance arrangements, can metagovern effectively and '... are not undermined by close links with powerful economic actors, but rely on them.' They (2009: 191) conclude their study by announcing that:

> Governments have *enhanced* their capacity to achieve goals by developing closer relationships with non-state actors. The move to governance with and through societal institutions has not weakened the power of the state and indeed may have given new opportunities to oversee society. [Emphasis in original]

The state-centric theory on which the Bell and Hindmoor thesis rests was itself a reaction to earlier literature that all too easily suggested that the power of the state had declined in the face of globalisation and powerful multinational corporations on the external side and lost autonomy to organised interests and democratic pressures on the internal side. Drawing on the range of writings on the capacity of the state (Evans 1997; Weiss 1998; Hobson 2000), Bell and Hindmoor join others in challenging this decline of the state thesis both empirically and theoretically. The empirical dimension stresses the relative nature of threats, such as globalisation and the variety of state and capitalist forms, which in turn create a multiplicity of responses to the external and internal demands on the state, some of which are considerably more successful than others. The conceptual work is done by challenging the idea that a state has to be autonomous from society and to be able to command societal actors in order to be strong. As Weiss (1998: 29) notes, such an 'unsubtle notion' of state capacity just does not make sense in complex industrial democracies. What we should rather be looking for is governed interdependence, '... a negotiated relationship, in which public and private participants maintain their autonomy, yet which is nevertheless governed by a broader set of goals set and monitored by the state ...' (Weiss 1998: 37). The essence of a strong state in the context of metagovernance is precisely to be able to undertake that steering role.

We need to engage in one final manoeuvre in order to provide a theoretically coherent account of the powers of a metagoverning state. We need an organising device and we propose to use a framework originally developed by Hood (1986) and enhanced further by Hood and Margetts (2007). Government is understood to have access to four specific tools – Nodality, Authority, Treasure and Organisation – and our proposition is that each of those tools, suitably adapted, could be a driving force for state-centric metagovernance. The concept of nodality refers to the position of an organisation within a network. For Bell and Hindmoor (2009), the state is the key nodal actor at the centre of the world of governance. Again, according to Bell and Hindmoor, the capable state has authority that stems from its control of regulatory and legislative systems and its ability to deploy force and its perceived legitimacy. Although the term 'treasure' is usually understood to refer to financial resources (Hood 1986), it can be expanded to include any form of asset that can be exchanged or transferred to others. Again, Bell and Hindmoor are clear that the capable state is still able to access many resources. The final element of the policy tools framework is organisational capacity. This refers to the ability of an organisation to utilise the resources it controls and the institutional structures that enable organisations to act in the first place. Again, the capable state in metagovernance mode will not always do things directly, but can bring substantial administrative and organisational capacity into play to influence others. We are now in a position to state boldly the theory of metagovernance we propose to test:

A capable state with access to the assets of nodality, authority, treasure and organisational capacity can metagovern effectively to achieve its policy goals with and through powerful economic actors.

The remainder of this chapter discusses the attempts of the British government to revive the nuclear industry through metagovernance against this proposition.

The background to the emergence of a commitment to nuclear renaissance

In 1990, as part of a wider programme of privatisation of the energy industry, the then Conservative Government began to privatise the British electricity industry (1989 Electricity Act). Although it succeeded in privatising the majority of the electricity industry, it was unable to sell the UK's nuclear power stations as nuclear power was unprofitable and private companies were unwilling to accept the financial liabilities associated with decommissioning the oldest stations (Estrin, Marin and Selby 1990). To support the nuclear industry and fund nuclear decommissioning, the government imposed a surcharge on electricity generated from fossil fuels (the Fossil Fuel Levy) and compelled electricity suppliers to purchase the electricity generated from nuclear power through the Non-Fossil Fuel Obligation. The Fossil Fuel Levy and the Non-Fossil Fuel Obligation were deemed to represent an unlawful subsidy by the European Union and were ultimately abolished in 2000. The government succeeded in privatising the UK's most modern nuclear power stations in 1996 as the wholesale electricity price was sufficient to allow these stations to operate at a profit.

In the privatised electricity market, the UK Government acted to establish barriers to entry to the electricity market in the form of licences and it regulated the market; it did not interfere with the investment decisions of the commercial companies. As such, the government effectively delegated the delivery of its energy policy to the market. This point was made by a senior policy adviser:

"Take North Sea oil. We didn't really do anything, we just sat back and issued the licences and permits and let the market get on with it." (Senior policy adviser A, personal interview, July 2009)

During the first decade of the twentieth century, the UK Government has come to believe that the country faces three interconnected problems in respect of its energy policy:

1. The UK has committed itself to stringent and legally-binding reductions in greenhouse gas emissions as part of the 2004 Kyoto Protocol.

2. Throughout the 1990s, the UK came to rely on natural gas from the North Sea for power and domestic heating, but these supplies started to dwindle (Department of Trade and Industry (DTI) 2003; Lovell, Bulkeley and Owens 2009) and Britain became increasingly dependent upon imported natural gas (DTI 2003; DTI 2007).

3. The UK's nuclear power stations are fast approaching obsolescence (Department Business Enterprise and Regulatory Reform (BERR) 2009; Department of Energy and Climate Change (DECC) 2009) and this may cause a shortfall in electricity-generating capacity. These power stations cannot be easily replaced without compromising Britain's commitments under the Kyoto protocol or by increasing its reliance on imports of natural gas.

The seriousness of these problems was expressed in comments by a senior policy adviser who argued that the UK's situation made it 'vulnerable'. A senior Environment Agency official went further: 'There is a great link between sustainability and security. If we were in the middle of a very cold winter, how long do you think those trees would last if we lost gas or electricity? Not very long.' (Personal interview, October 2008)

Given the gravity of the problems, the UK Government has come to see energy policy as a strategic issue (Scrase and Ockwell 2009) and is no longer content to rely upon networks of self-governing private sector companies. In the case of the nuclear renaissance, the government has decided it had better be a metagovernor. How is it going about that task and what are its chances of success? We use the NATO framework to come to a judgment.

Nodality

Government can claim nodal status because it has the ability to permit, forbid or restrict the actions of the participants in the network. In other words, it can exercise influence. As such, the intentions of government are carefully monitored by those within the network, a point that a parliamentary policy adviser drew particular attention to: 'Government has a voice. Simply by broadcasting its intentions government can change the risk profile that market assigns to particular energy technology.' (Policy adviser, personal interview, July 2009)

This understanding is consistent with the state-centric view of metagovernance outlined above. In an effort to promote its policy objective (a revival of nuclear power), the UK Government has sought to communicate to the private sector that it is supportive of nuclear power. This has involved a sustained attempt to highlight the steps that it has taken such as legislative reform or the streamlining of regulation. Civil servant A explained that the purpose of this communication exercise was to: 'provide certainty to business'. (Personal interview, December 2009)

The challenge has been to create a convincing long-term message. Nuclear power stations take many years to build and have life spans of more than fifty years. As such, would-be nuclear operators are keen to determine whether or not the UK Government is willing to establish and maintain a policy regime that will continue to support the nuclear industry (Cadoux-Hudson in Wood 2009). There are political divisions over nuclear power generation which are difficult to paper over. This point was made rather forcefully by a former Cabinet Minister:

> Parliament is very divided on this. Both the parties are divided. I raised a question on nuclear power and there were many members of the Tories cheering in support and many of my own side sitting there glumly or shaking their head vigorously.

> (Former Minister, personal interview, May 2009)

Prior to the 2010 general election, the then Labour Government carefully enlisted the support of the main opposition party (the Conservatives) in an effort to communicate to industry that the British body politic is largely united on the issue of nuclear power (Hendry 2008). In fact, senior policy adviser A went as far as to comment in 2009 that: 'there is not a cigarette paper between the government and the opposition'. Unfortunately for the metagovernance strategy, the outcome of 2010 UK General Election has led to a coalition government being formed between the Conservative and Liberal Democrat parties, with the latter having a much more negative stance towards nuclear power. The coalition agreement, however, does allow for the nuclear policy to remain on the table as long as the new build is driven by private investment and without public subsidy. There is probably now an enhanced prospect of mixed signals for the nuclear industry, a point confirmed by a senior Liberal Democrat MP: 'The Liberal Democrats are unique amongst the major parties in that policy is democratically constituted. A majority of the party is opposed to nuclear power. However there is a significant minority that is in favour.' (Personal interview, July 2009)

The government's communication strategy is most effectively understood as a story-telling exercise designed to establish a narrative that Britain is 'a good place to do business' because the political climate is supportive, the regulatory regime is not onerous and that substantial commercial opportunities exist. The initial success of this strategy can be gauged by the fact that in 2008 the nuclear industry's judgment was that Britain represented the most viable commercial opportunity after the United States (Ward 2008). Senior civil servant A even went as far as to argue that government has successfully: '... built confidence in the nuclear industry. EDF bought British Energy and we have sold the NDA sites and that was something like £4 billion. That is a huge sum of money with no possibility of return for ten years.'

The difficulty is that the UK Government is not the only government interested in nuclear power (Baker 2009). Moreover, nuclear technology is complicated and the skills and technology is controlled by a few multinational companies. In fact, civil servant B (personal interview, May 2009) commented: 'The nuclear industry is global. You wouldn't dream of building a nuclear power programme in isolation, so we are pretty much linked.' This has created a situation in which governments are scrambling to secure contracts with the nuclear industry. Ward (2008) characterises this situation as 'a race'. To secure its own position and attract the interest of the private sector, the UK Government has taken to emphasising the scale of the commercial opportunity the UK represents. However, nuclear industry expert A (telephone interview, December 2008) offered a rather more sceptical view: 'If you listen to presentations by the government, they talk about very large nuclear programmes – twenty to thirty reactor units and the creation of 100,000 jobs; it's just pie in the sky.' This scepticism can be explained by considering the nature of nuclear industry.

The manufacture of nuclear reactors is, as senior policy adviser A put it: '... a black art of the highest order and Japan is about the only country with the skills.' Therefore, the number of reactors that can be produced in any given year is limited by the industrial capacity of the manufacturers in Japan. In the race to secure contracts, the UK is competing with countries such as China, the United States and the Middle Eastern states, and these countries are prepared to spend vast sums on money. This point was acknowledged by senior policy adviser B (personal interview, February 2009) who noted: 'If other countries need to bounce the queue, if they need to accelerate their pace in the race, they just write a big cheque. Well, we're not in a position to be able to do that.' As such, it can be observed that the nuclear industry is embedded within a multinational network in which there are multiple centres of power competing with one another. The UK Government cannot credibly claim more than a modest degree of nodality in such a network and lacks the necessary resources to establish a dominant position. In other words, it is less far capable than it first appears.

Authority

By exercising authority, governments may permit or restrict actions or reconfigure institutions. Consistent with a state-centric understanding of metagovernance, the UK Government is using its legislative power to create an institutional environment that is supportive of nuclear power. It is widely believed that the UK's planning legislation poses a significant barrier to the development of nuclear power stations or any large infrastructure project. As a second nuclear industry expert commented:

> You get into the mire of planning difficulties. We have seen that in other major projects in the UK and you could be spending inordinate amounts of money on design and preparation and dialogue over the licensing only to find that the planning application gets bogged down.
>
> (Nuclear industry expert B, telephone interview, March 2009)

The fear was that local government would be asked to decide upon, on the basis on local politics, whether an infrastructure of national importance could be constructed. As senior civil servant B (telephone interview, May 2009) scathingly put it: 'The first three pages of a planning application go into global warming. That is not something for local councils to go into. Government needs to do that.'

The response was the enactment of the Planning Act 2008 and the creation of the centralised Infrastructure Planning Commission (IPC). The Planning Act 2008 (c. 29, Pt. 2, s .5, para. 1(a)–(b)) grants government the power to define particular infrastructure projects as national policies by Ministerial fiat. Civil servant C (personal interview, March 2009) was explicit on this: 'The intention is that you have one debate over whether or not you have nuclear power and a series of [local] debates that are site-specific.' However, it should be noted that throughout the UK's nuclear programme, local councils were supportive of the development of nuclear power stations (see O'Riordan, Kemp and Purdue 1988). As such, the government's belief that centralisation was necessary to bypass uncooperative local authorities is simply not supported by the historical record. If approached in state-centric metagovernance terms, the UK government's decision to centralise the planning system can be explained. To ensure a revival of nuclear power, the government must provide 'certainty' to the nuclear industry by demonstrating the existence of a benign policy regime. The senior Environment Agency official interviewed explained that: '… [n]o one is going to shell out the billions necessary to build nuclear reactors without been sure that there is a likely outcome of the planning process.' As such, the power of the state is deployed to remove 'any unnecessary obstacles', as civil servant A put it.

Some legal obstacles are more easily removed than others. Although the nuclear industry is subject to the domestic legal systems of the countries in which it operates, it is also subject to international legislation and regulation from the International Atomic Energy Agency and the European Union. Whilst a state can ignore international regulation (e.g. Iran), it is unthinkable that a modern democratic state would violate international law in such a manner. As civil servant C noted: 'European legislation requires governments to justify any major impact of any major project that has benefits and risks and justify that it makes sense.'

A second barrier to the UK Government's ability to metagovern by exercising authority is that it is subject to its own laws and is embedded within a system of checks and balances. In the UK, government decisions can be subject to legal challenge if it shown that the government has acted in a manner that is fundamentally incompatible with its own procedures, statutory duties or existing legislation. This is particularly relevant in the case of nuclear power as there are over 500 individual legislative instruments that govern the possession, use and disposal of radioactive and nuclear materials in the UK. As such, the sheer complexity of the legislation creates numerous opportunities for government decisions to be challenged because compliance with such complex and voluminous legislation is very difficult. As senior civil servant A acknowledged: 'Some of the decisions [we make] may be open to legal challenge but you can't do everything so perfect that there is no possibility of challenge.' The government's understandable mistakes will provide ample opportunity for those opposed to nuclear power to launch legal challenges. The woes of the metagovernance strategy in this area have increased since the 2010 election with the new coalition committed to dismantling the centralised infrastructure planning system, recently put in place by Labour, and replacing it with something that cedes greater powers to local and regional decision-makers, but ensures that projects of major national importance will be judged by ministers in the context of parliamentary-backed national policy statement. The government claims that the new arrangements are 'as robust as possible, and minimise the risk of successful judicial review' (Communities and Local Government 2010), but others may judge that they could be even more prone to judicial review.

Treasure

A state-centric view of metagovernance argues that a government has access to vast resources that it can use to promote its policies and resources a plenty are required in the nuclear field. Senior civil servant B commented: 'Nuclear new build is game for big companies. EDF is Europe's largest utility. It's a hundred-and-fifty billion euro company and RWA and E.oN who have bought the NDA sites are hundred billion euro companies.' The UK Government has access to resources such as land. The most attractive sites for the development of new nuclear power stations are former nuclear sites because these sites have pre-existing connections to the electricity grid. In the UK, former nuclear sites are owned by the Nuclear Decommissioning Authority (NDA). The NDA is a non-departmental agency controlled by the government (NDA 2009) and this has granted the government access to another form of treasure. As senior policy advisor B explained:

> [The NDA] owns a lot of land, and a lot of the land is prime site for nuclear new build in the UK. So it had a whole bunch of assets, and we were quite instrumental in trying to make sure that those assets became available for potential investors.

The ability of the government to metagovern through treasure is restricted by the physical structure of the electricity grid and the corporate operations of the private company that manages the grid. Britain's electricity grid is not a single unitary system, but is more accurately understood as several regional grids linked together (Chessire 1996). The grid itself is owned and managed by a private company – National Grid – which charges electricity supply utilities for access to the electricity distribution grid (National Grid 2008/9). The National Grid's fee structure is based on a complicated formula which levies charges upon electricity generators based upon the costs of managing the distribution of the electricity (National Grid 2009). As it is easier to manage the distribution of electricity within a single grid rather than across several regional grids, National Grid charges lower fees if the electricity does not have far to travel. This creates an incentive for electricity supply companies to build power stations as close as possible to regions where there is demand for electricity.

The south of England accounts for around one third of Britain's electricity demand and the highest population density (Office of National Statistics 2001; DECC 2008). Therefore, the most desirable land for building nuclear power stations is in the south of England. This led nuclear industry expert A to comment that: 'as soon as you start loading [new] combinations onto the grid in the south of England, you have a serious risk of destabilising the grid. OFGEM and National Grid are really worried about it.' As the UK electricity industry is a privatised system, the electricity generators are not responsible for the stability of the grid whilst the organisation(s) that are responsible for the stability of the grid are not responsible for the actions that may destabilise the grid. This leads to the rather ironic situation in which the government's attempts to assist the private sector to promote nuclear power to address an electricity shortage is effectively undermining the stability of the distribution system.

A state-centric view of metagovernance assumes that when a government exchanges treasure, the outcomes of these exchanges is progress towards the government's agenda. As such, it is assumed that treasure grants the government control. The empirical case study has suggested that the deployment of treasure – in the form of land – simply grants the UK Government an ability to influence (rather crudely) the decisions of private sector companies. However, the complexity of the electricity supply system requires a greater degree of control than the UK Government is capable of exercising with the policy instruments that it has to hand.

Organisational capacity

A capable state has access to considerable administrative and organisational capacity, which can be deployed in support of government policy by enabling the actions of those that government wishes to metagovern. In the United Kingdom, nuclear power is overseen by a multitude of different organisations ranging from the Health and Safety Executive (HSE), the Environment Agency, Office of Civil Nuclear Security and the UK Safeguards Office. Furthermore, prior to passage of the 2008 Planning Act, would-be nuclear operators also had to interact with local authorities to obtain planning permission. The transaction costs involved in interacting with all these different organisations is considerable. In an effort to simplify the number of different organisations that would-be nuclear investors must work with, the UK Government has created the Office of Nuclear Development (OND). As civil servant A put it, the OND is designed to serve as a 'one-stop shop for industry' and to 'act as a liaison between the different parts of government. We look to make the process work.' In other words, the nuclear industry interacts with the OND and the government incurs the transactions costs. As such, the UK Government uses its organisational capacity to reduce the costs the nuclear industry may face and by doing so makes the UK appear to be more attractive within the global market.

To operate a nuclear power station in the UK, a nuclear operator's licence is required. These licences are issued by the Nuclear Installations Inspectorate (NII), which is part of the Health and Safety Executive. The process of licensing a nuclear reactor is a time consuming, with the NII assessing each individual reactor on its own merits and considering every aspect of the reactor's design and proposed operation in an effort to determine if the design is as safe as possible. This requires that the reactor designer and the would-be nuclear operator engage in lengthy dialogues with the NII and if the NII is not convinced by the arguments, it can mandate that changes be made (Nuclear Installations Act 1965). However, the costs of altering an established reactor design are considerable as new equipment and parts must be purchased (O'Riordan et al. 1988). Thus, the nuclear industry is faced with an expensive and uncertain process.

To address these issues, the UK Government proposed a system of 'pre-licensing'. This would involve the NII examining and licensing a specific reactor design and allowing industry to construct future reactors 'off the shelf' without reference to regulation. However, as nuclear inspector A [personal interview, August 2008] explained: 'Politicians were talking about pre-licensing without knowing what it meant. They wanted a system of pre-licensing like the Americans and you could take a design off the shelf.' Nuclear inspector B [personal interview, August 2008] explained that British nuclear regulation is based on the principle of 'as low as reasonably achievable', so they push for higher and higher safety margins rather than set a threshold that an applicant just needs to pass. The UK's safety regulators require that everything is made as safe as it could possibly be. This is substantially different from most countries; they follow a prescriptive model of regulation, which mandates that a fixed standard has to be achieved. If the UK Government wished to make meaningful changes to the way in which the NII examines nuclear power stations, it would have to change the underlying ethos that informs national regulation.

Although pre-licensing is impossible, the UK Government pressured the NII to develop a similar procedure and this led to the development of the Generic Design Assessment (GDA). In the GDA process, the NII communicates to would-be nuclear developers the methodology and process under which their reactor and power station designs will be assessed. As nuclear inspector B explained:

What you see is a series of testings. We ask them: 'Why can't you go that bit further?' They will come back and say we have looked at it and it causes problems elsewhere or perhaps the cost is disproportionate.

This allows any serious problems to be detected and changes made before the power station undergoes the actual licensing assessment. As such, it is believed that the GDA process will reduce costs by reducing the risk of delay.

There are three barriers to the UK Government's attempts to leverage its organisational capacity in support of the nuclear industry:

1. the GDA process is unique in global nuclear regulation;
2. the NII is short of manpower; and
3. the relationships between the different government departments and agencies involved in nuclear regulation are far from harmonious.

The majority of countries operate prescriptive systems of nuclear regulation based on the United States model. Whilst the GDA process is not especially costly in and of itself, the NII has a tendency to demand information far beyond that which is required in most countries, given that they are seeking to reconstruct 'the decision-process'. In fact, Nuclear Inspector B explained that the nuclear industry has found it 'difficult to put [itself] in the place of the regulator' and that the GDA demands information that is 'very different to what they provide for their own regulator'. Therefore, it might be argued that the GDA actually increases the industry's transaction costs.

The NII is a small organisation and the majority of its inspectors are employees of the former nationalised nuclear industry. This gave the NII an unparalleled understanding of the operation of the British-designed reactors and power stations that form the majority of UK's existing nuclear industry. As no one has sought to construct a nuclear reactor in the UK since Sizewell B, there was no incentive for the NII to expand its recruitment (Weightman 2008). Nuclear inspector C (telephone interview, August 2008) commented 'there is a shortage of staff, it's well documented [and] it's exacerbated by the need to do these assessments.' Nuclear inspector B was more forthright: 'To put it in perspective, the American Nuclear Regulatory Agency has 430 people working on reactor assessment at the moment. We have sixteen so far and we are ramping it up to twice that.' Although the NII possesses an expert staff, it is hard to believe that thirty-two people could assess multiple power station designs quickly enough for the UK to begin construction of the nuclear power stations it needs to avoid an electricity shortage.

Although the OND is attempting to coordinate the actions of a multitude of different departments, these departments and agencies are actually involved in a classic bureaucratic competition for control. This is illustrated by the reactions of the Environment Agency and the NII to an event at the Sizewell A nuclear power station. The NII is formally responsible for the regulation of the operation of nuclear power stations (Nuclear Installations Act 1965) whilst the Environment Agency has authority over releases of radioactive material off-site (Radioactive Substances Act 1993). In 2007, a water pipe delivering water to a spent fuel storage pond developed a leak and an alarm that should sound in the event of falling water levels failed to activate (World Nuclear News 2009). The leak was swiftly detected and fixed and the incident was ranked at one out of seven (the lowest possible score) on the International Nuclear Event Scale. However, the NII deemed the event serious enough to investigate, but did not opt to prosecute given that the event was minor and very little radiation was released (HSE 2007). This decision was not supported by the Environment Agency, which considered its own prosecution under the Radioactive Substances Act 1993. This is despite the Environment Agency's lack of jurisdiction over a nuclear site. The NII claims that throughout its investigation, it worked closely with the Environment Agency (HSE 2009), but this is simply not supported by the fact that the Agency continued to investigate the operators of Sizewell A after the NII had decided not to take legal action (Channel 4 News 2009). It is hard to see how the OND can coordinate the different organisations involved in nuclear regulation for the benefit of the nuclear industry if they are in competition with each other.

Discussion and conclusion

The state-centric view that a capable state can 'metagovern' effectively as long as it has access to key assets would appear to be called into question by our case study. It was observed that the despite the UK Government's claim to nodality, its ability to exercise authority, deploy treasure and organisational resources, its capacity for metagovernance is limited by political conflicts, international pressures, legal requirements, limited resources and organisational complexities. These arguments are summarised in Table 6.1.

The UK Government remains committed to overseeing a revival of nuclear power but delivering this policy goal faces significant problems. Despite these problems, the nuclear industry clearly believes that the UK has some commercial potential given that it has been willing to submit reactor designs to the NII and has purchased land from the NDA. However, the case study suggests that there will be significant limits on the numbers of nuclear power stations that can be constructed. Therefore, it might be argued that a few new nuclear power stations may be built in the UK, but it is unlikely there will be a substantial nuclear revival. As the attempt to revive nuclear power is ongoing, it is worthwhile considering whether or not the problems highlighted could be overcome. The most realistic option is for the UK Government to subsidise the nuclear industry or pay for upgrades to the electricity grid. This would demonstrate a commitment to nuclear power. However, as the empirical evidence shows, the government lacks the necessary financial resources. Furthermore, such a move would prove politically and legally impossible in the face of divisions within Parliament and the European prohibitions on subsidies. An alternative option is that the UK Government could attempt to establish itself as a purchaser and distributor of electricity. Whilst this policy option would not represent a subsidy, the UK Government has not indicated that it has any desire to involve itself directly in the operation of the electricity market.

We have used a 'least-likely' case – the UK's nuclear renaissance policy – to cast doubt on the state-centric version of metagovernance theory. We have not provided a knock-out blow to the theory, but plainly we have demonstrated the need for it to be refined or qualified. What form should that refinement take? We do not need to replace a state-centric understanding of metagovernance with a more society-focused approach (Pierre and Peters 2000; Rhodes 1997; Sørensen 2006). The two perspectives are best seen as the sides of a coin rather than in conflict with one another. The key insight of Weiss (1998) remains in place: that state capacity relates to an ability to be both integrated with powerful economic actors and autonomous enough to steer the institutions of the state and those actors towards shared goals. Jessop (2002: 52–3; 240–3) drawing on the work of Dunsire (1996) refers to metagovernance as the 'organisation of the conditions of governance' and 're-articulating and collaborating different modes of governance' (Jessop 2002: 240–1). Jessop sees metagovernance as a 'containing process' undertaken by the state, but prone to failure. We need to understand better when that containing process is likely to hold and when it is likely to break down, as in our case, where there are major doubts about the capacity of the UK to metagovern

Table 6.1: Prospects for effective metagovernance – the case of UK nuclear renaissance

State capability	Opportunities	Limitations
Nodality	– Government is a prominent actor with regulatory power – it must be listened to. – Government can create a supportive narrative.	– Government is deeply divided and has a tendency to make policy based on factional politics. – The nuclear industry is multinational and other (richer) governments are competing with Britain.
Authority	– Ability to change the law to make construction of nuclear power stations easier.	– Nuclear energy is subject to multi-level governance. – Legislative complexity makes it difficult for the government to realise policy. – Government is subject to its own laws and policy decisions may be subject to legal challenge.
Treasure	– Government can sell land near nuclear sites.	– The ability to realise nuclear power is dependent on stability of the electricity grid. – Government lacks the control necessary to ensure the stability of the electricity grid.
Organisational capacity	– Government can create and use supportive institutional infrastructure and procedures to lower costs for the private sector.	– Generic Design Assessment (GDA) is unique and this increases the costs faced by the nuclear industry – The NII lacks the manpower to carry out the GDA process in a timely fashion. – There is serious division between the different agencies and departments within government.

its way to a nuclear renaissance. Yet as Weiss (1998) argues, it only makes sense to refer to state capacity in terms of specific policy or issue. What the UK lacks in its capacity to metagovern in the area of major energy infrastructure may not be a constraint or limitation in other policy fields. For theory to develop in this field, we need to refine its claims and develop a range of 'most difficult' tests comparable to the one offer here.

George and Bennett (2005: 123) explain: 'Generalising the results of case studies is not a simple function of the number or diversity of cases studied. Single cases can cast doubt on theories across a wide range of conditions.' Using qualitative methods requires a different approach to inference compared to quantitative methods. But too often theories drawing on insights from qualitative methods are supported by numerous illustrations rather than a focused examination of cases chosen for their relevance. The study of a multiplicity of events is often accompanied by a loose assumption of the more the better. But the connection between theory building and case studies needs to be seen in a sharper perspective than that. It requires the theory to be specified in a refutable manner and the case study to have the quality of providing a crucial test. Political scientists in the future could make greater use of crucial cases to test emerging bodies of theory.

Acknowledgements

This work was carried out as part of the SPRIng project, aimed at developing a decision-support framework for assessing the sustainability of nuclear power, led by the University of Manchester and carried out in collaboration with City and Southampton Universities. The authors gratefully acknowledge the Engineering and Physical Sciences Research Council (EPSRC) and the Economic and Social Research Council (ESRC) for supporting this work and to the interviewees who allowed us to quiz them about an unfolding policy. The views expressed in the paper are those of the authors alone.

References

Baker, K. (2009) 'Delivering nuclear power: Challenges for the Obama Administration', *International Journal of Public Administration*, 32: 747–52.

Bell, S. and Park, A. (2006) 'The problematic metagovernance of networks: Water reform in New South Wales', *Journal of Public Policy*, 26: 63–83.

Bell, S. and Hindmoor, A. (2009) *Rethinking Governance: The centrality of the state in modern society*, Cambridge: Cambridge University Press.

Channel 4 News (2009) *Revealed: The Unreported Nuclear Accident*. Online. Available http://www.channel4.com/news/articles/science_technology/revealed+the+unreported+nuclear+accident/3206757 (accessed 11 June 2009).

Chessire, J. (1996) 'UK Electricity Supply under Public Ownership', in J. Surrey (ed.) *The British Electricity Privatisation Experiment*, 14–39, London: Earthscan.

Chhotray, V. and Stoker, G. (2009) *Governance Theory and Practice. A Cross-Disciplinary Approach*, Basingstoke: Palgrave Macmillan.

Communities and Local Government (2010) *Localism Bill – Media Background Note*. Online. Available http://www.communities.gov.uk/news/newsroom/1794971 (accessed 6 January 2011).

Department of Business, Enterprise and Regulatory Reform (2007) *Meeting the Energy Challenge: A White Paper on Energy*, Cmd. 7124, London: TSO.

— (2008). *White Paper on Nuclear Energy*, Cmd. 7296. London: TSO.

— (2009) *Energy Trends, June 2009*. Online. Available http://www.berr.gov.uk/files/file51898.pdf (accessed 17 July 2009).

Department of Energy and Climate Change (2008) *Regional Energy Statistics*. Online. Available http://www.decc.gov.uk/en/content/cms/statistics/regional/regional.aspx (accessed 15 August 2009).

— (2009) *The UK Low Carbon Transition Plan*, London: TSO.

Department for Trade and Industry (2003) *Energy White Paper: Creating a low carbon economy*. Cmd. 5761, London: TSO.

— (2007) Meeting the energy challenge: a white paper on energy, Cmd. 7124, London: TSO.

Dunsire, A. (1996) 'Tipping the balance: Autopoiesis and governance', *Administration and Society*, 28: 299–333.

Estrin, S., Marin, A. and Selby, M. J. P. (1990) 'Conflicting aims in electricity privatisation', *Public Money and Management*. 10: 39–48.

Evans, P. (1997) 'The eclipse of the state? Reflections on stateness in an era of globalization', *World Politics Fiftieth Anniversary Special Issue*, 50: 62–87.

George, A. L. and Bennett, A. (2005) *Case Studies and Theory Development in the Social Sciences*, Cambridge (MA): MIT Press.

Gerring, J. (2007) *Case Study Research: Principles and Practices*, New York: Cambridge University Press.

Health and Safety Executive (2007) 'Enforcement Assessment Record', in J. Large (2009) *Sizewell A – Cooling pond recirculation pipe failure incident of 7 January 2007 Assessment of the NII decision making process.* Online. Available http://www.largeassociates.com/cz3179/R3179-A3.pdf (accessed 18 August 2009).

— (2009) *Supplementary notes on the HSE Board Paper 'Briefing on the Nuclear Programme' and subsequent media reporting.* Online. Available http://www.hse.gov.uk/foi/releases/nd060709supp.pdf (accessed 18 August 2009).

Hendry, C. (2008) Personal communication with the authors.

Hobson, J. M. (2000) *The State and International Relations*, Cambridge: Cambridge University Press.

Hood, C. (1986) *The Tools of Government*, Chatham (NJ): Chatham House.

Hood, C. and Margetts, H. (2007) *The Tools of Government in the Digital Age*, Basingstoke: Palgrave Macmillan.

Jessop, B. (2002) *The Future of the Capitalist State*, Cambridge: Polity Press.

Kickert, W. J. M., Klijn, E.-H. and Koppenjan, J. F. M. (1997) 'Introduction: A Management Perspective on Policy Networks', in W. J. M. Kickert, E-H. Klijn and J. F. M. Koppenjan (eds) *Managing Complex Networks: Strategies for the Public Sector*, London: Sage.

Koppenjan, J. F. M. and Klijn, E.-H. (2004) *Managing Uncertainty in Networks: A Network Approach to Problem Solving and Decision Making*, London: Routledge.

Lovell, H., Bulkeley, H. and Owens, S. (2009) 'Converging agendas? Energy and climate change policies in the UK', *Environment and Planning C: Government and Policy*, 27: 90–109.

National Grid (2008/9) *Annual Review.* Online. Available http://www.nationalgrid.com/NR/rdonlyres/A3842215-A6F6-499B-9FD5-A101EAE6D0D0/35022/8847_NG_Review.pdf (accessed 20 July 2009).

— (2009) Statement of the Connection Charging Methodology. Online. Available http://www.nationalgrid.com/NR/rdonlyres/44EB525A-D24-4141-8B07-982B819651CB/33165/GBCCMI5R0DraftvFINAL.pdf (accessed 15 August 2009).

Nuclear Decommissioning Authority (2009) *About Us.* Online. Available http://www.nda.gov.uk/aboutus (accessed 24 July 2009).

NVIVO, *Qualitative Data Analysis Software; QSR International Pty Ltd*, Version 8, 2008.

Office of National Statistics (2001) *Census 2001.* Online. Available http://www.statistics.gov.uk/census2001/population_data.asp (accessed 16 August 2009).

O'Riordan, T., Kemp, R. and Purdue, M. (1988) *Sizewell B: An Anatomy of the Inquiry*, Basingstoke: Macmillan.

Pierre, J. and Peters, B. G. (2000) *Governance, Politics and the State*, Basingstoke: Palgrave Macmillan.

Rhodes, R. A. W. (1997) *Understanding Governance*, Buckingham: Open University Press.

Scrase, I and Ockwell, D. (2009) 'Energy issues: Framing and policy change', in I. Scrase and G. MacKerron (eds) *Energy for the Future*, Basingstoke: Palgrave Macmillan.

Sørensen, E. (2006) 'Metagovernance: The changing role of politicians in processes of democratic governance', *The American Review of Public Administration*, 36: 98–114.

Sørensen, E. and Torfing, J. (eds) (2008) *Theories of Democratic Network Governance*, Basingstoke: Palgrave Macmillan.

Stoker, G. (1998) 'Governance as theory: Five propositions', *International Social Science Journal*, 50: 17–28.

Ward, T. Unpublished Presentation at the Nuclear Investors Conference, London, UK, June 2008.

Weightman, M. Unpublished Presentation at the Nuclear Investors Conference. London, UK, June 2008.

Weiss, L. (1998) *The Myth of the Powerless State*, London: Polity Press.

Wood, J. (2009) 'Hopes and fears of EDF's man on the nuclear frontline', *Utility Week*. 5th June 2009. Online. Available http://www.utilityweek.co.uk/features/interviews/the-hopes-and-fears-of-edfs-ma.php (accessed 6 June 2009).

World Nuclear News (2009) *Old Nuclear Event Out in the Open.* 12th July 2009. Online. Available http://www.world-nuclear-news.org/newsarticle. aspx?id=25415&terms=Sizewell+A (accessed 18 September 2009).

chapter seven	politicians as metagovernors – can metagovernance reconcile representative democracy and network reality?

Joop Koppenjan, Mirjam Kars and Haiko van der Voort

Introduction – the problematic position of representatives

Being a politician in our modern western network society is tough. To their electors, representatives have to account for policies produced in policy networks of administrators, civil servants and societal actors. The theorem of the 'primacy of politics' suggests that within representative democracy, elected politicians are in a position to decide upon critical societal issues. In reality, they lack the information, skills and resources to get grip on decision-making and, consequently, they find themselves in an uncomfortable position. Expectations regarding their capacity to determine policies for special interest groups, the media and electorate are high. However, their position *vis-à-vis* the networks in which policies are formulated and implemented is weak. Administrators, civil servants and network actors state that representatives act too much upon the daily worries of their electors by intervening and exercising micro-management, which disturbs their valuable but vulnerable interactions within networks. Or they are blamed for not committing themselves to network processes just to keep themselves free for formal decision-making moments. Interest groups, media and citizens may complain that politicians are outmanoeuvred by network actors and that the expected political steering and control actually becomes a symbolic exercise.

From a democratic viewpoint, this can be seen as problematic. It implies that there is a danger that the core institutions of the representative democracy, such as the representatives and representative bodies, lack the abilities to exercise and control political power by authoritatively allocating values within society (Easton 1965). Bovens *et al.* (1995) point at 'the shifting of politics' whereby key societal decisions are increasingly taken outside the influence domain of the vertical steering and accountability relations of representative democracy (see also Held, 1995; Thomassen and Schmidt 1999; Dryzek 1996; Van Kersbergen and Van Waarden 2004). In addition to a reduction in steering possibilities, there is an increase in asymmetry in relations between the representatives and executive power as regards the available information, knowledge, expertise and capacity (Scharpf 1999). Therefore, elected politicians find it difficult to influence the substance and implementation of policy (Klijn and Koppenjan 2000).

This shifting of politics does not result in the fading of representative democracy and the rise of network governance, in which new forms of horizontal democracy will prosper and replace the old ones; the old institutions of representative democracy do not perish, but are quite alive. As a result, two institutional practices coexist in what might be called 'parallel worlds', sometimes independently evolving according to their own logics and institutional rules, but occasionally coming together and colliding. The questions then are: can both practices be reconciled and how might this be achieved?

On the matter of reconciling institutions of classic representative democracy with the practices of network governance, authors like Sørenson and Torfing (2005) and Klijn and Skelcher (2007) speak of 'democratic anchorage of government networks', but there has been no authoritative answer. This chapter explores how the recent concept of 'metagovernance' might help to provide an answer. Metagovernance could be seen as a viable strategy for representatives to steer network processes. Taking up the role of metagovernor might provide representatives with a new repertoire of strategies to influence and steer network processes in such a way that the advantages of network governance and the anchorage of these practices in the institutions of representative democracy are simultaneously being realised.

However, 'metagovernance' is still ill-defined. It has been interpreted in many different ways. The aim of this chapter is to discover what we can learn about the added value of representatives as 'metagovernors' for democratic network governance. Therefore, the question is:

Can metagovernance help representatives and representative bodies redefine their role in such a way that they succeed in representing societal values, providing political steering and calling network actors to account for their behaviour and performance, without being outmanoeuvred or without disturbing the network processes, but rather facilitating and enhancing them?

We address the question as follows:

– provide clarification of the concept of metagovernance and observe how it relates to the attempts of representative bodies at steering and monitoring the policy-making process in network settings;
– observe metagovernance by representatives in practice.
– discuss the background of our explorative case study and methodological choices underlying it;
– provide a description of the case study;
– assess the role of representatives in the case study, asking to what extent they acted as metagovernors and with what results; and
– discuss the research findings.

Metagovernance – 'governance of governance'?

In public administration literature, the concept of 'network governance' is increasingly being used for analysing public decision-making and steering in complex settings. 'Networks' or 'policy networks' reflect the insight that the processes by which public policy is made and is implemented evolve in horizontal settings: complex sets of interactions between mutually dependent, but relatively autonomous public, private and societal parties. These networks cut across existing territorial, administrative and functional boundaries (Castells, 1996; Rhodes 1997, 2000; Kickert, Klijn and Koppenjan 1997).

'Steering' can be understood as deliberate attempts to influence the course of interaction processes within networks and their outcomes. Steering attempts of a single actor within a network is limited in its effects. This is mainly due to the variety of actors present, each pursuing their own objectives and applying their steering strategies, the mutual dependencies between these actors, and the dynamics of the context in which steering happens (Koppenjan et al. 2009; De Bruijn and Ten Heuvelhof 2008; O'Toole 1997). Because of these complicating factors, steering is best understood as a variety of steering efforts by various actors, referred to as 'governance' (Kooiman 1993; Pierre 2000). The increased acknowledgment of the complicating factors for steering is often presented as a shift from 'government' to 'governance'.

'Government', then, refers to a (public) hierarchical actor that has exclusive steering abilities, whereas 'governance' stresses the patterns of steering efforts by various actors. 'Governance' assumes that 'societies are governed by a combination of governing efforts by all kinds of actors and entities, public as well as non-public' (Kooiman and Jentoft 2009). In addition, governance also refers to a shift in the way government *as a public institution* steers. Because of the limitations of government's resources and capacities in the light of the complexities of its steering tasks and its dependency on other parties, forms of horizontal steering will be adopted. Government will be involved in a process of negotiation and collaboration with parties, pushing and pulling in order to have policy (and its implementation) proceeding in the intended direction or facilitating other parties to do similar. As such, governance refers to both the shift towards a horizontal style of steering by government, and to the fact that this horizontal steering is part of the larger pattern of steering efforts by the various actors within a network setting.

This raises the question whether these patterns as a whole might be deliberately changed in an intended direction, and if so, how. In the literature on governance, the concept of 'metagovernance' is reserved for this question. The way governance happens may be influenced by steering attempts from a higher level. Metagovernance is referred to as the 'governance of governance' (Jessop 2002, 2004).

Several scholars have defined some more specific activities as examples of metagovernance. Some describe metagovernance as a deliberate design-like activity, which could be an interaction process between actors about a specific problem. This is called 'process architecture' or 'process design' (De Bruijn et al. 2002;

Klijn and Edelenbos 2007). 'Governance', then, comprises of the actors that are involved in an interaction process or strategic game that addresses this problem. Metagovernance could also involve an 'institutional design'. In that case, rules, norms and habits that shape and constrain the behaviour of actors within a network are (re)designed (Sørensen and Torfing 2007: 175; Jessop 2003; Klijn and Edelenbos 2007). Such 'designing' implies active and deliberate metagovernance, which is then applied to a specific and definable 'governance network'. In this context, Triantafillou (2007) speaks of 'network formation'.

An important criticism on this literature is that it is quite optimistic about the governability of networks (Kelly 2006). It implicitly suggests a relatively determinable 'governance-system' and makes it possible to change systems deliberately. It seems to give little attention to the limitations of steering that may also be present at this level. In this way, the metagovernance literature is not so much about the '*governance* of governance', but rather about the '*government* of governance'. This approach appears to see metagovernance as a way for 'government-as-institution' to impose its goals on the network process simply by taking a meta-position.

Not all scholars subscribe to this 'government of governance'. They acknowledge that metagovernance has to be executed in the same complex and uncertain network context as government or governance. Some authors do not define a specific metagovernor (e.g. Kooiman and Jentoft 2009). O'Toole (2007: 219) writes:

> Public authorities may not be the only ones working at the metalevel. In fact, it becomes an empirical question as to whether public authorities are at all involved at the metalevel; an alternative might be that other social actors sometimes set the basic rules of the game that ultimately (at another level of action) produces outputs and outcomes.

An important suggestion from this quote is that there are more 'metagovernors'. This in turn suggests that, as governance, metagovernance cannot be understood from the perspective of a single actor. The outcome of metagovernance cannot be linked to the purposes of a single actor, but will be a result of several interventions from a number of actors that operates in a meta-arena at a metalevel (Compare Kiser and Ostrom 1982; Koppenjan and Groenewegen 2005).

But metagovernance strategies are not exclusively applied in a meta-arena or a meta-game. Trying to influence the conditions of the game may also occur in the game itself. From this perspective, metagovernors, whoever they are, are involved in the 'networked' governance processes. They may participate – more than a 'designers-perspective' assumes – in actual network interactions. This is why Sørensen and Torfing (2007: 181) distinguish 'hands off' (designing) and 'hands on' (participating) types of metagovernance. Examples of the hands-on type of metagovernance are formulating (public) policy, knowledge sharing and providing (organisation) capacity (Whitehead 2003; Sørensen and Torfing 2007: 176).

The similarity between these metagovernance efforts is that their metagovernors have the intention to have some impact on the 'metalevel'. They deliberately take a 'metaposition'. They intend to influence the network itself, rather than have some influence within the network. To be clear, this does not say a lot about the actual effects. It is perfectly possible, with hindsight, that steering efforts in a network had considerable impact on governance patterns. The main difference is that the 'design school' assumes some vertical relationship between the metagovernor and the network, whereas the 'participative' school suggests a horizontal, 'networked' relationship between several metagovernors and between metagovernors and other actors within the network.

Now that we have demarcated metagovernance as deliberate attempts to influence networks, we can distinguish two forms of metagovernance. More design-oriented metagovernance can be seen as 'government of governance', whereas more participative forms can be characterised as 'governance of governance' (see Table 7.1).[1]

Table 7.1: Metagovernance compared to government and governance

Steering Intended meta-position?	Vertical: hierarchical	Horizontal: networked
No	Government	Governance
Yes	Government of governance	Governance of governance

Building upon the above proposed distinction between these forms of metagovernance, we suggest that an important challenge for further research is to acquire knowledge about the following questions:

Under what conditions can each of these metagovernance forms be a successful in network settings?

- To what extent is our assumption that 'governance of governance' is more suited to be applied in network settings' than 'government of governance' correct?

Metagovernance by representatives?

How do the forms of steering relate to attempts of representatives and representative bodies to come to grips with the realities of network governance?

Attempts to re-establish the primacy of politics by imposing political decisions upon administrators, civil servants and societal actors, can be qualified as an attempt at restoration of *government*. If we assume that policy making happens in a network, we would not expect this to result in a reconciliation of representative democracy and network governance. Rather it is expected that these attempts

---

1. To be complete, we would have to distinguish also 'government of government' and 'governance of government'. Since we have assumed a shift from 'government to governance', we have decided not to consider these types.

reproduce the problematic effects of political interventions in network processes: disturbed interaction processes or representatives being outmanoeuvred by administrators, civil servants and network actors.

Participation of politicians in network processes might on the other hand be seen as forms of *governance*: representatives taking part in network processes (e.g. by participating in meeting with stakeholders), thus acting as actors among other actors, all pursuing their own strategies. In this way they may be successful in articulating problems and values, receiving information of problems and preferences of stakeholders and in influencing processes and outcomes. However, there are no guarantees that they will be able to steer these processes, hold actors accountable, nor that they will succeed in preventing capture by the network, making it impossible for them to exercise their formal rights to take authoritative decisions and to hold administrators accountable. So, metagovernance might be an alternative way for politicians to deal with network reality.

An interesting example of *metagovernance* by representatives is provided by the introduction of a dual system into local and provincial politics in 2003 by the Dutch national government. The aim was to strengthen the position of representative bodies *vis-à-vis* administrators. In this system, representatives have a 'framework-setting role', which formally implies that 'the representative body lays down beforehand what the aims and the desired societal effects of a particular policy should be. The Executive sees to the implementation of the policy within the scope of these frameworks' (Association of Provincial Authorities and Ministry of the Interior 2006). This idea of framework setting builds on popular ideas from the New Public Management School. Concepts successfully applied in private businesses, e.g. 'management by objectives' and 'performance management', are also prescribed for governments (Osborne and Gaebler 1992; Behn and Kant 1999; Osborne and Plastrik 2000; Pollitt 2003).

It is unclear how this form of metagovernance deals with the requirements of network governance. Actually, it can be argued that the idea that the provincial and municipal representatives lay down beforehand unilaterally the aims and desired social effects of policies, neglects network characteristics like complexities, interdependencies and dynamics. Framework setting as defined above, therefore, can be seen as a form of 'government of governance'. It is expected that this type of metagovernance will not contribute to reconciling representative democracy with network governance, but rather will encounter similar limitations as the government-inspired attempt at re-establishing the primacy of politics.

This brings us to the question of what the repertoire of representatives that use 'governance of governance' strategies would look like. We assume that government policies are developed and implemented in networks in which the Executive interacts with representatives of other governments, businesses, interest groups, users and citizens. This implies that metagovernance strategies of representatives and their representative bodies would have to:

- find a way of dealing with the complexities of the issues dealt with in these networks, thus overcoming the problems of information asymmetry and overload;

- take interdependencies that characterise these networks into account. Understanding that administrators are dependent for their performance upon other actors, may for instance result in negotiating frameworks and performance measures rather than imposing them;
- cope with uncertainties and dynamics of network processes. Instead of simply defining frameworks upfront, this requires strategies that allow flexibility while keeping actors committed to agreed upon goals (Compare Koppenjan, Kars and Van der Voort 2009).

As formulated in the introduction above, this chapter aims at examining to what extent metagovernance and, more specifically, governance of governance applied by politicians in a network setting can contribute to the reconciliation of representative democracy and network governance. In order to do so, and building upon the above reasoning, our case study is guided by the following questions:

- How was the representative body involved in the networked policy process?
- How can their involvement be qualified: as government, governance, government of governance or governance of governance?
- What were the effects of these attempts at steering and how can these be explained?
- What can be learned from these findings regarding the contribution of metagovernance by representatives to reconciling representative democracy and network governance?

Methodology and case study selection – the reconstruction of agricultural areas

To answer the above questions, we will analyse the role of politicians in the reconstruction of agricultural areas in the Dutch Province of North Brabant. This reconstruction was required by the national government as a reaction to the swine flu epidemic of 1997. Zoning was supposed to reduce the risk of further outbreaks. The province governed the reconstruction process by drafting and implementing the 'Reconstruction's Move' (*Reconstructie aan Zet*) policy paper. The evaluation of this policy process formed part of the broader study 'Steering with frameworks', which we conducted in 2006 (Koppenjan *et al.* 2006). First, we describe the context of the 'Steering with frameworks' research and how the case study into the drafting and implementation of the 'Reconstruction's Move' policy paper was performed. We then discuss why we chose to focus on this policy paper.

'Steering with frameworks' studied the provincial practice of framework setting, which took place at a time that a so-called 'dual system' had just been introduced in the Dutch provinces. This system, introduced in 2003, implied that the Provincial Executive (PE) and the elected Provincial Council were 'unbundled'. In 2003, on instigation of the Dutch Ministry of the Interior, a separation has been made between the Provincial Council (PC) and the Executive Board regarding their composition, powers, and function. Earlier a 'monistic' relationship prevailed: the members of the Executive Board were also members of the PC. This was seen as problematic, leading to a weak position of the Council, not being able to steer the Executive Board or to call it to account. Consequently, the roles between the Board and PC had to be reallocated. In the new, dualistic situation, the PE deals with administration. The role of the PC is to set the frameworks for the administration, to monitor the PE, and to represent the citizens. As noted in the introduction above, the framework-setting role of the PC means that 'the Council lays down beforehand what the aims and the desired societal effects of a particular policy should be. The Executive sees to the implementation of the policy within these frameworks' (Association of Provincial Authorities and Ministry of the Interior 2006). In order to carry out its steering and monitoring role, the PC makes use of framework-setting policy papers such as 'Reconstruction's Move'.

The case study regarding the reconstruction of agricultural areas in the Province of North-Brabant was conducted as follows:

1. The content of the policy paper 'Reconstruction's Move', the framework for the rest of the process, was analysed.

2. We interviewed members of the PC and PE, representatives of non-governmental organisations, and civil servants. These interviews focused on the content of the framework in the specific policy paper, the process of setting and implementing the framework during the phases of agenda setting, and preparation, adoption and implementation.

3. We organised a workshop in which members of the PC discussed their framework-setting and monitoring role during these three phases.

4. We proposed an arrangement for framework setting and monitoring by means of framework-setting policy papers.

We believe the provincial practice of framework setting and, more specifically, 'Reconstruction's Move' to be a relevant case in the light of our theoretical framework. First, the reconstruction process was consciously organised as an interactive process, in which stakeholders were involved in the formation and implementation of the policy. As such the case provides a good example of network governance: administrators, civil servants and stakeholders collaborating and negotiating. Secondly, the policy affected the core interests of farmers in the province, an important group within the constituencies of the political parties, and this guaranteed a high level of political attention, resulting in an active involvement of representatives and the PC in the process. As such the process provides ample data on how elected politicians operated in this network governance process. Thirdly, the simultaneous introduction of the dual system makes this case study even more interesting, since it may be regarded as an attempt to improve the coupling between vertical politics and horizontal networks by means of metagovernance through framework setting.

The reconstruction of agricultural areas in the Dutch province of North Brabant[2]

In reaction to the swine flu epidemic in 1997, the Dutch national government decided that areas with intensive livestock industries should be reconstructed. Zoning should reduce the risks of new epidemics. This would require relocation and closure of farms. These radical interventions in agricultural areas would at the same time provide opportunities for new economic developments, nature development, improvement of environmental conditions and improvement of the well-being and viability of these areas. These reconstructions were imposed by the National Reconstruction Act (*Reconstructiewet Concentratiegebieden*) of 2002.

Policy design of the reconstruction of the agricultural areas

In 1999, the Province of North Brabant anticipated the implementation of this law. It initiated an interactive process in which stakeholders, like municipalities, farmers and environmental groups, participated in drafting the provincial White Paper, 'Reconstruction's Move' (*Reconstructie aan zet*) of June 2001. This White Paper presented the framework that would guide the further process of making reconstruction plans. It stated that sustainable development within agricultural areas requires dynamics, especially as far as economic activities are concerned. These dynamics should be governed by a framework in order to ensure the sustainability of developments.

The White Paper focused on seven agricultural areas to be reconstructed. Plans regarding these areas had to be ready by 2005 and would be the result of an interactive process, managed by the reconstruction commissions. In the reconstruction commissions, various stakeholders would be represented: farmers, inhabitants, business, environmental and nature groups, and municipalities. Representatives of the province and national government would participate as advisors. The White Paper formulated the goals that had to be realised by 2015, which is ten years after the plans would have been accepted and implemented.

The White Paper provided actors with substantive guidelines to be used in (re)allocating functions and activities in the reconstruction area. Goals assigned to reconstruction commissions referred to good environmental conditions (water, surface, air, nature and landscape) and to the creation and use of opportunities for sustainable social-economic development (agriculture, recreation and tourism, socio-economic policy and transport).

In addition, the White Paper specified requirements for the process, rules to be followed, steps to be taken, parties to be involved, instruments to be used, and products to be delivered. In doing so, the province did not intend to dictate all activities. By emphasising goals, not means, the province intended to challenge stakeholders in the area to generate innovative ideas and solutions. It took

---

2.   The information on the case is based on Koppenjan *et al.* 2006.

the network-like setting of the process as a point of departure: it encouraged collaboration among involved stakeholders and bottom-up initiatives, which would result in tailor-made plans. At the same time, this approach provided guidance by specifying constraints, conditions and goals.

The roles of the province would be: formulation of the policy framework, managing the overall process, facilitating the reconstruction commissions by the creation of favourable conditions, providing subsidies, and alignment with other provincial policies.

The processes promised to be quite complex, not just because of the various interests to be reconciled, but also since the province required that plans should result in speeding up and enhancing various other provincial policies. Furthermore, the plans had to comply with the regulations of various governments (municipalities, national government and the European Union) over a number of topics.

The plans would overrule the planning responsibilities of municipalities, to make sure that they would be implemented; it was serious business. The province would take the final decision on the plans. The province promised beforehand to accept the reconstruction plans as far as they complied with the formulated conditions in the White Paper. It would not depart from the plans without an adequate motivation.

Since the plans would be developed under the regime of the National Reconstruction Act, eventually national government would have the final say. It would also co-finance the implementation of the plans, as long as they were realised within the legally-determined time framework.

Role of the Provincial Council

Agriculture is an important sector within the Province of North Brabant. Since the vital interests of farmers were at stake in this process, the policy was highly significant, with a potential for conflicts and politicisation. In 1999 and 2004, the newly-inaugurated Executive, a coalition of political parties with a majority in the Provincial Council (PC), had depicted the revitalisation of agricultural areas as one of its priorities. What political parties and especially the governing coalition definitely did not want to happen was an outbreak of protest by farmers, for instance by blocking the entrance of the provincial government building, as had happened a few years earlier. Given the political significance of the issue, it was obvious that the PC, with its seventy-five elected part-time members, would play a role in this process, one way or another. What role did it play and, more specifically, to what extent did it succeed in fulfilling the role of framework-setter and metagovernor in the network process? In this network process, the Executive, consisting of six full-time members of the Executive Board, chaired by the Queen's Governor and supported by the public service, consisting of about 1,300 civil servants, fulfilled a prominent role. The Executive closely interacted with the wide set of actors and provided metagovernance by setting up and managing the interactive processes resulting in the White Paper and its implementation in the seven reconstruction areas. Below, the role of the PC in this process is analysed by specifying its involvement in the various phases of the process: the drafting of the White Paper between 1999 and 2001, the design of the reconstruction plans between 2001 and 2005 and the decision-making on these plans between 2005 and 2006.

Role of the Provincial Council in the start-up process

Provincial politicians were involved in the interactive processes by which the 'Reconstruction's Move' White Paper was drafted. The White Paper was decided upon by the Provincial Council (PC) and draft versions had been discussed in its specialised commissions. Members of the PC considered the White Paper to be theirs. It gave the Executive the assignment to govern the process, to inform the PC and to come up with good plans. The PC would take the final, formal decision on the reconstruction plans. Other responsibilities, such as the fulfilment of the role of responsible authority for environmental impact assessments, were delegated to the Executive, in order to speed up the process.

Although the PC considered the White Paper to be *its* framework, it had not actually formulated the framework itself. The content was formulated by the civil service and the Executive in collaboration with stakeholders. Also, it was observed that members of the PC were surprised by the complexity of the topics addressed. Despite this complexity, according to observers, the debate in the PC on the White Paper maintained its focus on the main topics at stake.

In addition to this formal trajectory, individual members of the PC, especially members of governing parties, were informally consulted by the Executive about the composition of the reconstruction commissions and especially about the appointments of the chairs. On the one hand, this indicates that elected politicians were influential in the network process. On the other hand, the informal nature of this consultation might also be regarded as the Executive undermining attempts at framework setting and metagovernance by the PC, co-opting politicians, outmanoeuvring the members of the opposition, and preventing debate in the PC.

Role of the Provincial Council in the drafting of reconstruction plans

In the period between 2001 and 2005, the seven reconstruction commissions drafted their plans in collaboration with the stakeholders in the areas. The Provincial Council was informed about the progress of the processes by quarterly reports. In this period, members of the PC were regularly invited to visit the reconstruction areas.

In 2002, a deadlock arose between the province and the farmers. Complying with all the conditions and rules and regulations meant that new developments and business expansion ware impossible. More specifically, the province urged the farmers to reduce the size of the existing locations for agricultural businesses. The space used would remain available for these farms, but space that was reserved and not yet used would no longer be available. New enlargements of existing farms would only be allowed by permits. Although the organisation representing the farmers, the ZLTO, stated that this was unacceptable, neither civil servants nor members of the Executive were responsive to these signals. Subsequently, the ZLTO withdrew from the reconstruction processes. Without the farmers participating, it was unclear how the processes could proceed. Next, members of the PC stepped in, making statements on the need to break the impasse and urging the Executive to be more flexible. This lead to the introduction of a new, informal rule of the game: from then onwards, the existing rights of farmers would be respected, except in the most vulnerable locations within the reconstruction areas. Thanks to the mediating activities of the members of the PC, the ZLTO returned to the negotiation table. More importantly, this intervention led to a turn around in the provincial approach: a strict maintenance of upfront conditions was replaced by a more flexible approach, judging new initiatives in the light of the objectives and values underlying concrete goals and conditions.

Role of the Provincial Council in the formal decision-making process

Although the reconstruction commissions were supposed to comply with the framework set by the Province of North Brabant and to comply with the various policies and regulations that applied, the plans that were eventually submitted did not do so in all respects. For example, they included a proposal for expansion of agricultural activities in vulnerable areas. Since the plans were binding, legal procedures of consultation and appeal had to be followed. Citizens would experience the effects of the plans and therefore formal procedures of objection and appeal had to be followed in the phase of decision-making. During the consultation phase, 3,000 objections against the plans were put forward. If these subsequently resulted in 3,000 appeals to the court, the success of the reconstruction process would be jeopardised. So the province had to judge the plans in the light of the framework, objectives and existing policies and regulations, while at the same time accommodating the objections. The Executive Board dealt with this problem by not simply rejecting the plans, but by judging them in the light of the objectives and intentions underlying the framework. It explored how conflicting interests could be accommodated by a different way of implementing the proposals or by introducing mitigating or compensating measures. If exceptions on the framework were agreed upon, they were made valid for all the areas, in order to increase the chance that the plans would hold in court. The amended plans in the end resulted in 167 court cases, which were not considered a problem for their acceptance and implementation.

Although members of the Provincial Council (PC) had been involved during the interactive process, in this phase, in which they were supposed to take the final decision on the plans, it was especially difficult for them to have an overview of the various regulations and policies that were involved. It was not easy to understand the context in which the plans had to be judged and which frameworks, objectives and agreements had to be applied. What made things even more complicated was that during the process new objectives and insights had been added to the earlier framework.

To cope with this complexity, the PC decided to organise hearings during the consultation phase. These hearings provided an overview of the state of affairs in the seven interactive processes, the backgrounds of the compromises that had been negotiated and the logistics that had governed these negotiations. At the same time, the hearings fulfilled an important symbolic function, by articulating the engagement of the politicians with the process and their concern with the way the interests of the various stakeholders would be affected. At the same time, the politicians did not yield to the temptation to make promises to specific stakeholders for electoral gain, thus deranging or even jeopardising the reconstruction process. Here the PC seems to have functioned as an institution, rather than as an arena for party politics (Andeweg and Irwin 2002).

After the Executive had adjusted the plans of the reconstruction commissions, stakeholders and, especially, nature and environmental organisations started a lobby towards members of the PC in order to adjust the plans further in the direction of their preferences. Being informed on how the plans had been negotiated, the members of the PC decided to react in a reserved way, not wanting to overthrow the delicate compromises the Executive Board had negotiated. Not all political parties within the PC agreed with this attitude though. The opposition initiated a debate in the PC on the extent to which the plans would damage what was called 'the vulnerable provincial interests', especially in the field of nature development and the environment.

Table 7.2: The interactive process of the reconstruction of agricultural areas in North Brabant

1997	Swine flu epidemic in the Netherlands Government announces a bill to reconstruct agricultural areas
Drafting of the framework	
1999	Province announces reconstructions and starts consultations
2000	Parliament accepts the Reconstruction bill
2001	Framework-setting White Paper 'Reconstruction's Move' accepted by Provincial Council
Implementation of the White Paper: the development of reconstruction plans	
2001	7 reconstruction commissions established in seven agricultural areas
2002	Deadlock: ZLTO leaves the reconstruction commissions Members of Provincial Council mediate
2003	Province makes turn from forbidding to development: process continues
Decision-making on reconstruction plans	
2004	Consultations of stakeholders in context of formal procedures Hearings by Provincial Council
2005	Renegotiations of plans Decision of Provincial Council on plans 167 court cases

Assessing the role of the Provincial Council in the interactive process – metagovernance?

In this section, the metagovernance of the Provincial Council (PC) in network governance is assessed by identifying role of the PC and its members in the interactive process aimed at the reconstruction of agricultural areas and examining the effects of this role fulfilment.

Reconstruction as an interactive process – metagoverned by the province

The process of the reconstruction of agricultural areas can be seen as a form of network governance. Stakeholders, various governments, representatives of businesses and their umbrella organisations, interest groups and residents collaborated and negotiated in developing plans for the reconstruction of agricultural areas. The choice for an interactive process meant that the province restrained from a government approach, but acknowledged the importance of governance, given the complexities, interdependencies and dynamics involved. However, the process was not a purely a bottom-up or self-regulatory process. Within the legal framework provided by the national government, the Province of North Brabant took up an active role as metagovernor by initiating the process, providing a framework for the processes and by actively guiding and supervising the processes and their results.

A first look at the Council's role – metagovernance

Within this provincial metagovernance approach, the Provincial Council and its members tried to fulfil a meaningful role by representing the interests of the provincial inhabitants, by providing political steering and by holding network actors and, especially, the Executive accountable. In doing so, the PC and its members undertook a set of activities.

During the processes of policy formation and consultation by which the White Paper and the reconstruction plans were interactively drafted, members of the PC participated in the governance processes. They did so by being present, doing site visits, exchanging information and ideas and building relationships. We consider these to be governance activities – the participation of politicians in the interactive process as actors among actors.

The main part of the activities of the PC and its members, however, had the nature of metagovernance: setting frameworks for the network process and the Executive Board and facilitating processes to arrive at frameworks or aimed at coming up with solutions within the scope set by the frameworks. Certainly, the PC did not carry out the metagovernance in isolation; rather it supported the Executive in its metagoverning, thus providing co-metagovernance (compare Kooiman (1993), who speaks of co-governance). The perception of the PC as being in control, actually being the metagovernor of the process, as claimed by some politicians, is a clear exaggeration. To a certain extent, the PC merely sanctioned frameworks developed by the network and the Executive in collaboration, delegated responsibilities to the latter and eventually had a limited influence on the plans developed by others. It would not be fair to take an opposite stand though, and declare that the PC was set aside by the other actors. The PC was involved in the formulation of the framework, it supported the governance processes that led to the framework, and it conducted a political debate on the main topics involved, not getting lost in details. So the PC contributed to the metagovernance process by providing co-metagovernance.

Metagovernance by the province – government or governance of governance?

The type of metagovernance the province originally used can be seen as somewhere in between 'government of governance' and 'governance of governance'. The argument for governance of governance is supported by the way the frameworks were set: by a process of consultation and negotiation rather than by frameworks being imposed by government. On the other hand, the formulation of the frameworks was not simply a bottom-up process, but governed by the province, within the larger legal framework set by national government, requiring reconstruction. This inequality between government and stakeholders may lead to the conclusion that instead of governance of governance, the steering style used by the province was predominantly that of government of governance. Another indication in this direction is provided by the inclination of the province to keep reconstruction commissions to the framework set beforehand.

A shift towards governance of governance

Due to the impasse resulting from the prevalent government-of-governance approach and the subsequent intervention by the Provincial Council, the metagovernance approach shifted in 2002 towards governance of governance. The dynamics within the process have been acknowledged, new topics and considerations have been incorporated and rather than persevering with the upfront goals and constraints, ways of accommodating conflicting interests have been explored. This approach became a guiding principle, especially in the formal phase of decision-making.

If we focus on the interventions of the PC and its members, it can be concluded that they reflected the characteristics of governance of governance rather than government of governance. It was the PC that urged the province to change its metagovernance style, thus exercising a major influence on the reconstruction process as a whole. In the phase of formal decision-making, the PC did not use the upfront framework as a departing point for the assessment of the reconstruction plans, but chose a process-like approach: organising hearings to cope with information problems, familiarising itself with the logistics and rules that had been developed in the governance processes, articulating provincial values, and acting as a last resort for stakeholders. Also in this phase, the metagovernance of the PC was complementary to the metagovernance of the Executive, adding to it and providing the process with democratic legitimacy by being involved.

Attempts at steering and an explanation of the effects

It might be concluded that the Provincial Council succeeded in internalising the logic of the interactive reconstruction process, supporting it rather than disturbing it, coping with the information overload, and focusing on the main problems rather than losing itself in details, micro-management and party politics. The fact that members of the PC did not engage in party politics may be seen as an indicator of the quality of the contribution of the politicians to the process.

However, the actual contribution of the PC in this phase may also be assessed differently. It may be argued that its involvement was merely symbolic, express-ing its engagement rather than steering or holding parties accountable. Certainly the PC did not succeed in keeping parties to upfront formulated goals, due to the complexity of the process. It may also be stated that the PC merely accepted the compromises negotiated in the network, rather than influencing them. The re-served attitude towards nature and environmental group lobbies might also be interpreted as politicians being co-opted by the Executive, not daring to go against the dominating coalition of farmers and the Executive, thus trading off provincial values. The late debate on provincial values, initiated by the opposition parties indeed supports this interpretation. However, the lack of overall political conflict, the continued support of stakeholders for the process during the whole trajectory and the absence of party politics during the hearings all suggest that in the process, rather than the PC being captured and the opposition parties being outmanoeu-vred, various interests were taken seriously and were accommodated, and Council members were fulfilling their role as metagovernors adequately. The PC fulfilled a modest but consistent role, coping with the challenges that result from the network characteristics of the governance setting by using governance of governance rather than government of governance. It acted as an institution rather than as an arena, articulating provincial values, mediating between conflicting interests and safe-guarding the quality of the process, thus providing the Executive with meaningful complementary metagovernance and performing the role of framework-setter and co-metagovernor successfully.

Conclusions – governance of governance and framework setting

The aim of this contribution was to examine how metagovernance might help representatives and representative bodies to redefine their role in such a way that they succeed in representing societal values, providing political steering and call-ing network actors to account for their behaviour and performance, without being outmanoeuvred or without disturbing the network processes, but rather facilitating and enhancing them.

A first conclusion is that although both in theory and practice doubts exist as to whether politicians are actually prepared and capable of engaging in me-tagovernance in the case of network governance processes, the findings show that examples of such practice do exist and can be successful in metagoverning these processes. The case study simultaneously shows that, given the limited resources of representatives, the expectations of the effects of their metagoverning activities should be modest. It seems unrealistic to expect them to control the network process. Rather the case study shows how representatives align their steering attempts with those of the Executive Board, providing co-metagovernance. Nevertheless, by doing so, they may succeed in influencing the process, providing it with political steering and holding network actors accountable, thus effectively increasing the democratic legitimacy of the network process.

A further conclusion is that although the case shows that metagovernance can be successful, it does not imply that all forms of metagovernance will do. More specifically, the case provides indications that in network settings attempts at government of governance are difficult to maintain on the long run, because of the very characteristics of these settings. The same characteristics underlying the shift from government to governance are also apparent at a metalevel, complicating 'government of governance', and requiring governance of governance instead.

Given the single case-study approach used, it is not possible to generalise too much. It is unclear to what extent the conditions underlying the success in this case study are specific and would be repeated in other cases. For instance, the awareness of the politicians with regard to the political risks at stake in the process may have resulted in a willingness to collaborate as an institution rather than as an arena. This could be unique rather than generic. Also, the shadow of hierarchy hanging over the process may have shaped and mitigated the behavior of network actors, thus making the job of metagovernance relatively easy. And, of course, the characteristics of provincial representatives in the Dutch context and the institutional context in which they operate may have been specific, again reducing any general lessons applicable other sectors, governmental levels and countries.

So, further theoretical thinking and systematic empirical research is needed into the forms and effects of metagovernance used by politicians and into the conditions under which these strategies can successfully be selected and applied.

References

Association of Provincial Authorities and the Ministry of the Interior (2006) *Vernieuwingsimpuls Dualisme en provinciale democratie*. Online. Available http://www.vernieuwingsimpulsprovincies.nl.

Andeweg, R. D. and Irwin, G. A. (2002) *Governance and Politics of the Netherlands*, London, New York: Palgrave MacMillan.

Behn, R. D. and Kant, P. A. (1999) 'Strategies for avoiding the pitfalls of performance contracting', *Public Productivity and Management Review*, 22 (4).

Bovens, M. A. P., Derksen, W., Witteveen, W., Kalma, W. P., and Becker, F. (1995) *De verplaatsing van de politiek: Een agenda voor democratische vernieuwing*, Amsterdam: Wiardi Beckman Stichting (in Dutch).

Castells, M. (1996) *The Rise of the Network Society*, Oxford: Blackwell.

Dryzek, J. S. (1996) *Democracy in Capitalist Times*, Oxford: Oxford University Press.

de Bruijn, H., Heuvelhof, E. F. ten and Veld, R. J. In 't (2002) *Process Management: Why Project Management Fails in Complex Decision Making Processes*, Dordrecht: Kluwer.

de Bruijn, H. and Heuvelhof, E. F. ten (2008) *Management in Networks: On Multi-actor Decision Making*, London: Routledge.

Easton, D. (1965) *A Systems Analysis of Political Life*, New York: Wiley.

Held, D. 1995. *Models of Democracy*, Cambridge: Polity Press.

Jessop, B. (2002) *The Future of the Capitalist State*, Cambridge: Polity.

— (2004) 'Multi-level Governance and Multi-level Meta-governance', in I. Bache and M. Flanders, *Multi-level Governance*, Oxford: Oxford Press.

Jessop, R. 'Governance, Governance Failure, and Meta-Governance', paper presented at the International Seminar on Policies, Governance and Innovation for Rural Areas, Università della Calabria, 21–23 November 2003.

Kelly, J. (2006) 'Central regulation of English local authorities: An example of meta-governance?', *Public Administration*, 84 (3): 603–21.

Kickert, W. J. M., Klijn, E. H., Koppenjan, J. F. M. (eds) (1997) *Managing Complex Networks*, London: Sage.

Kiser, L. and Ostrom, V. (1982) 'The Three Worlds of Action: A Meta-theoretical Synthesis of Institutional Approaches', in E. Ostrom (ed.) *Strategies of Political Inquiry*, Beverly Hills: Sage: 197–222.

Klijn, E. H. and Edelenbos, J. (2007) 'Meta-governance as Network Management', in E. Sørensen and J. Torfing, *Theories of Democratic Network Governance*, New York: Palgrave MacMillan.

Klijn, E. H. and Koppenjan, J. F. M. (2000) 'Politicians and interactive decision making: Institutional spoilsports or playmakers', *Public Administration*, 78 (2): 365–88.

Klijn, E. H. and Skecher, C. (2007) 'Democracy and network governance: Compatible or not?', *Public Administration*, 85 (3): 587–608.

Kooiman, J. (ed.) (1993) *Modern Governance: New Government-Society Interactions*, London: Sage.

Kooiman, J. and Jentoft, S. (2009) 'Meta-governance: Values, norms and principles, and the making of hard choices', *Public Administration*, 87 (4): 818–36.

Koppenjan, J. F. M. and Groenewegen, J. (2005) 'Institutional design for complex technological systems', *International Journal for Technology, Policy and Management*, 5 (3): 240–58.

Koppenjan, J. F. M, Kars, M., van der Voort, H. G. and Heuvelhof, E. F. ten (2006) *Sturen met kaders*. Onderzoek in opdracht van de Commissie Beleidsevaluatie van de Provinciale Staten van Noord-Brabant. (Research commissioned by the Committee for Policy Evaluation of the Provincial Council of Noord-Brabant) Delft/Den Bosch (in Dutch).

Koppenjan, J., Kars, M. and Van der Voort, H. (2009) 'Vertical politics in horizontal policy networks: Framework setting as coupling arrangement', *Policy Studies Journal*, 37 (4): 769–92.

Osborne, D. and Gaebler, T. (1992) *Reinventing Government*, Reading MA: Addison-Wesley.

Osborne, D. and Plastrik, P. (2000) *The Reinventor's Fieldbook: Tools for Transforming your Government*, San Fransisco: Jossey-Bass.

O'Toole, L. J. (1997) 'Treating networks seriously: practical and research-based agendas in public administration', *Public Administration Review*, 44.

— (2007) 'Governing Outputs and Outcomes of Governance Networks', in E. Sørensen and J. Torfing, *Theories of Democratic Network Governance*, New York: Palgrave MacMillan.

Pierre, J. (ed.) (2000) *Debating Governance. Authority, Steering and Democracy*, Oxford: Oxford University Press.

Pollitt, C. (2003) *The Essential Public Manager*, London: Open University Press/ McGraw-Hill.

Rhodes, R. A. W. (1997) *Understanding Governance: Policy Networks, Governance, reflexivity and accountability*, Open University Press, Buckingham/Philadelphia.

— (2000) 'Governance and Public Administration', in *Debating Governance: Authority, Steering and Democracy*, J. Pierre (ed.) Oxford: Oxford University Press.

Scharpf, F.W. (1999) *Governing in Europe: Effective and Democratic?*, Oxford: Oxford University Press.

Sørensen, E. and Torfing, J. (2005) 'The democratic anchorage of governance networks', *Scandinavian Political Studies*, 28 (3): 195–218.

— (2007) *Theories of Democratic Network Governance*, New York: Palgrave MacMillan.

Thomassen, J. and Schmidt, H. (eds) (1999) *Political representation and legitimacy in the European Union*, Oxford: Oxford University Press.

Triantafillou, P. (2007) 'Governing the Formation and Mobilization of Governance Networks', in E. Sørensen and J. Torfing, *Theories of Democratic*

Network Governance, New York: Palgrave MacMillan.

van Kersbergen, K. , and van Waarden, F. (2004) 'Governance as a bridge between disciplines: Cross-disciplinary inspiration regarding shifts in governance and problems of governability, accountability and legitimacy', *European Journal of Political Research*, 43: 143–71.

Whitehead, M. (2003) 'In the shadow of hierarchy: Meta-governance, policy reform and urban regeneration in the West Midlands', *Area*, 35(1): 6–14.

chapter | metagovernance by numbers –
eight | technological lock-in of australian
| and danish employment policies?

Peter Triantafillou

Introduction

Over the last two or three decades, the handling of unemployment has changed dramatically.[1] In general terms, Keynesian-inspired demand management and so-cial security mechanisms have been altered, supplemented and partly replaced by employment policies that target the supply of labour at both the individual and collective levels (Jessop 1993). At the individual level, the attempts to make work pay and increase the so-called 'employability of the unemployed' are working to reconstitute the unemployed as an active job seeker (Dean 1995). At the collective level, tax regimes and public infrastructures are redesigned with a view to create competitive workfare states (Cerny 1997; Peck 2001). Accordingly, work in the form of regular, paid labour is no longer only a means to the economic survival of households and national wealth, but also increasingly regarded as a vehicle for individual self-esteem and being a full citizen (Walters 1997). This change in the governing of unemployment has also been associated with important transforma-tions of the employment services in many OECD countries (OECD 1999). Despite many significant variations in this transformation, two elements seem to be part and parcel of this process. First, we find a range of measures seeking to move the unemployed into work as fast as possible regardless of her or his (other) needs and problems, an approach often termed 'work first'. Secondly, in the process of adopting this approach, the employment services have been infused with more or less comprehensive performance measurement systems seeking to gauge the ef-fectiveness, efficiency and, at times, the quality of these services. The broad ques-tion driving this chapter is: what, if any, interactions can be identified between the work-first approach and performance measurement techniques?

This chapter addresses the metagovernance of the interactions between policy goals and policy instruments. My assumption is that in order to properly under-stand metagovernance, it is necessary to address not only how the interactions between societal actors are more or less directly governed, but also to address how the interactions between policy goals and policy instruments are governed. If it is correct that the metagoverning of the interactions between policy goals and policy

---

1. This chapter is indebted to the generous advice and discussions offered by Mark Considine. The responsibility for any errors or dubious assertions rests solely with the author.

instruments somehow shapes the choice of policy goals, then it also sets certain limits to the freedom for agency experienced by the individuals and organisations engaged in interactive policy making. For this reason, it may be worth examining the possible interactions and linkages between policy goals and instruments. In order to address the interactions between policy goals and performance measurement instruments, we may first note the existence of a rapidly growing literature that has paid attention to the unintended consequences of performance measurement systems (Smith 1995; Van Thiel and Leeuw 2002; Bevan and Hood 2006). Some research also exists on the more or less unintended consequences of measuring employment policies such as creaming of the strongest client, parking of the weakest clients, and reducing local discretion in service provision (Considine 2005; Marston 2006). What this literature succinctly demonstrates is that performance measurement techniques may contribute to all kinds of non-intended results. More generally, this literature shows that often there is no direct link between policy goals and the instruments adopted to pursue these goals. Yet, in order to make this point, we are necessarily forced to retain a Weberian-inspired distinction between performance measurement systems and means deduced from pre-given political intentions or ends. If not, it would hardly make sense to talk about non-intended effects.

There are, however, at least two problems associated with applying the Weberian ideal of means or policy instruments as something deduced – via rational expert knowledge – from pre-existing political goals as a framework for analysing the interactions or the relations between the performance measurement techniques and employment policy approach. First, as scholars of implementation processes have argued for some time, ends and means are often extremely difficult to disentangle in real life. This may be so because political goals are vaguely defined, if not absent (Hjern and Hull 1982: 114), change during the political process (Majone and Wildawsky 1978), or because such goals are formulated before the identification of the problems they are addressing, i.e. according to some contingent 'garbage-can process' (Cohen *et al.* 1972). Secondly, the analytical distinction between ends and means at times leads to the conclusion that eventual unintended effects brought about by the use of certain means, such as performance measurement, can be more or less easily rectified by selecting other more appropriate means (Smith 1995: 301–5). However, two decades of New Public Management-inspired reforms in many OECD countries indicate that such side effects are not so easily removed. Accordingly, it seems worth entertaining the suggestion that ends and means are somehow more intimately related than normally assumed in much of the 'side effect' literature.

Another way to shed light on the interactions between performance measurement and the employment policy approach is to address what could be termed the *constitutive effects*, i.e. the consequences of adopting a particular policy instrument for the problem identification, policy objectives or policy design. Michael Power and others have argued that in the process of making practices auditable, calculable and/or measurable, these practices are changed (Power 1997: 87–9). In other words, instead of the Weberian ideal of means being determined by the calculation of the ways in which we may most rationally pursue a given end, it may be that the means somehow influences the ends chosen. This seems to me a fruitful avenue for addressing how performance measurement interrelates with the problem identification, policy objectives and design. Such an analytical avenue has been developed by Bruno Latour, who regards objects and technologies not merely as means to given human ends, but as devices that enable and thereby shape human actions, deliberations and goals in particular ways (Latour and Venn 2002). While the suggestion found in some Actor-Network Theory studies that objects and technologies per se have the capacity to act is dubious, I find it worth pursuing the idea that the availability of technologies and practical implements makes a difference to the ways in which a political problem is addressed and tackled.

To assume that the choice of means is somehow related with and limits the scope of possible ends does not amount to simply reversing the causal relationship between ends and means, i.e. to claim that means somehow determines ends. In order to avoid such causal reductionisms, we may turn to Foucault's notion of *regime of practice*, which suggests that we study political interventions as the contingent relations between an epistemological axis (ways of producing true knowledge about a problem to be governed) and a moral axis (desirable goals and codes of conduct) (Foucault 1991: 75). In the present case, this implies that we study the interactions between two elements. First, the ways of producing true knowledge about unemployment. A number of studies have suggested that the governing of unemployment is underpinned by an ideological or epistemological infrastructure that may broadly be dubbed 'neo-liberalism' or 'advanced liberalism'. While this may have a lot of credence, we cannot simply deduce or read off actual political interventions from such wider intellectual infrastructures (Howard 2006). We need to be more specific by turning our attention to the tangible forms of knowledge pertaining to the governing of unemployment, notably the knowledge created through solid performance measurement techniques. Secondly, we should study the political goals and desirable conduct of the unemployed and the job services. Apart from the general ambition of reducing unemployment, just what sort of goals and codes of conduct are deemed desirable? What are the expectations imposed on the unemployed and how should the employment services conduct themselves in order to reduce unemployment? It is the strategic and irreducible interactions between these two axes that are studied below.

This chapter therefore explores the interplay between the calculative devices for the monitoring of the employment service on the one hand and the problem identification and the formulation of goals on the other. Such an understanding may supplement the suggestion that the New Public Management reforms in general and contracting out in particular favour a work first approach (Bredgaard and Larsen 2007). Based on a comparative study of Australia, Denmark and the Netherlands, they argue that the making of a market of private providers competing for delivering employment services in the most effective and/or efficient manner makes it difficult to deviate from policy goals focusing on short-term measurable results. While this argument does seem to have some credibility in the Australian case, where the employment services have gone through wholesale outsourcing, the Danish case does not fit so easily. While the employment services in Denmark have been extensively contracted out over the last few years, it is the municipalities that are held politically responsible for the services, not the private providers. Accordingly, this chapter examines the hypothesis that it is less the privatisation and contracting out of employment services per se and more the systematic monitoring, evaluation and comparison of the service provision that spurs on a work-first approach. In brief, my argument is that *the calculative techniques seem to contribute to reinforce a work-first approach to the handling of unemployment in both Australia and Denmark.*

The Australian and the Danish employment policies have been chosen because in many ways they represent very different cases. First, Australia has perhaps the world's most comprehensive contracting out of employment services, which has been subjected to a comprehensive system of performance measurement since 1998. In contrast, the employment services in Denmark are still by and large public, even if a certain level of outsourcing has taken place during the last few years. Similarly, a comprehensive and systematic performance measurement regime pertaining to the employment services was only established in 2006. Secondly, Australia has a national (uniform) employment services system controlled by a single public authority, namely the Department of Employment, Education and Workplace Relations (DEEWR). Denmark, until very recently, has had a dual system tackling unemployment: a state-run system for the insured and a municipal system for the uninsured unemployed. Finally, the social partners have had very limited influence on Australian labour market policy over the last two decades. In contrast, Denmark has a long tradition of including social partners in the design and implementation of employment policies at all administrative levels.

If, despite these significant historical and institutional differences, we see a certain convergence in terms of problem identification and policy goals towards the work-first approach, it may provide an indication of the hegemonic strength of this approach. We may also have an indication of the role of monitoring of the performance of employment policies that cuts across different institutional contexts. In order to illuminate the possible interactions between performance measurement and the employment policy approach, I have gone through a number of Australian and Danish policy documents, government homepages publishing performance results, expert reports and newspaper articles. These written sources have been supplemented by interviews with key bureaucrats in the DEEWR during the latter months of 2008.

The emergence of the work-first approach

Both Australia and Denmark have experienced quite fundamental changes to the ways unemployment is addressed and governed. While a work-first approach has become increasingly dominant in both countries, the historical development and institutional shape of this approach has been played out quite differently in the two countries.

Australia

During the 1980s and early 1990s, Australia witnessed a significant shift in the dominant intellectual framework for tackling unemployment. Keynesian-inspired demand management combined with more or less extensive social security schemes were replaced by a framework informed by international competitiveness discourses (emphasising the role of domestic institutions) on the one hand and structural macroeconomics (emphasising price stability) on the other (Bryan and Rafferty 1997; Harris 2001). This new framework meant that the governing of unemployment was regarded less a question of regulating domestic demand and consolidating social security mechanisms, and more a question of improving international competitiveness and reducing structural barriers on the labour market. The Labor Government, which held office between 1982 and 1996, increasingly insisted that improving Australia's competitiveness necessitated developing its human capital. From the late 1980s onwards, the unemployed had to participate in various training, education and on-the-job programmes to allow the long-term unemployed and other disadvantaged groups to be included in the labour market once economic growth and demand recovered.

The Coalition Government, which came into office in 1996, seriously questioned the efficacy of the of human capital approach and essentially replaced it with a work-first approach. According to the new government, the extensive training programmes previously launched by Labor were not only highly expensive, but also ineffective in helping people find jobs. The employment services had to be reformed, they argued, by cutting training programmes and creating incentives both for the job seeker and the employment service to find the former a job as soon as possible. This was to be achieved by creating a competitive market of employment services. Following two reforms between 1994 and 1998, the Australian system for handling the unemployed was contracted out to private organisations through the Job Network, which in turn was regulated by the federal Department of Employment and Workplace Relations (DEWR – the predecessor to DEEWR) (Considine 2003). In order to facilitate the creation of a market for employment services and gauge the performance of the new providers, an elaborate payment system together with a comprehensive monitoring was put into place (see below).

Also in 1998, public support for training and education programmes for the unemployed was drastically reduced. Whereas the previous Labor government had found that skilling, re-skilling and education of the labour force were crucial to remain internationally competitive, the Coalition Government came to office in 1996 determined to adopt a work-first approach in which the primary goal was a speedy placement of job seekers into paid employment. Any training of the unemployed was to be based on market needs and very limited public funding. A predominantly human capital development approach was therefore replaced by a predominantly work-first approach designed to get as many unemployed into paid employment as fast possible. While this approach was widely criticised by academics, social organisations and the employment providers for being, among other things, ineffective, socially unfair and unable to meet the demands that international global competition puts to the skills of Australian labour, it remained essentially unchanged until 2008.

When Rudd's Labor Government entered office the role of human capital development was emphasised once again and substantial public money was put into training programmes and places. Yet it would be too superficial to see this as simply as the abandonment of the work-first approach in favour of human capital development. Even if employment providers now have wider possibilities of offering training to job seekers, providers are still evaluated on the basis of the number of job placements made and the time taken. It seems that the work-first approach, with various modifications, has come to stay in Australia regardless of the party in government. Before addressing the role played by performance management in this, I turn to the recent changes in Danish employment policy.

Denmark

The historical development of the Danish employment policy approach shows a number of similarities to the Australian policy. In Denmark, too, economic discourses on structural unemployment and international competitiveness became highly influential in shaping the understanding of how best to deal with unemployment (Torfing 2004). Apart from insisting on a monetary policy favouring price stability, the Liberal-Conservative Government, which held office between 1982 and 1993, insisted that unemployment be tackled, not by stimulating demand, but by increasing the competitiveness of Danish industry and other commercial sectors *vis-à-vis* other countries. The strengthening of Danish competitiveness was pursued through a combination of cutting public subsidies to labour market training and education, reducing unemployment benefits, and suspending automatic salary rises.

During the same period, education and training was seen as an increasingly important factor for ensuring the competitiveness of the Danish labour force. However, it was only when the Social Democrats and the Social Liberal party entered into government in 1993 that training and education began to play a really significant role in the attempt to 'activate' the unemployed. In order to remain eligible for unemployment benefit, the (insured) unemployed or the so-called 'job seekers' had to subject themselves to an individualised action plan, made up of a variety of activities such as CV and job application writing, network utilisation, job training and more general education. By the same token, the maximum period for receiving unemployment insurance was reduced from seven to four years. The reason given by the Social Democratic Government for boosting investments in training and education for the unemployed was that not only did it help maintain the competitiveness of the Danish labour force, but it also reduced the so-called 'frictions' or 'structural barriers' in the labour market (Torfing 2004: 187 *et seq.*). The Danish trade unions hesitantly accepted to moderate claims for wage rise in favour of comprehensive training and education programmes for both those in work and out of work. Consequently, the activation-cum-human capital approach would dominate the Danish employment policies throughout the 1990s.

With the return of a government made up by the Liberal and the Conservative Party in 2001, the human capital approach would gradually but surely be replaced by an emphasis on 'work first'. Public funding for job training and labour market education programmes for the unemployed and the employed was significantly reduced. In a vein remarkably similar to that of the Australian Coalition Government, the new Danish Government argued that education and training is necessary, but that it must also be tailored to the needs of Danish industry (*Beskæftigelsesministeriet* 2002). Far too many programmes, they argued, did not really improve the chances of finding a job. Moreover, the benefits for both the insured and the non-insured unemployed were gradually reduced in order to increase the economic incentive to look for work.

The Liberal-Conservative Government also found outsourcing a promising avenue for improving the effectiveness of the employment services. In 2003, an uneven process of outsourcing employment services was initiated. Within the municipal system, which offers services for the non-insured, outsourcing has developed very modestly. By 2006, only one quarter of the municipal Job Centres had purchased a private employment service and even fewer of these were a result of a tendering process leading to longer-term outsourcing (Skou *et al.* 2009: 12). In contrast, the outsourcing of the (state) public employment service for the insured unemployed rose rapidly to around 50 per cent by the end of 2005. Yet, from this level it dropped steadily to 11 per cent by the end of 2008 because of a series of regulations forcing the private contractors to take on 'special target groups' and ensure a certain level of activation of the unemployed (Skou *et al.* 2009: 12–13).[2]

While these regulations are frequently violated by the private actors, the government has so far imposed few, if any, sanctions. Just how committed the Liberal-Conservative Government is to privatisation may be further indicated by its reaction to a recent evaluation showing that private actors are much more costly than public services (Skou *et al.* 2009: 167–8). Instead of a cautious retreat, the government (recently) issued a Bill in Parliament whereby the state will cover 50 per cent of the municipalities' costs when using a private contractor (Minister of Employment 2009b: remarks 2.2.9).

Finally, the Liberal-Conservative Government found that the dual system for handling the unemployed – one for the insured run by the state and one for the uninsured run by the municipalities – was too bureaucratic and did not adequately attend to the needs of the unemployed. Accordingly, new Job Centres attending to the needs of both the insured and the uninsured unemployed were created in (nearly) all 98 Danish municipalities in 2007. This physical merging of the job service was subsequently supplemented by an administrative merging of the two systems. By 2010, the municipalities would be politically and financially responsible for the employment services for both types of unemployed. Sustained criticism raised by the both the employers association and the trade unions of the inability of

---

2. Subsidised job placement has been the main service outsourced to private actors, while supervision and job training has been outsourced much less (Deloitte 2008: 4).

the new single-entry system to attend to the needs of the insured unemployed and to impoverish the so-called 'Danish model', whereby the social partners have a large say in the regulation of employment issues, has been dismissed as irrelevant to the aim of delegating the full responsibility for the employment services to one authority only, namely the municipalities. More generally, this immunity to criticism from what are usually very influential societal interest groups, may be taken as an indication of the strength of the work-first approach. The two previously dominant approaches to the governing of unemployment, namely making labour supply meet demand (the state-run service for the insured 'unemployed') and providing social security (the municipal service for the uninsured 'aid clients'), seem to have been more or less wholly replaced by the unilateral quest of spurring the effectiveness of the employment services to make 'job seekers' find a job as fast as possible. As in Australia, this shift has raised the fundamental question of how to govern the performance of the employment services. It is the political attempts to address this last question to which I will now turn.

Metagoverning the performance of labour market policies

The changes in Australian and, more recently, Danish employment policies described above have in both cases implied the introduction of comprehensive and systematic performance measurement systems. Both countries are seeking to metagovern the employment policies and services by, on the one hand, allowing service providers a relatively wide room for manoeuvre in determining local policy goals and the shape of the services rendered and, on the other hand, deploying an increasingly comprehensive monitoring system to gauge the performance of these services. In order to address the interactions between performance measurement and policy approach, I focus on three issues, namely:

1. the employment service practices rendered *visible* by the performance measurement techniques;

2. the *standards* for the processes and procedures invoked to govern unemployment; and

3. the *public debates* over the problems linked to the ability of performance measurement to tackle unemployment.

Australia

Systematic monitoring and evaluation of the performance of employment policies was introduced relatively early in Australia. Evaluations were carried out by the Bureau of Labour Market Research in the early 1980s and by the DEET in the late 1980s, although the policies were not really designed with the intention of being susceptible to systematic monitoring and evaluation (Stretton and Chapman 1990: 34). Comprehensive post-evaluation of employment policies was inaugurated in 1991 with the establishment of the Evaluation and Monitoring Branch in the

DEET (Evaluation and Monitoring Branch 1992). From then on, the Evaluation and Monitoring Branch in the DEET embarked on a series of evaluations of its various labour market programmes (Evaluation and Monitoring Branch 1993; 1994). The background for this innovation was the increasing influence of 'public choice thinking' and the drive for increasing public sector effectiveness, which was most clearly codified in policy terms in the much quoted Hilmer Report (Hilmer *et al.* 1993), which subsequently resulted in the establishment of performance measurement regimes across a range of Australian policy areas.

With Labor's reform programme, *Working Nation*, Australia appears to enter an era in which systematic evaluation is part and parcel of employment programmes (Government of Australia 1994: 140–1). Without much notice, *Working Nation* inaugurated the practice of linking the formulation of a labour market programme with a programme measuring the effectiveness of the former (Evaluation and Monitoring Branch 1995). Some of the results from the evaluation of the reforms were soon used by the Coalition Government to argue that Labor's policies had been a failure, not least because less than one third of those completing the Job Compact training programme had found regular, paid jobs afterwards (Evaluation and Monitoring Branch 1995: 9). Evaluation data published by the Department of Employment, Education, Training and Youth Affairs (DEETYA 1996) suggested that Job Compact, into which the majority of clients were directed, was very expensive and not effective (Evaluation and Monitoring Branch 1995: 54). This first systematic measuring of the employment programme paved the way for a new kind of terrain in which the problem of unemployment would be identified and addressed less in terms of the aggregate demand for labour or social security and more in terms of the capacity of the employment service to enable the unemployed into paid jobs as soon as possible.

The new terrain for identifying unemployment problems was further bolstered through the outsourcing of the employment services in 1998 and the launching of a comprehensive monitoring system designed to enable systematic comparison (benchmarking) of the performance of the private providers (DEWRSB 1999). A new grid of visibility was created with the nationwide Star Ratings system, which graded all providers one to five stars depending, above all, on their relative effectiveness (number of unemployed persons placed in job in a certain period) and efficiency (duration between registration as unemployed and placement in a regular paid job).

The initial system was deliberately designed to focus mainly on outputs (job placement) in order to leave the providers with as much room for manoeuvre in bringing about the desired results. Even at this early stage, the employment contractors were obliged to provide quite extensive and standardised data to a complex federal computer system that would allow the calculation and comparison of provider performances. On the one hand, this implied that job seekers were categorised according to standardised groups and the provision of standardised, quantifiable indicators on effectiveness and efficiency. On the other hand, the requirement that the employment services be made both calculable and comparable meant that all dimensions of the employment services remained invisible.

Yet, together with a payment system that emphasised speedy job placement, the Star Rating system instigated a number of dubious provider practices, notably the parking of clients who were deemed unlikely to be placed in job (Productivity Commission 2002: 11.37). Many such clients received few or no services at all and many providers did not bother to check whether their clients were actually applying for jobs as required.

After criticisms from several non-governmental organisations (NGOs) and academics of these practices, the Coalition Government decided to expand the monitoring of the providers to include not only the output (the number of people getting a job or entering a recognised education), but also parts of the processes leading to that output. The Active Participation Model reform implemented in 2003 aimed to secure that all unemployed persons were activated throughout their unemployment period and that provider 'malpractices' were reduced. This meant that the grid of visibility was expanded. Now the 'quality' or the process of the service was to be monitored too, in the sense that providers were obliged to document and report to DEWR all the meetings and activities held with the unemployed in order to ensure that the latter remained an active job seeker. Similarly, the Star Rating system was now expanded to include not only indicators of effectiveness and efficiency, but also quality indicators (job seekers' satisfaction with their provider, provider facilities, provider's adherence to the contract and eventual fraud).

The Active Participation Model was soon also subjected to critical debates, this time above all by the providers. The new model, they argued, reduced choice not only for providers who had to adhere to strict regulations for conducting job search activities and reporting these, but also for clients who now had to stick with the same provider until he or she found a job. The many procedural requirements imposed on the employment services allegedly left little or no room for job search innovation. Moreover, the indicator for measuring quality was criticised for being unclear and/or subjective (Sinclair 2008; Thompson 2008). Moreover, the quality indicators were criticised by the providers for being subjective and ambiguous and therefore unsuitable for measuring performance. Ironically, public choice thinking, which had once served as the main intellectual ammunition for outsourcing and closely monitoring the performance of the employment service, was now turned against the attempts to exercise closer government supervision and control of the processes involved in the services rendered.

Notwithstanding such criticisms, getting as many people into work as fast as possible remained the key strategy to tackle unemployment. Other strategies, such as work-sharing, negative income tax, citizens' living allowance, were mostly not debated at all or, if so, rejected as being unrealistic (e.g. Bell 2000). The only significant change was the attempt by the Labor Government, which took office in 2008, to recuperate human capital development by investing substantially in training through the Productivity Places Program and other measures. However, such measures have so far remained subservient to the work-first approach. Employment providers are still paid and evaluated according to the number and the speed of placements. Recent talks about evaluating the 'social outcomes' of the employment services have so far been stranded because of the lack of practical indicators

(Caldwell and Bowen 2008). In fact, the new government further tightened the job seekers' obligations by introducing the rule that every day missed out from a planned activity is sanctioned by an equivalent loss of benefits. Unemployment, therefore, is still essentially tackled by monitoring and exerting economic incentives (sanctions) over both the employment services and the unemployed in order to get the latter into work as fast as possible.

Denmark

Danish labour market and unemployment programmes have been subjected to more or less comprehensive evaluations since the 1980s (Albæk and Winther 1990: 101; 1993: 34). Yet these evaluations remained rather ad hoc and were clearly not integrated into the design of employment policies. A first change to this can be seen in the comprehensive public sector reform programme, *Denmark as leading nation* (*Danmark som foregangsland*), launched by the Social Democratic-Social Liberal Government in 1998. The reform programme tried to gauge the performance of Danish society through a series of benchmarking analyses and use these as a vehicle for spurring on the effectiveness and efficiency of public services. By the same token, we see the emergence of a more systematic monitoring and evaluation of the employment services conducted by the Labour Market Board under the Ministry of Employment (Triantafillou *et al.* 2005).

Yet, it was not until 'structural' reform was introduced, which fundamentally altered the jurisdiction between state, counties and municipalities in 2006/07, that the systematic measurement of the performance of Danish employment policies was implemented. With the gradual delegation of the full political and financial responsibility of the employment services to the ninety-eight new municipalities, it became possible to introduce systematic comparison (benchmarking) of the employment services. This possibility should not come as a surprise in as much as one of the key motivations behind the structural reform was to enable more systematic measuring and comparison of the municipal public services, which comprise around two-third of total public spending in Denmark.

Since 2006, the municipal Job Centres have been obliged to produce a wide range of standardised employment data (Law 522, 24th June 2005) in order to make their relative performance visible. One group of baseline indicators show month for month the number of people on different types of social benefit and unemployment insurance in each municipality, in each comparative cluster of municipalities and at the national level. A second group of data try to measure the performance of the municipality in meeting the goals defined annually by the Ministry of Employment. With few variations these goals have implied reducing the unemployment rates of particular segments, namely persons who have been unemployed for more than three months, persons on sick leave for more than 26 weeks, and young persons. The performance of each and every municipal Job Centre in meeting these goals is publicly available at a homepage administered by the Ministry (see: http://www.jobindsats.dk). Finally, a third group of indicators show how well Job Centres attend to the procedural requirements involved in activating the unemployed such as the rate of job interviews and activation proposals provided to various groups of job seekers within stipulated time limits (Arbejdsmarkedsstyrelsen 2009a). While many of these procedural requirements are not new, placing them into a comparative ranking system suggests that they are no longer so much a question of ensuring the rights and duties of the unemployed, but more a question of ensuring the performance of the Job Centre. This new comparative grid of visibility thus portrays the Job Centres as competitors in a game in which the winners are supposedly the best to get people into jobs. While some municipalities may be sceptical about the suitability of this game in generating new jobs, they are strongly urged to adhere to it in as much as the Ministry regularly reports on the amount of money that can be saved by each Job Centre if they perform according to the average on the aforementioned indicators (Arbejdsmarkedsstyrelsen 2009b).

The new performance measurement regime seems hard to change let alone roll back. A recent evaluation of this system for measuring the performance of the Job Centres questioned both the usefulness and the large resources necessary to feed the system with data (Arbejdsmarkedsstyrelsen 2008: 5–9). However, the Ministry of Employment insisted on advancing the use of performance measurement as a central instrument in tackling unemployment. According to a new law (due to be fully implemented in January 2010), the municipalities will be partly compensated by the state for payment of unemployment insurance (Minister of Employment 2009a). However, in order to give the municipalities an incentive to get the unemployed into work, the *economic compensation from the state will partly be based on the Job Centre's performance* compared with the performance of other Job Centres within the same province.[3] If the Job Centre is performing above the average of the province, it is economically rewarded; if it slips below, it is sanctioned.[4]

This radical reform of the employment services based on intense performance monitoring did not pass without protest. At least two different critiques have been articulated by the political parties in opposition, the Danish Social Counsellor's Association, social scientists and others. First, they feared that training, education and other more costly measures with more long-term effects would be further reduced. Training and education of the unemployed have so far played a significant part in the state-financed efforts of motivating the insured unemployed. When these costs are taken over by the municipality, the latter will have a strong incen-

---

3. For the purpose of this policy only, Denmark has been divided into eight provinces, each made up by one to 15 municipalities (http://www.folketinget.dk/doc.aspx?/samling/20081/lovforslag/1184/index.htm).

4. More precisely, the 50 per cent of municipal employment service (including benefits) expenses are compensated (by the state) in case of 'passive' unemployment and 75 per cent in case the unemployed is activated. Municipalities are compensated on the basis of the national average unemployment rate and the rate of the local employment region to which it belongs. If the local unemployment rate increases by more than 5 per cent point above the national average, it is compensated through a separate insurance mechanism financed by all the municipalities (http://www.bm.dk/sw34377.asp).

tive to minimise training and education in favour of cheaper solutions, such as CV writing. Secondly, a labour market think tank (*Arbejderbevægelsens Erhvervsråd*) and several researchers have criticised the new model for unfairly punishing or rewarding municipalities (see Gjertsen 2009). Lumping together municipalities simply according to geographical proximity rather than for example socio-economic indicators is hardly providing a fair ground for comparison. They also point out that the closure of local workplaces – thereby increasing unemployment – will result in the economic punishment of municipalities due to forces over which they have little if any control, such as fluctuations in domestic or international demand for a specific commodity. In brief, the merger of the employment services combined with the introduction of complex and rigorous benchmarking of performance has created a new problem area in which the central quest is to improve the capacity of Job Centres to help the unemployed back into work as fast as possible. The Danish Social Counsellor's Association has criticised the new employment service system for overlooking the unemployed and their actual chances of finding a job (Gjertsen 2009). However, the political reform and associated criticisms focus mainly on the kind of financial incentives and indicators that enable the most fair and effective way of improving the performance of the municipal Job Centres.

Conclusion

Despite significant historical and institutional differences between the Australian and Danish employment policies and services, I have tried to demonstrate that the recent reforms show important similarities in the interactions between the performance measurement techniques and the employment policy approach, i.e. work-first. By latching on to the Latour-inspired analytical framework, I have tried to go beyond the ends-means debate (what is the causal relationship between ends and means?) and illuminate some of the ways in which these performance measurement techniques interact with and favour particular policy priorities. In both countries, the metagovernance of the interactions between policy goals and policy instruments seem to create a technological lock-in favouring the work-first approach in at least three ways. First, the computer-based knowledge produces a particular *visibility* focusing on objective and quantifiable performance data (Marston 2006). The requirement that the employment services be made both calculable and comparable in order to gauge their relative performance favours an approach to tackling unemployment that is based on objective and quantifiable practices. This clearly resonates strongly with the work-first approach's emphasis on effectiveness and efficiency. Other approaches are either not measurable or, if so, would come out as a poorly-performing policy according to current indicators of success. The current subordinate position of the human-capital approach in both countries may partly be due to the tensions – if not outright contradictions – between training and education measures on the one hand, and a performance regime that by default gauges any time spent on anything else than job placement as counter-productive on the other.

Secondly, the performance measurement techniques seem somehow, paradoxically, to produce an increased emphasis on *process standards*. In Australia, we have seen a development from an almost exclusive focus on output that triggered several undesirable effects such as 'creaming' and 'parking'. This led to a renewed political focus on a number of operational elements in the employment services, elements that were subsequently standardised and closely monitored. In Denmark, the political requirement that the unemployed are activated as fast as possible, and remain active throughout the unemployment period, has similarly resulted in specific process standards that are closely monitored if not always enforced. Thus the current way of metagoverning the employment policies in Australia and Denmark, which aim at giving local policy makers and employment service providers enough room for manoeuvre in determining the form of services rendered, seems actually to reduce this room for manoeuvre. At least, it has proven politically unacceptable and economically unfeasible for the employment service providers in both countries to address unemployment in ways that substantially differ from the work-first approach.

Thirdly, the performance measurement techniques and the regime they constitute seem to a wide extent to deflect more fundamental *debates* on or problems associated with the work-first approach. At least in Australia, much of the critique of the employment services has revolved around whether DEEWR's way of monitoring the providers is adequate (to prevent fraud), too burdensome (imposing costs on provision), or badly designed (creating incentives for 'parking' and 'creaming'). In Denmark, where the performance regime was implemented much more recently, we seem to find more substantial criticism of the uniform work first-inspired policy. Critics of the current work-first approach have argued that if the Danish labour force is to remain able to meet the challenges of global competition, then education and human capital development should play an important role both for those inside and outside the labour market. Others have criticised the work-first approach on the grounds that it seems to leave little role for the social partners, who traditionally have had a significant influence on job training activities. Yet neither of these critiques seriously questions the work-first approach. Even the most ardent proponents of human capital development have to acknowledge that education and training are simply a means to a given end, namely to get the unemployed into jobs. If the human capital approach appears to have a little more patience than the work-first approach in reaching that goal, it is simply because there is a belief that education and training provide more sustainable employment. In brief, this debate between work first and human capital development is not a debate over goals, but about suitable means to a given and, apparently, unquestionable goal. In this debate, proponents of the human capital approach seem always to be on the defensive because they have to prove that education and training really do produce (more sustainable) jobs.

If the current way of metagoverning the employment policies in Australia and Denmark implies that the human capital approach sits somewhat uneasily with the current measurement techniques, then other more 'radical' approaches to tackling unemployment seem completely at odds with this regime. Marxist- or Classical Greek-inspired ideals of citizenship, for example, entail an understanding of the good life in which (paid) labour is supposed to be minimised in favour of other creative activities. Clearly, any policy approach informed by such ideals of citizenship would emerge as a complete disaster in the current measurement regime. This negative evaluation of alternatives to the work-first approach is problematic because labour today seems under increasing pressure. On the one hand, the current financial-cum-fiscal crisis has been followed by increasing unemployment and fear among those in work of losing their jobs; to try to push people into jobs that are not there is obviously problematic. On the other hand, those who do have a job increasingly suffer from work-related stress, apparently because more things have to be achieved in shorter time and because of the imminent danger of being fired. If this diagnosis is correct, it may be time to seriously reconsider the desirability of the work-first approach and, not least, the performance measurement techniques supporting it.

On a more conceptual level, this chapter indicates that the metagoverning of employment policies by way of numbers may (unintentionally) reduce the room for manoeuvre by local policy makers, social partners and others in determining local policy goals and the design of the employment services rendered. In this way, policy arenas and the policy processes and interactions taking place within these arenas might be significantly altered by metagoverning through performance measurement regimes. Yet how the governing of numbers actually shapes policy interactions has not been examined in this chapter or elsewhere. Accordingly, there is a need for expanding the current research agenda on metagovernance to include not only the more or less direct governing of the interactions between actors, but also how performance measurement regimes and other policy instruments may (indirectly) shape the arenas and success criteria circumscribing such interactions and processes.

References

Albæk, E. and Winther, S. (1990) 'Evaluation Research in Denmark: The State of the Art', in R. C. Rist (ed.) *Program Evaluation and the Management of Government*, New Brunswick: Transaction Publishers.

Albæk, E. and S. Winther, S. (1993) 'Evaluering i Danmark: Rationalitet eller politisk våben?', *Politica*, 25 (1): 27–46.

Arbejdsmarkedsstyrelsen (2008) *Evaluering af resultatrevisionen*, Copenhagen: Arbejdsmarkedsstyrelsen.

Arbejdsmarkedsstyrelsen. (2009a). 'Resultatrevision; Scorecard, rettighed'. Online. Available http://www.jobindsats.dk/jobindsats/resrev/scorecard/2009/2009Q01/Jobcenter_alle_2009Q01.html (accessed 20 July 2009).

— (2009b) *Vejledning til udarbejdelsen af resultatrevisionen, 12 marts 2009*, Copenhagen: Arbejdsmarkedsstyrelsen.

Bell, S. (2000) 'Unemployment, inequality and the politics of redistribution', *The Unemployment Crisis in Australia: which way out?*, Cambridge: Cambridge University Press, pp 252–70.

Beskæftigelsesministeriet (2002) *Flere i arbejde*, København: Beskæftigelses-ministeriet.

Bevan, G. and C. Hood, C. (2006) 'What's measured is what matters: Targets and gaming in the English public health care system', *Public Administration*, 84 (3): 517–38.

Bredgaard, T. and Larsen, F. (2007) 'Implementing public employment policy: What happens when non-public agencies take over?', *International Journal of Sociology and Social Policy*, 27 (7/8): 287–301.

Bryan, D. and M. Rafferty (1997) 'Still Calling Australia Home? International Integration and the Framing of National Economic Problems in Recent Official Reports', *Australian Journal of International Affairs*, 51 (1): 5–24.

Caldwell, J. and Bowen, G. (2008) Interview with Group Manager Jo Caldwell and Branch Manager Garvin Bowen, DEEWR, Canberra.

Cerny, P. G. (1997) 'Paradoxes of the competition state: the dynamics of political globalisation', *Government and Opposition*, 32 (2): 251–74.

Cohen, M. D., March, J. G. and J. Olsen, J. (1972) 'A garbage can model of organizational choice', *Administrative Science Quarterly*, 17 (1): 1–25.

Considine, M. (2003) 'Governance and competition: The role of non-profit organisations in the delivery of public services', *Australian Journal of Political Science*, 38 (1): 63–77.

— (2005) 'The Reform that Never Ends: Quasi-Markets and Employment Services in Australia' in E. Sol and M. Westerweld, *Contractualism and Employment Services – A New Form of Welfare State Governance*, The Hague: Kluwer Law International.

Dean, M. (1995) 'Governing the unemployed self in an active society', *Economy and Society*, 24 (4): 559–83.

DEETYA (1996) *Working Nation: Evaluation of the Employment, Education and Training Elements*, Canberra: Department of Employment, Education,

Training and Youth Affairs.
DEWRSB (1999) Job Network Member Performance Information, October 1999, Canberra: DEWRSB.
Evaluation and Monitoring Branch (1992) *The Management of evaluation in DEET: a guide*, Canberra: DEET.
—   (1993) *The SkillShare network: an evaluation*, Canberra: Department of Employment, Education and Training.
—   (1994) *Client Surveys Report: National survey of employer satisfaction with CES services*, Canberra: DEET.
—   (1995) *Working Nation Evaluation Strategy*, Canberra: Department of Employment, Education and Training.
Foucault, M. (1991) 'Questions of method', in C. G. G. Burchell and P. Miller (eds) *The Foucualt Effect*, London: Harvester Wheatsheaf: 73–86.
Gjertsen, M. (2009) 'Borgerlig drøm: Og ingen taler om den arbejdsløse'. *Information*: 4–5.
Government of Australia (1994) *Working nation: policies and program*, Government White Paper, Canberra: AGPS.
Harris, P. (2001) 'From relief to mutual obligation: welfare rationalities and unemployment in 20th-century Australia', *Journal of Sociology*, 37 (1): 5–26.
Hilmer, F., Rayner, M. and Taperell, G. (1993) *National Competition Policy: Report by the Independent Committee of Inquiry*, Canberra: AGPS.
Hjern, B. and Hull, C. (1982) 'Implementation research as empirical constitutionalism', *Journal of European Political Research*, 10: 105–16.
Howard, C. (2006) 'The new governance of Australian welfare: street-level contingencies', in P. Henman and M. Fenger (eds) *Administering Welfare Reform*, Bristol: The Policy Press, pp 137–59.
Jessop, B. (1993) 'Towards a Schumpeterian Workfare State? Remarks on post-Fordist political economy', *Studies in Political Economy*, 40: 7–39.
Latour, B. and Venn, C. (2002) 'Morality and technology: The end of the means', *Theory, Culture and Society*, 19 (5/6): 247–60.
Majone, G. and Wildawsky, A. (1978) 'Implementation as evolution', in H. Freeman (ed.) *Policy Studies Review Annual*, Beverly Hills: Sage.
Marston, G. (2006) 'Employment services in an age of E-government', *Information, Communication and Society*, 9 (1): 83–103.
Minister of Employment (2009a) *Forslag til Lov 184 om ændring af lov om arbejdsløshedsforsikring m.v., lov om retssikkerhed og administration på det sociale område og forskellige andre love, fremsat 31. marts 2009.*
—   (2009b) *Forslag til lov 185 om ændring af lov om ansvaret for og styringen af den aktive beskæftigelsesindsats, lov om en aktiv beskæftigelsesindsats*, fremsat 31, marts 2009.
OECD (1999) *Implementing the Jobs Strategy: Assessing Performance and Policy*, Paris: OECD.
Peck, J. (2001) *Workfare States*, New York: Guilford Press.
Power, M. (1997) *The Audit Society: Rituals of Verification*, Oxford: Oxford

University Press.

Productivity Commission (2002) *Independent Review of the Job Network: Inquiry Report*, Canberra: Commonwealth of Australia.

Sinclair, S. Interview with National Employment Services Australia, CEO Sally Sinclary, 22nd October 2008, Melbourne.

Skou, M. H., Winter, S. C. and Beer, F. (2009) Udlicitering af sagsbehandling. Andre aktører i beskæftigelsesindsatsen, Copenhagen: SFI.

Smith, P. (1995) 'On the unintended consequences of publishing performance data in the public sector', *International Journal of Public Administration*, 18 (2&3): 277–310.

Stretton, A. and Chapman, B. (1990) *An Analysis of Australian Labour Market Programs*, Canberra: Australian National University.

Thompson, D. Interview with CEO of Jobs Australia, David Thompson, 17th October 2008, Melbourne.

Torfing, J. (2004) *Det stille sporskifte i velfærdsstaten. En diskursteoretisk beslutningsprocesanalyse*, Aarhus: Aarhus Universitetesforlag.

Triantafillou, P., Hansen, T. and Christensen, A. (2005) 'Benchmarking i den offentlige sektor i Danmark', *Nordisk Administrativt Tidsskrift*, 86 (2): 132–50.

Van Thiel, S. and Leeuw, F. L. (2002) 'The performance paradox in the public sector', *Public Performance and Management Review*, 25(3): 267–81.

Walters, W. (1997) 'The 'Active Society': new designs for social policy', *Policy and Politics*, 25 (3): 221–34.

PART III

DEMOCRACY

chapter nine | institutional evolution within local democracy – local self-governance meets local government

Jurian Edelenbos and Ingmar van Meerkerk

Introduction

In the Netherlands, citizens have the formal opportunity to put issues – under certain conditions – on the political agenda. This has been possible since May 2006 at the national level and at the local level since March 2002. In addition, people increasingly engage in an informal way, on their own initiative, to draw from their expertise, experience and knowledge to formulate ideas for policy that they may offer to government. Such 'citizens' initiatives' can be seen, in addition to interactive policy making as a form of citizens' participation (Edelenbos *et al.* 2008). Citizen participation is often initiated by government; it is a bottom-up development started by citizens themselves (Edelenbos *et al.* 2008).

In this chapter, we elaborate on the institutional implications of the 'citizens' initiatives' within local democracy. These initiatives could be described as forms of self-governance, leading to the emergence of 'proto-institutions' (Lawrence *et al.* 2002). These proto-institutions interact with established institutions of representative democracy. This interaction is a co-evolving process in which both types of institutions react to each other in certain ways. In this contribution, we describe this institutional evolution and try to find determining factors in this process. We want to provide explanatory factors of processes of institutional co-evolution. We argue that these factors are of major importance with regard to processes of citizen participation and co-operating mechanisms between proto-institutions developed by citizens' initiatives and established institutions of representative democracy.

We will treat one in-depth case study: the citizens' initiative in the municipality of Vlaardingen. At this moment there is an initiative for the (re)development of Broekpolder, an area southwest of Vlaardingen. For the case study, we used two main research methods: document analysis and semi-structured interviews. The Broekpolder case was selected for scientific research is because it is unique in the Netherlands – here we see that a formal right to put something on the government agenda through citizens' initiative developed to a form of self-organisation. In general, citizens' participation is initiated and organised by government, but in this case it was organised by the local community. In the research, all relevant written documents, such as memos, reports and political documents, were subjected to accurate study. In addition, eleven key players were interviewed, some several times, and these were made up of civil servants, council members, aldermen and citizens. The interviews were semi-structured and main themes were used to structure the interview – process development, institutions, co-operation, and change. We reconstructed the process and history of the case, and then asked questions about the coordination and co-operation between the federation (citizens) and government (council, civil servants, administrators).

The structure of this chapter is as follows:

- set out the theoretical perspective in which we place the case of Broekpolder Vlaardingen;
- examine the concepts of institutions, citizens' initiative and adaptive capacity;
- introduce the Broekpolder case study;
- analyse the institutional implications and tensions;
- describe the institutional evolution in the case study;
- provide an explanation of this evolution; and
- draw conclusions.

Theoretical perspective

A sociological perspective on institutions

The institutional approach in the functioning of public administration has received much attention in recent years (March and Olsen 1989; Goodin 1996). The institutional theory has a versatile 'body of knowledge' (Peters, 2005). This theory involves roughly three streams: economic, political and sociological (Edelenbos, 2005), which do not exclude each other. This chapter introduces the concept of 'institution' in accordance with the sociological perspective.

The sociological perspective focuses on rule systems and roles of (organised) individuals who shape interaction patterns between actors in a certain policy area (policy arena or policy situation) (Giddens 1984; Eggertson 1990). We then speak of 'rules *of* the policy game' and 'roles *in* the policy game' (Kiser and Ostrom 1982; Goodin 1996). Goodin defines (1996: 52) institutions as 'organised patterns of socially constructed norms and roles'.

Interactive policy making as self-organisation

Local citizens' initiatives and interactive policy making can be seen as processes of self-organisation where (organised) citizens and social interest groups spontaneously come to a common action (Edelenbos *et al.* 2008). Informal citizens' initiatives often arise from dissatisfaction with the actions of governments and function as a response to proposed government policy. Citizens and social groups often see that resistance is useless and then switch to a more proactive way of resistance by developing plans on their own initiative. Self-organisation is the internal capacity of elements within systems to adjust and develop (e.g. Cilliers 1998; Heylighen 2002). The concept focuses on how processes come about, develop and change. Processes evolve out of events, actions and interactions and build an institutional structure (Benson 1977; Teisman *et al.* 2009). Through interaction and bonding among citizens and public officials, information exchange, learning and mutual experience develop, which may promote new patterns of relationships (Meek 2008: 420; Morçöl 2008). Processes of self-organisation in turn might lead to new relationships between governmental institutions and civil society. A form of participatory democracy enters a representative democracy, which could lead to a reorientation of existing democratic institutions (Edelenbos 2005).

The interaction process between institutions and proto-institutions as a source of institutional evolution

Although many definitions and descriptions underline the sustainable, regulatory and stable character of institutions (Kiser and Ostrom, 1982; Giddens 1984), here we also want to emphasise the volatility and transience of institutions (Lawrence *et al.* 2002). The institutions that are now stable and sustainable all had an origin in which they were capricious in nature and were experienced as a new institution. Institutions do not only regulate the act, but are also found in that act and brought to further development (Eggertson 1990). In this chapter, we approach institutions as being processes of social interaction that could become the object of transformation when different, interrelated but sometimes incompatible social arrangements meet (Benson 1977; Seo and Creed 2002).

As a result of the application of citizens' initiative, new institutional arrangements could be constructed that interact with the existing institutions of representative democracy. This interaction can produce tensions or 'incompatible institutional processes' (Seo and Creed 2002). It leads to pressure on both institutional arrangements. The 'proto-institutions' (Lawrence *et al.* 2002) in participatory democracy can be understood as temporary, and these short-term institutions can provide a 'de-institutionalisation' of existing institutions that have a stable and long-term character (Edelenbos 2005). Old and new institutions influence each other, and from this co-evolutionary process, both can mutually adapt themselves into a search for new operation logic. 'Ongoing social construction produces a complex array of contradictions, continually generating tensions and conflicts within and across social systems, which may, under some circumstances, shape consciousness and action to change the present order' (Seo and Creed 2002: 225).

Finding a balance between the old institutions of representative democracy and the proto-institutions of participatory democracy asks for adaptability of both institutions. The interaction between the different institutions is therefore of major importance. However, in practice, this interaction process is difficult to bring about and in many cases does not lead to institutional evolution. 'Interactive governance is often organised as an informal process with different rules and roles than the existing institutional representative system, which runs parallel or prior to the formal institutions of negotiation and decision making' (Edelenbos 2005: 128). This could easily result in the evaporation of emerging proto-institutions in participatory democracy and the reestablishment of existing patterns of behaviour within the institutions of representative democracy.

In the literature on adaptive capacity of systems, different factors are mentioned which are important with regard to processes of adaptation, innovation and uncertainty. These factors are grounded in interaction processes between different institutions or systems and could therefore stimulate institutional co-evolution.

Factors of adaptability grounded in interaction processes

In the literature on adaptive governance and processes of institutional change, several factors are mentioned that may affect the evolution of institutions (Edelenbos 2005; Folke *et al.* 2005; Granovetter 1973; Koppenjan and Klijn 2004; Maguire *et al.* 2004; Seo and Creed 2002; Teisman *et al.* 2009; Williams 2002). Three important and interrelated factors are: informal networks, trust and boundary spanning.

Informal networks: interactions between actors within informal networks outside the realm of formal institutions could enhance the chance of the emergence of innovative policies and arrangements (Bekkers *et al.* 2010). This factor is about networks with an informal character that connect agents operating within traditional institutions of representative democracy and agents operating outside these institutions. The informal character of the networks provides room for involved actors to think and behave outside their established roles and rules according to their formal position within established institutions. People are not directly pinned down to or held accountable for certain statements. Informal networks give room for experimentation and could lead to change. However, not all informal networks facilitate institutional evolution. Important in this matter is the structural 'embeddedness' of the networks (Granovetter 1973). 'Structural embeddedness is critical to our understanding of how social mechanisms coordinate and safeguard exchanges in networks, for it diffuses values and norms that enhance coordination among autonomous units ...' (Jones *et al.* 1997: 924). For institutional evolution to happen, it is important that different parts of the social system representing the institutional processes of representative democracy are connected to one another.

Trust: besides the structure of the networks, the quality of social relationships (Granovetter, 1973) is a determining factor for change. Trust is seen as an important facilitating mechanism for cooperation between different parts of social systems (Edelenbos and Klijn 2007; Nooteboom 2002; Ring and Van de Ven 1992). This could ultimately lead to changes within existing, established patterns of behaviour. Because trust helps people to tolerate uncertainty and make decisions where there is uncertainty (Luhmann 1979; Bachmann 2001), it is especially important in horizontal and emerging partnerships (Edelenbos and Klijn 2007; Koppenjan and Klijn 2004). In the interaction between the emerging institutions of participatory democracy and the institutions of representative democracy, there is uncertainty regarding the rules and roles of individuals. Representatives of both institutions must have trust in the partners' intentions and competences for accepting their views and their influence.

Boundary spanning: as stated above, the existence of informal networks and processes in which new forms of governance are developed is not enough for the institutional evolution of the involved governmental entities to occur. Institutional change could happen when new practices are linked with existing routines (Maguire *et al.* 2004). Meaningful connections have to be made with the existing institutions of representative democracy (Edelenbos 2005). Individuals who are able to connect emerging rules and roles within these informal networks with established rules and roles within the institutions of representative democracy could therefore be described as key persons. These so-called 'boundary spanners' understand '…both sides of the boundary, enabling them to search out relevant information on one side and disseminate it on the other' (Tushman and Scanlan 1981: 291–2). Boundary spanners have a feeling for different institutional arrangements (cf. Williams 2002) and could therefore make connections between these institutional arrangements, which could lead to institutional co-evolution.

Framework for approaching and analysing the case

We describe and analyse the developments in institutions in the encounter between representative democracy (municipal institutions) and participatory democracy (citizens' initiative). We speak of institutional evolution when new ways of working emerge. With regard to this case, this means that existing municipal institutions show resilience: they are able to connect (new) participatory forms of democracy with their institutional practices, developed within representative democracy. New forms of citizen participation are incorporated, leading to new patterns of behaviour. For actors in those institutions, it means that they are able and willing to change their roles and rules of behaviour. We speak of 'institutional rigidity' when municipal institutions resist new ways of working. This is the case when actors are not able or willing to change their roles and rules of behaviour: changes or new developments are delayed, resisted or absorbed in existing institutional procedures.

Our research examined the interaction processes between the emerging proto-institution (citizens' initiative) and the (three) institutions of representative democracy within the municipality of Vlaardingen (see the three arrows in Figure 9.1). In these three interaction processes, we looked at how the institutions of both citizens' initiative and the local government developed in time (from 2005 to 2010). We depict institutions as the roles people play in practice, as argued above. We therefore looked closely at how representatives of the citizens' initiative, the City Council, the Civil Service, and the board acted, analysing their daily activities in performing their jobs.

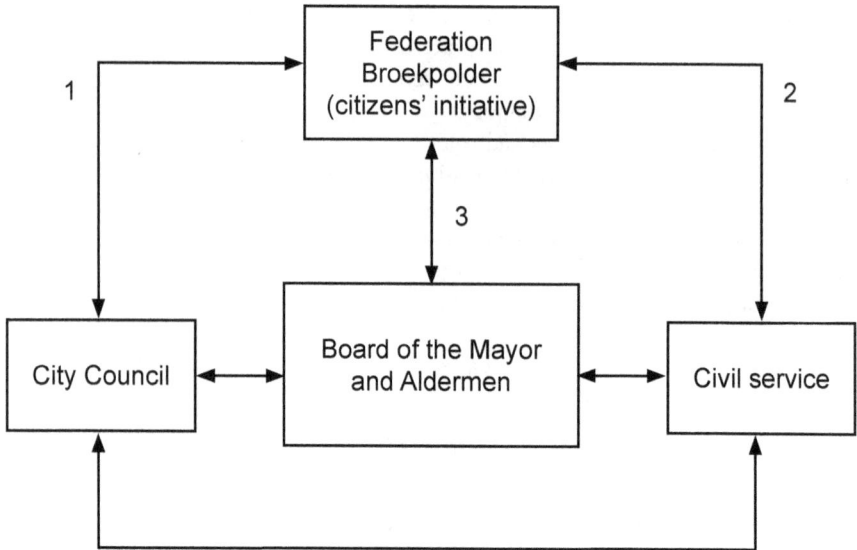

Figure 9.1: Relations between citizens' initiative and existing municipal institutions

Case study: introduction

The origin of the citizens' initiative in Broekpolder

The Broekpolder is an old recreational area of approximately 300 hectares in the north-western part of the city of Vlaardingen. In early 2000, the city and the province of Zuid-Holland had plans to build houses in the area. The Broekpolder was designated as a search location for 'rural living' by the regional government. This caused a large protest in the local community, which resulted in 10,000 signatures against the arrival of country houses in the Broekpolder. The regional government decided not to take any initiatives until 2010.

Meanwhile, a group of thirty citizens of Vlaardingen had gathered with the aim of maintaining the open and green character of the area. At the end of 2002, this group organised a number of meetings where citizens were invited to consider the future of the Broekpolder. It looked for co-operation with the council, Mayor and Aldermen (administrative body), and civil servants (see Figure 9.2).

The agreement between the municipality and federation

This citizens' initiative was formalised on 5th October 2006 in the Foundation Federation Broekpolder. The Foundation has two goals:

1. In the broadest sense, to develop and maintain the Broekpolder area through sport, recreation, culture, cultural history, nature and education.
2. To take care of the common interests of the users of the Broekpolder on a voluntary basis.

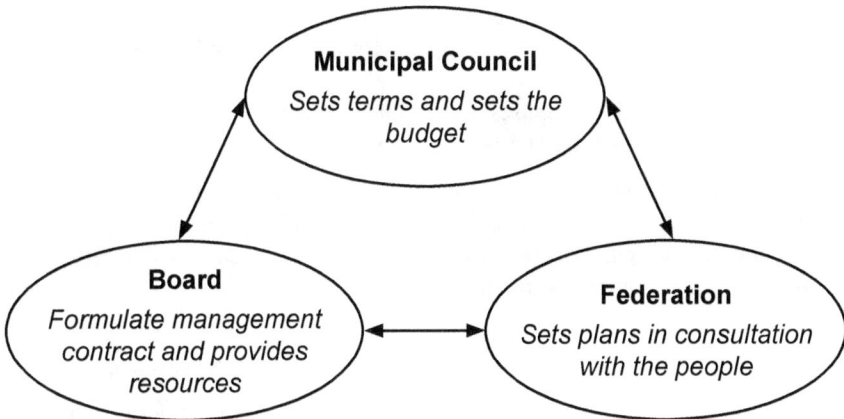

Figure 9.2: The model of Vlaardingen

The municipality (the administration) and the Federation jointly developed a policy note that later became a social contract in which the citizens' initiative and its
relationship with the municipality were elaborated. Special attention was paid to
the degree and the extent of citizen participation and initiative of the Federation.
With respect to participation possibilities, a distinction was made between *area
maintenance* and *regional development* of the Broekpolder. With regard to the
maintenance activities, the Federation was allowed to give *qualified advice* on
the contract extension of the Board, which is the basis of the performance of daily maintenance in the Broekpolder. The municipal administration can only differ
from the advice if there is a strong argument against it. However, the Federation
should refrain from a direct interference with the normal daily maintenance.

With regard to the regional development, two categories are distinguished:
small enhancements and large development projects. With regard to small enhancements, the Federation gives *binding* advice to the Mayor and Aldermen.
With regard to the large development plans and projects, the Federation takes *the
initiative* in generating ideas and subsequently develops in cooperation with the
municipality those projects. However, there is the precondition that the Federation
provides societal support for their ideas and plans – it should make enough effort to bring all the interested parties and stakeholders together that reflects the
population of Vlaardingen. The Federation receives a budget for their organisation
and the maintenance and development of the area. This budget is approved by the
council. The Federation is bound by this budget, by the overall structure plan for
the region and by legal requirements.

Practice of the Federation

The Federation has the ambition, while practicing its initiating role, to serve as a
platform where all citizens are able to get in contact with each other. A number of
chambers are created in which several themes, such as recreation, sport and envi-

ronment, are elaborated. The Federation sees its added value in acting as a loosely coupled organic network, where participants form linkages and alliances with others to obtain their goals.

The Federation also proposes to arrange the communication with the city council through the creation of a political portal:

> If some ideas are beginning to show maturity in the Federation or if council members like to raise something, then an orientation meeting between Federation and (parts of) the city council can take place. These meetings are informal in the sense that the municipalities' members are free to bring their ideas.
>
> (Municipality of Vlaardingen 2007: 6)

With regard to its representativeness and creating support for ideas and plans, the Federation is focused on creating linkages to municipality (council, administration and Civil Service) and the broader society in Vlaardingen. It has several informal links to key players in the Civil Service, the Mayor and Aldermen. The vision document for the area is developed with the consent of the council and administration. The Federation will also involve the broader public in the development of the vision document and the specific projects it embraces. The Federation continuously tries to reach and involve the citizens of Vlaardingen through advertisements, presentations and (public) meetings and events. In this way, the Federation responds to the demand of the city council to represent the population of Vlaardingen as much as possible.

Analysis: Institutional implications in three relationships

Relationship 1: Board of Mayor and Aldermen – the Federation

From the beginning, the relationship between the Federation and the Board of Mayor and Aldermen has been positive and productive. People with management experience participated in the Board. The chairman of the Federation was a former council member and knew her way in the municipal organisation. At the time of the citizens' proposal, one of the aldermen (Mr Versluijs of the Labor Party), had a (personal) connection with the group of citizens. He had been actively involved in the design of the citizens' initiative. This seems to be a crucial aspect. Through this connection, support for the citizens' initiative was embedded in the Board of Mayor and Aldermen. The involved alderman played an important role in convincing the Board and the city council to support the citizens' initiative.

The Board parties – Labour, Christian Democrats and Green Party – attached relatively great value to the citizens' initiative. Citizen participation was included in the Coalition Agreement (2006–2010) as an explicit theme and political ambition. The citizens' initiative fitted in well here.

Nevertheless, the Board had to get used to the new (co-operative) structure. This was especially expressed in the preparation of the strategic vision for the Broekpolder region. After a motion of the council, in article 2 of the Covenant, it was determined that, first, a financial framework should be developed, offering clarity about the conditions that related to the ideas proposed by the Federation. This vision should be jointly prepared by the Federation and the municipal board. However, the Board had given this task to the Civil Service, but without taking the new role of the Federation into account. Hereby, a regular internal work approach was activated contradictory to the covenant that proposed co-operation between municipality and Federation. Through well-timed and appropriate responses by an involved and committed civil servant and the involved alderman, a vision in collaboration with the Federation was finally drawn up.

Relationship 2: Municipal Council – Federation

The institutionalised role of the council (setting the terms and controlling the Board on these terms) was (to some extent) challenged by the citizens' initiative. There was uncertainty about the future role of the council. To what extent would the council still be involved in the decision-making process concerning the Broekpolder? Implementing such projects was politically sensitive in the Broekpolder area, where competing political interests were at stake. The councils' discussion about the citizens' initiative proposal on 19th January 2006 (Gemeente Vlaardingen 2006a) shows that the council had reservations. For example, some council members feared making a decision from which they could not later withdraw. The council was afraid of losing its grip on the citizens' initiative that matters may be seen as a *fait accompli*. Some councillors wanted clear rules provided in advance, while the council as a whole was reluctant to create an extra organisational layer that could not be democratically controlled.

There are also some criticisms about the representativeness of the Federation. The strong involvement of some prominent Labor members (PvdA) in the initiative caused scepticism with some political parties. This led the Federation to involve more people with other (political) backgrounds (such as the VVD, liberal party).

The politicised situation in the city council frustrated the development of a council portal, ardently desired by the Federation. The political portal would accelerate the decision-making process by ensuring a timely alignment with politics on specific project proposals. However, the political parties had insufficient confidence in each other to create this portal. Who can we trust to represent the council in this portal? Do we like to prematurely commit ourselves to specific project proposals? The council wanted to retain the freedom and opportunity to have the final say at the end of the policy process, as they always had. It was, therefore, decided to operate in accordance with traditional political procedures to deal with project proposals; that the council would be involved through the whole Council Commission and would be informed by the Municipal Board on this issue.

Despite a reluctant and critical attitude, the citizens' initiative proposal was approved by the council with a large majority. What we observed in this case was that the political system was on the average positive about the initiative, but did not change its own patterns of behaviour. The council absorbed the initiative into its existing institutionalised practices. For example, the political portal is subjected to the treatment of new developments regarding the Broekpolder area (and therefore the citizens' initiative) takes place according to the usual procedures in the Council Commission on urban development. (This Commission meets two times each year.)

Later in the process, around the beginning of 2010, one political party (Christian Democrats) was very negative about the way the plans were developed out of sight of the council. This party was not happy with the way the council had no democratic role anymore in the process.

Relationship 3: Civil Service – Federation

The arrival of the Federation as a new partner to the Civil Service caused some consternation. Previous negative experiences with a citizens' initiative did not help. Because of a lack of professional expertise among citizens, civil servants feared that the involvement of the Federation would only delay implementing any projects. According to some respondents, the proposed co-operation implicitly felt as if the functioning of the Civil Service was questioned. Until the decisive council meeting (in 2006), the attitude among officials was mainly passive and negative. Previous investments in the relationship would count for little if the plans of the Federation for the city council were to be rejected.

With the formal acceptance of the covenant between the city council and the Federation, civil servants had to take their new partner more seriously. Article 10 of the Covenant provides for assistance and support to be given to the Federation – something that had not occurred before. Civil servants are obligated to provide this through information or advice, in the same way they are obliged to assist the Mayor and Aldermen. Article 10 is made with regard to a lack of resources available for the Federation, such as time, procedural experience and finance. However, both Federation and Civil Service experienced difficulties with putting this into practice. For civil servants, the system became diffuse and unclear. Civil servants now have to deal with two principal players: the Board and the Federation. Who do they have to serve, especially when there are conflicts of interests between the two principals? The obligation to assist the Federation was something of a problem. A lot of effort would now have to be expended, which would take up valuable time and money from the Civil Service. Its view was that assistance could mainly be used when ideas were fully developed, and soon be turned into projects. Civil servants were afraid that the official assistance could be overstretched. In practice, the arrangement led to an appeal to the administrative capacity, which was not always available at the desired moments.

The Federation, on the other hand, complained about a lack of administrative support. Some of this can be explained by the informal way in which the Federation acts and approaches civil servants. In the 'normal' case, whereby administrators can ask for support and advice, the interaction between administrator and civil servant was clearly regulated and institutionalised. Both parties knew, for example, how to arrange such an interaction and the extent of the support. However, this was not the case with regard to support for the Federation. Officials were not sure to what extent they could support the Federation and they did not see this service as 'part of their normal job'.

Civil servants responded by making the new situation as manageable and clear as possible, through regulations (as much as possible) and the development of a project organisation, in which tasks and responsibilities are clearly divided and defined. The proposed project organisation structure consisted of a programme manager, a steering committee and project groups. Directors of both the municipality and the Federation would participate in the steering committee. At first there was an explicit distinction between different project groups, both from the town and the Federation in order to create a workable situation in the eyes of the civil servants. The Federation was approached as a separate organisation with its own structure.

However, at the end of 2009 things were moving in the Civil Service. A programme manager was appointed from within the city council. This person was given the explicit task of assisting the Federation and creating connections to the city organisation. Also, project groups were formed in which both civil servants and members from the Federation (from the various chambers) were involved. Within these project groups members from the Federation and civil servants work together in making feasible plans that fit within the vision of the Federation. The programme manager plays a very different role in comparison with his or her colleagues, who are responsible for other areas: he or she coordinates, connects and facilitates instead of directing and steering.

Evolution of established institutions

What does the analysis to date indicate with regard to institutional evolution? We distinguish three periods of institutional evolution. The different periods of institutional evolution are summarised in Table 9.1.

In Period 1 of the institutional evolution, there is a tendency for the city council to keep the proto-institution at a distance. There are sceptics within the civil service, as well as among councillors. Councillors are critical about the representativeness and there is uncertainty with regard to the future role of the council with regard to this project. The attitude of civil servants could generally be characterised as reluctant. Civil servants were passive and sceptical towards the citizens' initiative. The proponents of the citizens' initiative (an alderman, an active civil servant and the chairman of the Federation) explore the way in which they could make a fruitful co-operating mechanism. They seek political support and broaden the participation within the Federation with members from different political parties.

We observe a change in Period 2 when the covenant is accepted by the council. Not surprisingly, it was this judicial arrangement that was creating an awareness, 'acceptance' and acknowledgement of the Federation's work and ideas within the Civil Service. Civil servants tried to make the new situation as manageable and as

Table 9.1: Periods of institutional evolution within the Broekpolder case study

Period of institutional evolution	Characteristics	Involved institutions	Focus on
Period 1 – dissociation (2002-2006)	Exploration, keeping other's institutions at a distance, awaiting, aversion	Civil Service, Federation, Council, Board of Alderman	Controlling, experimentation, seeking for political support
Period 2 – parallelisation (2007–2008)	Institutions are running and working in parallel, there is not enough coordination	Civil Service, Federation, Council, Board of Alderman	Searching for certainties, established institutions seek to absorb the initiative in existing institutionalised practices
Period 3 – synchronisation (2009 and running)	Institutions are to a large extent interwoven, leading to new ways of working together	Civil Service, Federation, Board of Alderman	Searching for effective co-operation mechanisms, embedding within different institutions

clear as possible. They were doing this in their established way of working: formulating rules and dividing clear responsibilities and tasks. However this is sometimes difficult when confronted with the informal way the Federation works. The council also tries to absorb the initiative into its existing institutionalised practices. It does not accept the formation of an informal political portal and sticks to the usual procedural arrangements with regard to area development. Also, the Board of Aldermen reacted in its practiced way with regard to the development of the vision by activating a regular internal work approach. So, although the covenant was an administrative novelty, it did not cause change within the different institutions. The established institutions of representative democracy and the proto-institution still worked separately, in parallel, according to their own established ways of working.

This changed in Period 3 (see Table 9.1), which is still running. The Civil Service and the Federation are more interwoven with the emergence of project groups made up of members from both organisations. In this period, the rules and the roles (Goodin 1996) within the Civil Service changed significantly in comparison with other development projects. We could speak of institutional change within the Civil Service. The responsible Alderman for area development supports the relationship between the programme manager and the Federation. The co-operation between the two organisations is in this way embedded within the Board. However, this clearly is not the case with the council. The consequence of the clear separation of Federation activities and council activities is that projects and plans are developed out of sight of the council.

Institutional evolution and institutional embedding – explanatory factors

The explanation for the evolution of existing institutions in this case was closely connected to the way in which the new 'proto-institution' was linked with the existing institutions. What was the role of the three factors mentioned in our theoretical framework?

The functioning of the *informal network* between members of the Board of Aldermen, the Civil Service and the Federation played a crucial role in the whole process. In the first phase (around 2004), the group of citizens made connections with the Board of Aldermen in an informal way to show their intentions and competences, to test the reaction, and to develop knowledge regarding important procedures and sensitivities within the political arena. After the acceptance of the proposal by the council (end of Period 1, see Table 9.1) a direct connection between the group of citizens and the civil service emerged. The involved civil servant in this matter noticed that contacts with the group of citizens 'were frequent and mainly informal'. He became part of the informal network and the structural 'embeddedness' with the established institutions of representative democracy increased. In co-operation with the group of citizens, he wrote a policy document aimed at orgainising the relationship between the Federation and the city council.

The Federation tried to expand the informal network with members of the council by proposing a council portal. The council rejected this proposal and this hindered a connection with the informal network. Regarding the latest developments in the council and the coming elections (March 2010), this might be problematic for the future development of the initiative. Because of the weak connection with the city council, one of the major parties – the Christian Democrats – complained about a lack of democratic control.

The *boundary spanners* between the different institutions played an important role in organising the linkage between the proto-institution and the existing institutions. In the civil service, the Federation and the Board of Aldermen there was such a boundary spanner. At the end of the first phase (2006), there was a committed civil servant who took care of the connection between the administration and the Civil Service. He took on the role of a 'guide of the initiative through the civil service' and he was able to translate the ideas, proposals and informal patterns of behaviour from the Federation into internal procedures, which fitted more with existing patterns of behaviour within the Civil Service. He also organised internal workshops for civil servants aimed at the issue of 'how to deal with two different principals' (the Board and the Federation). When this particular boundary spanner ceased involvement after 2006, the link between the Civil Service and the Federation deteriorated and the aims of the Federation and the Civil Service began to diverge. This is also expressed in Period 2 of institutional evolution (see Table 9.1) which is characterised by 'parallelisation'. At the end of 2009 this connecting role is picked up again by the newly appointed program manager. He adapted his role as program manager in accordance with the partnership. He described his role as 'coordinating', 'facilitating' and 'connecting' instead of directing and steering, which is the regular role of a program manager within the civil service. He facilitated the interaction process between civil servants ('experts') and members of the Federation which was aimed at developing policy proposals for the area. Together with the chairman of the Federation, he organised the formation of the joint project groups, which increased the interaction between both organisations (Period 3, see Table 9.1).

The Federation also had such a boundary spanner in the person of the chairman. With her working experience as a councillor, she was well aware of some important formal procedures and institutions in the municipal organisation. She realised that it was necessary to make connections to existing institutional practices of the city council in order to put the citizens' initiative into practice. In order to obtain the necessary support of councillors and civil servants, the Federation should adopt, to some extent, the municipal institutional habits, procedures and routines. Together with the boundary spanner in the civil service, she wrote the covenant. This harmonisation with the working methods of the Civil Service provided the necessary clarity among civil servants and councillors. Her approach to the formal procedure of public consultation regarding the strategic vision was also helpful. Before starting this procedure, she ensured that the governmental entities agreed upon the Federation's approach. The Federation took the formal procedure as point of departure for the public consultation, but changed the process of this consultation according to its own working principles. Instead of seeing this formal procedure as a 'necessary evil', the Federation took advantage of the situation to communicate with the local population and obtain new ideas and projects.

The third boundary spanner involved was an alderman. He played a crucial role in convincing the council that this experiment with citizen participation should be given the opportunity to go forward on a trial and error basis. As a policy advocate, he convinced other parties of the added value of this initiative. With regard to the civil service, he focused on 'avoiding the emergence of detailed rules' concerning the initiative and the relationship between the Federation and Civil Service: 'This is a typical reaction of civil servants, but is at the expense of the needed flexibility. For it is about a process and that needs room for development' (interview Alderman, 2009).

The different boundary spanners connected the logics of the three different entities and played a crucial role in organising and embedding new patterns of behaviour into existing institutional structures. Together they harmonised the differences between the administrative structures and processes of the Civil Service and the informal self-organising ways of the Federation. There was no such boundary spanner active within the city council.

What can be said about the role of *trust*? The increasing interaction between the city council and the Federation enabled the creation of familiarity, joint understanding and trust. Representatives from the citizens' initiative, Civil Service and the Board got to know each other's intentions and competences and this developed a growing trust. This was important for reducing the scepticism surrounding citizens' participation among civil servants (within the first phase of the interaction process). The committed civil servant 'was touched by the enormous drive and spirit of the involved citizens' (Interview Program Manager, 2010). This indicates intentional trust. As an experienced civil servant in this matter, the boundary spanner noticed that many civil servants did not have a high degree of trust in citizens concerning their participation in projects. The growing co-operation between the Civil Service and the Federation led to a growing trust in the capabilities and application of the volunteers working within the Federation. This was important for the willingness of civil servants to co-operate and to modify their dominant role in formulating policy proposals with regard to the area.

Within the council, a lack of trust is an important factor hindering the realisation of an effective link between the Federation and council. In the beginning, there was a lack of trust because of the strong involvement of Labor Party sympathisers. After broadening the network of citizens and the withdrawal of some Labor councilors, the intentional trust of the councillors in the Federation increased sufficiently to accept the proposal. However, council members were still eager to keep control over their formal roles, tasks and activities. They were very sceptical with regard to the Federation's abilities to produce sound democratic proposals. This indicates a lack of competence trust. There is, however, also a lack of (intentional) trust between council members, which hindered the formation of the political portal. According to the different respondents, some council members are afraid that other council members will try to use this portal for their own political aspirations.

Conclusion and discussion

Our research indicates the difficulty of putting participatory forms of democracy into practice within established institutions of representative democracy. Proto-institutions of participatory democracy have to be connected with these established institutions in order to prevent evaporation. Making an effective connection and realising embedding is dependent on different factors, of which trust, informal networks and connective capacity through boundary spanning is of major importance. These factors provide *institutional interaction*, which could be described as a co-evolving process wherein existing institutions slightly change or evolve by interacting agents, operating at the boundaries of these institutions. The boundary spanners connected the logistics of the three different entities and played a crucial role in organising how to embed new patterns of behaviour into existing institutional structures. They merged new ways of organisation with existing institutional procedures. This is a difficult task and requires individuals who are committed and have the necessary experience.

However, the absence of a boundary spanner within the council and a lack of trust between council members hindered the realisation of the political portal or another form of institutional linkage with the council. The complaint regarding a lack of democratic control in the council is an expected reaction from the viewpoint of the representative institutional settings and relationships where there is little opportunity for participatory democracy. It shows the tension when new forms of participatory democracy meet highly institutionalised forms of representative democracy.

In the case study, we found different periods in the process of institutional evolution. The importance of *institutional design* with regard to changes in the processes is addressed in the literature (e.g. Koppenjan and Klijn 2004). The result of this research emphasises the difficult *processes of institutional evolution*. The co-evolving process of institutional interaction is hard to grasp and could hardly be controlled, designed and directed. Different, interacting factors, come into play: boundary-spanning persons, informal networks and trust come together in a co-evolving process. It is a process characterised by learning, trial and error and is highly dependent on the interacting actors and specific contextual and cultural conditions of the case. If one of the factors (trust, boundary-spanning actors, informal networks) disappears, the evolution process could be brought to a halt.

We found that besides management and meta-governance (Sørensen and Torfing 2009), trust building was especially important (in Period 3, see Table 9.1) for opening up the established institutions, exploring and developing new interaction processes and behavioural patterns, and synchronising different institutional patterns. Trust provided an acceptance of the citizens' initiative and the input from involved citizens in formulating and developing policy plans. Different aspects and effects of trust have been stressed in the literature (Lane and Bachmann 1998; Edelenbos and Klijn 2007). In this study, we observed intentional and competence trust. From this growing trust, the actors were willing to take risks and therefore possibilities for change emerged. In the literature, the relationship between institutions and trust is mostly studied from the perspective of the stability of institutions and institutional design, which may enhance trust (Farrel and Knight 2003; Koppenjan and Klijn 2004). This study supplements a view that the presence of trust is an important factor for institutional evolution. It creates the confidence for 'stepping out of the box' and exploring new processes and institutions. This reverse relationship has not been studied widely. Further research should provide more insights in this relationship and the next step is to focus on adaptability (factors) and evolutionary aspects of governance networks.

References

Bachmann, R. (2001) 'Trust, power and control in trans-organizational relations', *Organization Studies*, 22 (2): 337–65.

Bekkers, V., Edelenbos, J. and Steijn, B. (eds) (2011), *Innovation in the Public Sector: Linking Capacity and Leadership*, London: Palgrave McMillan.

Benson, J. K. (1977) 'Organizations: A dialectic view', *Administrative Science Quarterly*, 22: 1–21.

Cilliers, P. (1998) *Complexity and postmodernism: Understanding complex systems*, London: Routledge.

Edelenbos, J. (2005) 'Institutional implications of interactive governance: insights from Dutch practice', *Governance*, 18 (1): 111–34.

Edelenbos, J., and Klijn, E. H. (2007) 'Trust in complex decision-making networks: A theoretical and empirical exploration', *Administration and Society*, 39 (1): 25–50.

Edelenbos, J., de Hond, L. and Wilzing, J. (2008) 'Op initiatief van de burger. Over de werking van het gemeentelijk burgerinitiatief', *Bestuurskunde*, 17 (2): 88–101.

Eggertson, T. (1990) *Economic Behavior and Institutions*, Cambridge: Cambridge University Press.

Farrell, H. and Knight, J (2003) 'Trust, institutions, and institutional change: industrial districts and the social capital hypothesis', *Politics and Society*, 31: 537–66.

Folke, C., Hahn, T., Olsson, P. and Norberg, J. (2005) 'Adaptive governance of social-ecological systems', *Annual Review of Environment and Resources*, 30: 441–73.

Giddens, A. (1984) *The Constitution of Society: Outline of the theory of structuration*, Los Angeles: Berkely.

Goodin, R. E. (1996) *The Theory of Institutional Design*, Cambridge: Cambridge University Press.

Granovetter, M. (1973) 'The strength of weak ties', *The American Journal of Sociology*, 78 (6): 1360–80.

Heylighen, F. (2002) 'The science of self-organization and adaptivity'. Online. Available http://www.eolss.net.

Jones, C., Hesterly, W. S. and Borgatti, S. P. (1997) 'A general theory of network governance: Exchange conditions and social mechanisms', *The Academy of Management Review*, 22 (4): 911–945.

Kiser, L. and Ostrom, E. (1982) 'The Three Worlds of Action: A Meta-Theoretical Synthesis of Institutional Approaches', in E. Ostrom (ed.) *Strategies of Political Inquiry*, Beverly Hills: Sage.

Koppenjan, J. and Klijn, E. H. (2004) *Managing Uncertainties in Networks*, London and New York: Routledge.

Lawrence, T. B., Hardy, C. and Phillips, N. (2002) 'Institutional effects of interorganizational collaboration: The emergence of proto-institutions', *Academy of Management Journal*, 45: 281–90.

Luhmann, N. (1979) *Trust and Power*, Chichester: Wiley.

Lane, C. and Bachman, R. (eds) (1998), *Trust Within and Between Organizations; Conceptual Issues and Empirical Applications*, Oxford: Oxford University Press.

Maguire, S., Hardy, C. and Lawrence, T. B. (2004) 'Institutional entrepreneurship in emerging fields: HIV/AIDS treatment advocacy in Canada', *Academy of Management Journal*, 47 (5): 657–79.

March, J. G. and Olsen, J. P. (1989) *Rediscovering Institutions The organizational basis of politics*, New York: Free Press.

Meek, J. W. (2008) 'Adaptive Intermediate Structures and Local Sustainability Advances', *Public Administration Quarterly*, 32(3): 393–414.

Morçöl, G. (2008) 'Complexity of Public Policy and Administration: Introduction to the Special Issue', *Public Administration Quarterly*, 32 (3): 305–13.

Nooteboom, B. (2002) *Trust: Forms, Foundations, Functions, Failures and Figures*, Cheltenham: Edgar Elgar Publishing

Ring, P. S. and van de Ven, A. H. (1994). 'Developmental processes of cooperative interorganizational relationships', *Academy of Management Review*, 19 (1): 90–118.

Seo, M. and Creed, W. E. D. (2002) 'Institutional contradictions, praxis and institutional change: A dialectical perspective', *The Academy of Management Review*, 27 (2): 222–47.

Sørensen, E. and Torfing, J. (2009) 'Making Governance Networks Effective and Democratic through Metagovernance', *Public Administration*, 87(2): 234–58.

Teisman, G. R., van Buuren, M. W. and Gerrits, L. G. (2009) *Managing Complex Governance Systems*, London: Routledge.

Tushman, M. L. and Scanlan, T. J. (1981), *Boundary Spanning Individuals: Their Roles in Information Transfer and Their Antecedents, Academy of Management Journal*, 24(2): 289–305.

Williams, P. (2002) 'The competent boundary spanner', *Public administration*, 80 (1): 103–24.

chapter ten | reconnecting representative and participatory/deliberative democracy in italy – the cases of tuscany and trentino

Simona Piattoni

Introduction

Interactive governance is about citizen involvement in policy making on a continuing and substantive fashion. It contains both a policy and a democratic recommendation, and is based on a growing body of analysis and reflection on governance practice (Pierre 2000; Pierre and Peters 2000; Kohler-Koch and Eising 1999; Marcussen and Torfing 2007; Sørensen and Torfing 2007). The upshot of this reflection is that the involvement of citizens improves democratic governance on several counts.

To start with, some policies could not be implemented at all without the direct involvement of the citizens (think of differentiated garbage collection as a good example), but even in those cases in which governments could deliver services through their agencies, they have become increasingly reluctant to do so. New Public Management (NPM) has suggested that delivering services by subcontracting them to for-profit companies or by transforming government branches into profit-making units might improve public finances as well as boost citizens' satisfaction. Under these new arrangements, citizens are supposedly treated like 'customers' to be satisfied rather than as mere 'users' to be serviced. Customer satisfaction becomes, in theory, an indicator of the quality of the service and governments may use market mechanisms to select providers offering the best (most cost-effective) service (Rhodes 2000).

Although NPM is considered by some to be the original inspirer of the 'governance turn' in public administration and political science (Stoker 1998), scholars have come to believe that the quality of policy making and policy delivery is improved not so much by introducing market-like mechanisms in public administration, but by soliciting the views, knowledge, and continuous evaluation – if not direct involvement – of citizens in what is aptly called 'interactive governance'. In addition to the attempt to reduce financial overload and pursue cost-effectiveness in public administration, it is believed that governments should also seek to involve citizens, both as a way of receiving first-hand knowledge of existing problems and possible solutions and as a way of explaining to an ever more exigent public the complexity of service delivery. If citizens could gain an appreciation of the logistical and financial problems associated with service delivery, they would contribute to policy solutions both intellectually and practically.

In addition to these practical grounds for pursuing interactive governance, there are several normative reasons as well:

1. Citizens have grown detached and disenchanted with partisan politics and representative democracy, and have since long requested to be more directly involved in policy making (Zittel and Fuchs 2007). Interactive governance appears to answer both requests. However, the way in which this involvement is accomplished is relevant for the equilibrium that may be attained between representative democracy and participatory/deliberative democracy.[1]

2. By participating interactively with government officers, citizens gain a better knowledge and appreciation of the complexity of government, hence close, at least in part, the cognitive and 'affective' gap with government institutions.

3. Citizen involvement in governance increases their civic and republican expertise and is widely assumed, at least since de Tocqueville, to have positive spill-over effects on to representative democracy in terms of their better capacity to evaluate government action and to reward or punish their elected representatives.

Interactive governance, in sum, may be both a direct and an indirect solution to democratic disaffection and ineffective government.

The move to market orientation in the public sector leading to greater cost-efficiency inspires NPM, but far from being a solution to political disaffection, it runs, paradoxically, against some of the same problems that also affect conventional political participation. One way of rendering the malaise of conventional political participation today is to say, with Rudy Andeweg (2003), that political representation has shifted from an *ex ante-ex fundo* mode (typical of post-war mass parties) to an *ex post-ex alto* mode (typical of today's electoral parties). The representation contract, thanks to which representatives obtain from the represented authorisation to represent their interests and values in the political process, may have its founding moment before (*ex ante*) or after (*ex post*) the representational activity. While, from a factual point of view, electoral authorisation must obviously be granted before the representational activity, from a more substantive point of view, it may also take place afterwards. Voters often choose their representatives on the basis of flimsy cues (party labels, catchy messages, good looks, etc.) and sometimes do not even get to choose them at all (as when parties decide to close lists of candidates selected by the leadership and unknown to the wider public). Voters may make up their minds as to whether they were in fact represented by these representatives only at the end of the mandate, when they must decide whether to confirm their choice or to 'throw the rascal out' (Mansbridge 2003).

---

1. I will explore the relationship between these two terms in the next section.

Similarly, while the content of the decisions that the representatives will contribute was once (in times of mass parties) supposed to be the result of a long process of consultation between candidates and voters during which the rank and file could convey their desires to the leadership (*ex fundo*), now the content of these decisions is often the result of the personal ideas of the individual candidate (in personality parties) or, more frequently, of the party leadership (in electoral parties) offered to followers and sympathisers at election times (*ex alto*). Voters are increasingly asked to choose, simultaneously, message and messenger without knowing much about either one. The result is the same kind of relationship as that which exists between supermarket products and customers, with the latter trying out various products only on the basis of brand name, packaging and the degree to which the producer could guess correctly the latest social trend, and confirming or modifying their choice only after having tried the products. The relationship between represented and representative is, thus, reduced to a series of bids and of reactions that do not amount to any real dialogue or representational relationship, pretty much like in a market. Under the circumstances, NPM cannot be the solution, but interactive governance can.

Interactive governance: participatory or deliberative?

Which type of democracy – 'participatory' or 'deliberative' – is embodied in interactive governance, and what relationship does either of them have with representative democracy? Political theorists discuss the relationship between participation and representation, which may be both conflictual and complementary, according to whether participation is seen as weakening or strengthening representative democracy.

Some theorists of democracy theorise direct political participation as a threat to representative democracy. According to the 'classical' theory of democracy,[2] identifiable with the works of Schumpeter, Dahl and Sartori, 'high levels of participation and interest are required from a minority of citizens only and, moreover, the apathy and disinterest of the majority play a valuable role in maintaining the stability of the system as a whole' (Pateman 1970: 7). Quite logically from this standpoint, 'an increase in political participation by present non-participants could upset the stability of the democratic system' (Pateman 1970: 3). These classical theorists are rather cynical about the interest of the masses in politics and pessimistic of their capacity to participate knowledgeably and reasonably in deliberative processes. These theorists at most acknowledge the *protective* function of participation, i.e. the usefulness of mass mobilisation only when democratic institutions are in danger.

The *educational* function of political participation is, instead, at the core of 'contemporary' theories of democracy: for Rousseau, G. D. Cole and J. S. Mill,

---

2. 'Classical' and 'contemporary' theory of democracy are Pateman's labels, which she uses as shorthand and, admittedly, somewhat imprecise expressions for the sake of exposition.

democracy is premised on the equality of all citizens in the political process. In this view, participation ensures that 'the general will is, tautologically, always just (i.e. affects all equally) so that at the same time individual rights and interests are protected and the public interest furthered' (Pateman 1970: 23–4). In reality, individual citizens will have a hard time participating directly and participation through 'tacit associations' (interest groups) will be the rule. Yet, through direct or indirect participation, 'the individual is educated to distinguish between the demands of the public and the private sphere ... he is forced to deliberate according to his sense of justice' (Pateman 1970: 25). Through participation, then, the individual learns to be 'one's own master'. Therefore, participation increases the value of individual freedom. But since all individuals are free and yet they are all 'equally dependent on each other and equally subjected to the law', the third *integrative* function of participation is that 'it enables collective decisions to be more easily accepted by the individual' (Pateman 1970: 27). As Mills puts it: 'through political discussion the individual "becomes consciously a member of a great community"' (Pateman 1970: 33).

According to the contemporary theory of democracy, participation, whether direct or indirect, individual or mediated through tacit associations, contributes to democracy because it protects it from the tendency of the representatives to deliberate in their own interests or in the interests of few (*protective function*), because it teaches individual citizens that they are free and equal (*educational function*), and because it gives substance to the idea that each individual is free and equal insofar as he/she accepts to be part of a larger community (*integrative function*). Are these theoretical expectations are borne out by facts? What is the relationship between participatory/deliberative democracy and representative democracy in our contemporary democracies?

As the cases described below will show, experiments with interactive governance may reveal different metagovernance strategies. On the one hand, they may be attempted in order to revive that civic engagement and trust in public institutions that should underpin representative democracy, but that may have evaporated following the dissolution of mass-party linkages between citizens and politicians characteristic of the postwar period. They may be seen as attempts to reconnect citizens and institutions by allowing bottom-up deliberation and contribution of that information, good will and feedback that even powerful executives need in order to govern effectively and legitimately. On the other hand, they may be used as complements to traditional corporatist consultation meant to keep under control popular disaffection, growing government isolation and escalating contentiousness. They may thus result in fairly conventional 'consultation' exercises and in the managed creation of additional institutional structures of interaction between citizens and regional authorities that further regiment the interaction between the two.

In both cases, interactive governance is resorted to only when representative democracy appears to falter. Insofar as direct participation in policy making is perceived as a more genuine experience – that creates trust in the process of identifying the problems and finding the solutions – than conventional electoral participation, the trust that gets created in the new governance arrangements may revitalise the trust that was once placed in governmental institutions (Hajer and Wagenaar 2003: 12). But insofar as it creates additional institutional layers of governance, it may further undermine that trust. The relationship between participatory/deliberative and representative democracy, therefore, is perhaps not as static as it would appear from the theoretical discussion, but rather fluid and dependent upon the specific circumstances of each polity and the political vision of its leaders.

The relevance of the Italian case

Experiments in participation and deliberation are spreading throughout Europe, particularly at the local level (Saward 2000; Heinelt, Sweeting and Getimis 2006). The local level is, across European state models (Hendriks, Lidstrom and Loughlin forthcoming), the one at which citizens have traditionally engaged in direct mobilisation, participation, and self-government. Therefore, the local level is most apt to test the relationship between representation and participation/deliberation.

Owing to the reduced territorial scale, citizens can best contribute their first-hand knowledge of the problems – and perhaps of the solutions – at the local level. Direct participation and deliberation are, therefore, particularly viable and rewarding at this level, so much so as to overshadow the importance of more conventional mechanisms of representative democracy. However, these same arguments also make representative democracy particularly strong at this level. If we accept the Tocquevillian thesis (de Tocqueville 1988[1848]), representative democracy is most vibrant at this level precisely because of active citizen participation in governmental affairs.[3] In other words, the local level is an excellent ground for testing the relative merit of the 'contradiction' versus 'complementarity' theses of participation and representation – or, if preferred, the relative merit of the 'classical' versus 'contemporary' theory of democracy – sketched out above and for analysing the complex relationship between participatory/ deliberative democracy and representative democracy.

At the same time, the crisis of representative democracy has not spared the local level. In recent years this level has experienced a dramatic decrease in institutional trust and government popularity, leading scholars to hypothesise a general decline in 'social capital' in as diverse contexts as the United States and Sweden (Sirianni 2009; Putnam 2000, 2002). The case of Italy makes no exception. While in the 1980s, the local level enjoyed the highest level of trust amongst all governmental levels, this trust plummeted during the first decade of the new century. Institutional specificities and historical contingencies naturally give the Italian

---

3. 'This type of collective endowment cannot but also reflect onto the quality of political institutions and onto the development of market relations, determining the moral fabric within which economic transactions and citizens-institutions relations take place: actor reliability *vis-à-vis* the rules, low incidence of opportunistic behavior, loyalty towards institutions' (Cartocci 2007: 52–53).

case a particular twist, but the basic story remains the same: levels of satisfaction with and trust in representative democracy are declining even at the local level. Indeed, Italy constitutes a particularly good example of a 'critical' case.

Historically endowed with vibrant and highly diversified local communities, Italian municipal, provincial and regional governments have become places of political rejuvenation, particularly after the national political class was swept away by the 'Bribesville' (*Tangentopoli*) scandals of the early 1990s. Captive for forty years of the byzantine equilibriums forged at the centre among the main post-war parties, in the early 1990s the local and regional tiers freed themselves of that tutelage and became sites of political innovation and political independence in their own right (Baldini and Legnante 2000; Caciagli and Di Virgilio 2005). After the fall of the Berlin Wall and the end of the ideological divide that had paralysed Italian democracy for forty years, the cure to the Italian malaise – extremely short-lived and non-responsive governments – was identified with the reform of the electoral system. The aim of the reform was to facilitate the transformation of the political system from an extreme form of 'consensus democracy' to a more clear-cut instance of 'majoritarian democracy' (Lijphart 1999) in which all parties could have a real chance to govern (in turns). To this end, the national electoral law was changed in 1992 from a rather extreme form of proportional representation to a mixed, but mostly majoritarian, system that was supposed to reduce the number of existing parties, bring about a healthy government-opposition dynamic and, most importantly, alternation in power.

At the local level, this same result was sought by allowing the direct election of mayors and of provincial and regional presidents, and by giving them an artificially constructed majority that would last for the entire legislature. By giving mayors, provincial presidents and 'governors' (as the regional presidents are sometimes called) a solid majority and extensive decision-making powers, it was hoped that also local and regional governments would become more directly responsive and accountable to voters, as they would be forced to deliver on electoral promises rather than pursue their own political perpetuation. The 1993 and 1995 electoral laws (for municipal and regional and provincial elections, respectively) were extraordinarily successful. Mayors and 'governors' became almost overnight first-rate political figures, while national politicians were suffering from a lack of credibility and notoriety (70 per cent of the national parliament had been renewed by 1994). Yet these apparently positive and much wanted effects hid some unexpected ones as well, which ultimately contributed to weaken local and regional representative democracy.

The effect of the 1993 and 1995 electoral laws was to strengthen the regional and municipal executives and to correspondingly weaken the representative assemblies. While mayors and governors could now pursue their own political agendas 'unencumbered' by the opposition, they also yielded greater power *vis-à-vis* the party leaders of the coalition that had supported them at election time. This gave rise to a paradoxical situation: strong mayors and governors ('strong' because directly legitimated by the popular vote and enjoying a solid governmental majority) began to feel increasingly isolated because they were forced to meet a societal demand that was no longer filtered – aggregated, prioritised and pack-aged – by political parties (Floridia 2007). These latter had become considerably weaker because they were often new and fragmented, and had lost that 'blackmail-ing potential' that they once wielded *vis-à-vis* the executive that they supported or opposed. Societal demands, therefore, increasingly took the form of ex-post reactions to government decisions and, often, of protest and contentious mobilisa-tion against government projects. Even the parties that had supported the winning candidate could do little more than claim resources for their particular constituen-cies as a way of keeping themselves alive. At the same time, government action had become potentially more incisive, but worryingly less responsive.

Under these circumstances, the virtuous circle – thanks to which the social capital abundantly present in some Italian areas could sustain a vibrant representa-tive democracy that in turn delivered those types of public goods that made trust and reciprocity (i.e., social capital) even more profitable – was broken. Next to a problem of weakening party-voter linkage, a problem of regenerating social capi-tal also emerged. In some regions, geographically circumscribed 'political subcul-tures' (Bagnasco 1977; 1988; Bagnasco and Trigilia 1984, 1985) began to erode (Ramella 2005; Almagisti 2008), party volatility to increase, and accountability to be reduced to a mere ex-post confirmation or rejection of the executive. In this context, regional and municipal executives began to feel the need to get back in touch with the citizens through channels different from the conventional (and by now weakened and unusable) party channels.

'Participation' and 'deliberation' became increasingly used buzzwords, par-ticularly at the local level. *Participation* takes a number of different forms, from the right to access public administration documents (which increases bureaucratic transparency, hence potentially accountability, but does not directly translate into interactive governance) to participation in important public decisions about ter-ritorial management, environmental choices, public service quality, etc. (which signals some sort of interaction or direct participation of citizens into governmen-tal choices) through referenda and other forms of popular consultation (town hall meetings, social forums, consultation, etc.).

'Partnership' is the term normally used to denote modes of societal partici-pation in which the citizens do not participate directly, but through non-govern-mental organisations (NGOs) and civil society organisations (CSOs). Partnership arrangements are normally stable and involve only a subset of local NGOs/CSOs, normally selected by the government itself. The innovative potential of these forms of participation is rather limited, as they tend to reproduce existing power relations and acknowledge only those organisations that already wield locally a significant economic, social or cultural power. Even when non-profit, voluntary associations are invited in, they are normally selected amongst the more established and 'reli-able' ones. The rules of participation are also normally dictated by the institutional actors; hence the potential for innovative, truly interactive governance is limited. Rather, what might happen is that, thanks to the relationships established in these rather formal and limited forums, some CSOs may get to know government people on a more informal basis and thus have informal access to and influence over the policy-making process that way (Piattoni 2005).

However, there are also forms of direct participation that favor genuine *deliberation* experimented with at the local level. Luigi Bobbio (2007) offers an overview of the various participatory practices by dividing them into three groups:

1. Those participatory practices that are particularly apt at registering in a participative way the problems and the needs of the citizens, e.g. information offices, consensus building, e-forums, focus groups, 'social' tables, open-space technology, etc.

2. Those instruments that should lead to shared projects, e.g. working groups and workshops, 'technical' tables, project laboratories, action planning, goal-oriented project planning, etc.

3. Those formats that facilitate debate among participants and allow them to reach a shared decision, e.g. citizens' juries, town meetings, deliberative polling, etc.

The goal of soliciting this type of participation/deliberation is rather simple: through direct participation of selected expressions of civil society, executives try to break the sense of isolation and perhaps even shift part of the responsibility (and eventual blame) for public decisions on to the citizens themselves. Moreover, in this way, they tend to recoup that political support that has become ever more elusive. That the representativeness of these forums is limited and normally biased towards the socially and civically active is inevitable, although positive measures are normally taken to solicit the 'widest possible participation'. These participatory arrangements are meant to support an ailing representative democracy, not to fundamentally supplement or replace it. When deliberation, i.e. informed, reasoned and principled argumentation, takes place, regional and local governments wish to tap into the surplus of legitimacy that such exercises normally yield.

Interactive governance, then, should imply more than simple rubber-stamping of decisions over which citizens have little control; it should aim at influencing, through consultative and deliberative mechanisms, a decision-making process that is ultimately the responsibility of the executive. Real deliberation should imply openness by government actors towards authentic citizen influence on both the problems to be tackled and the solutions to be pursued. Participation/deliberation has the potential to close that widening gap between the represented and representatives, and to recreate that social capital of trust in public institutions that is being eroded by apathy and disenchantment.

A tale of two regions: Tuscany and Trentino[4]

Tuscany and Trentino are two interesting cases because they are both regions endowed with high levels of social capital, as conventionally measured by the density of voluntary associations and networks of reciprocity (Putnam 1993), and in which regional and local governments play a pivotal role in its production and regeneration. At the same time, they are situated in two rather different geo-political parts of the country – in the north-east (Trentino) and in the centre (Tuscany) – and, therefore, belong to two rather different political subcultures – the 'white' (Christian Democratic) subculture, Trentino, and the 'red' (Communist, Socialist) subculture, Tuscany. While the Catholic tradition puts civil society ahead of the state, in Trentino government action plays an absolutely primary role. This is mostly due to the heightened political significance of its special Statute of Autonomy, in turn linked to the particular circumstances under which it ended up becoming part of the Italian state (after World War I) and of how its constitutional arrangement was linked to that of the neighboring German-speaking area of South-Tyrol (after World War II). Tuscany, in its turn, is a region in which the action of the regional government has been particularly forceful, as one would expect from a Communist-Socialist partisan tradition.

In view of testing whether the Italian political crisis, and the ensuing institutional changes, of the early 1990s affected regions in which social capital was not only abundant, but also governmentally sustained, Tuscany and Trentino provide two very apt examples for comparison. In these two regions, Christian Democratic and Communist hegemony was particularly strong, anchored in and reinforced by a host of flanking organisations that organised non-political activities such as charity work and leisure activities, youth sports and holiday trips, popular education and culinary events, production and consumption activities. Given the high density of co-operative forms of economic activities, particularly in the agricultural and the commercial sectors, and the habit of consulting with the social partners on most decisions, we could say that both Tuscany and Trentino enjoyed a strong tradition of *participatory forms of governance, at least of the conventional consultative (corporatist) form.* What happened to these forms of participation after the collapse of the large post-war parties and the new regional and municipal electoral laws that granted the executive (and the chief executive, in particular) the power to decide almost unilaterally? Did they manage to sustain representative democracy or were they forced to transform? Did they resort to the *deliberative form of participatory democracy embodied by interactive governance*?

---

4.   Formally, Trentino is an Autonomous Province. Together with Alto-Adige/Süd Tirol, they form the Region Trentino-Alto Adige/Süd Tirol. In practice, however, because of their special statutes, both Autonomous Provinces enjoy powers that are even more far-reaching than those of most Italian regions. Hence, it is totally appropriate to compare it to a region like Tuscany. For terminological simplicity, therefore, I will refer to Trentino as a 'region' and indicate its government as 'regional'.

Tuscany

Often described as a 'corporatist' political system (Piattoni and Smyrl 2003), Tuscany appeared at the beginning of the 1990s particularly well-equipped to weather the national political storm with a minimum of disruption. And yet, the problems befalling the Tuscan executive – their sense of isolation, impotence and surrounding hostility – are no different from those felt in other parts of the country. Party channels and functional associations no longer ensure that linkage that once connected represented and representatives (Profeti 2010). As distance breeds distrust, even a certain feeling of hostility can be explained. When citizens mobilize, they normally do so *against* a government project (Della Porta 2004, Della Porta and Piazza 2008). The social capital embedded in the 'red' subculture began to fray and to acquire a less partisan and more particularistic character (Floridia 2007; Almagisti 2008). When associations mobilise, it is more to defend their particularistic interests than to contribute to the formulation of organised and well-ordered societal demands. Society appears to play the role that once was of the opposition.

In this new context, the Region Tuscany decided to create direct links with the citizenry and passed a regional law aimed at fostering direct interaction between citizens and authorities.[5] Regional authorities recognise that the citizens' willingness to participate actively in governance mechanisms has not evaporated, but that it needs to be filtered, organised and capitalised upon. The aim of this law is to create the institutional and financial context within which 'new models for the construction of decision-making processes and new mechanisms for the production of collective choices can be experimented' (Floridia 2007: 621). The regional government neither decides the issues to be discussed nor the format that such interactive governance may take – both can be proposed by the citizens themselves – but it can, nevertheless, suggest issues and formats of its own.

The hope is that such an experiment will start a 'virtuous cycle' and will replenish the endowment of social capital still present in the region in ways that will simultaneously reward the citizens' desire to participate, train them to do so con-

---

5. The regional law *Norme per la partecipazione alle scelte politiche regionali e locali* (l.r. 30 luglio 2007) is available on the website of the Region Tuscany (*www.regione.toscana.it*) following the link 'participation'. This law was itself the outcome of a long process of participation, deliberation and continuous interaction between the regional ministry in charge with these matters (*Assessorato alle riforme istituzionali, federalismo, attuazione dello Statuto; rapporto con gli Enti Locali, aree metropolitane e città metropolitana; rapporti con i cittadini e promozione della partecipazione*) and various expressions of organised civil society. The main milestones of this process included an international conference (2006) and an *ETown-meeting* (November 2006) with more than 400 participants, which then selected 40 delegates that reconvened regularly in the following months to assess various drafts of the law. At the end of this participatory/deliberative exercise, the 'usual' consultative meetings were also held with the representatives of Tuscan local governments (provinces and municipalities) and of the social partners (employers' associations, trade unions), as is customary for the approval of any piece of regional legislation (Bobbio 2007: 91–98).

structively, and give the authorities the input that they need to govern.[6] More than twenty public debates have been so far financed and sustained by the Regional Authority.

How well-grounded is such hope? Will disenchanted citizens believe that their suggestions, as they emerge from these public debates, will effectively be acted upon and, therefore, accept the opportunity to participate in these deliberative exercises? Or will they see this as another attempt at window-dressing? The legal framework of the Italian state means that laws must and can be adopted solely by governmental authorities. However, according to the Tuscan law, if the regional agency approves a public debate, regional and local authorities must commit themselves to taking into account the recommendations that emerge from it. In practice, this means that governmental authorities must *at least* publicly justify why the recommendations are accepted, modified or rejected – as the case may be. This may not seem much in the way of progress *vis-à-vis* conventional consultation or even no consultation, but both the scope and the nature of the actors involved make these public debates significantly more diversified and inclusive than the regular 'corporatist' consultations. Also, the fact that the promoters must have a direct involvement in the problem to be debated ensures that public debates are not just opportunities for philosophical discussions. Citizens may be disappointed if their suggestions are not taken up, but they will have experienced genuine deliberation and will have improved their democratic skills in the process.

Trentino

Trentino experienced many of the same transformations as Tuscany did. Here, too, the dominant post-war party disappeared quickly as a political entity after the 'Bribesville' (*Tangentopoli*) scandals at the beginnings of the 1990s, but the 'white' political subculture remained strong. Trentino is still characterised by numerous and strong local associations – in a host of fields from agriculture to commerce, from banking to welfare, from education to culture – and by church-inspired civic involvement.

Although the regional fabric of associations was not shaken by the political

---

6. The law establishes the Regional Public Debate (*Dibattito pubblico regionale*) through which regional authorities commit themselves to hearing the citizens' voice on major issues and decisions. Guarantor that such public debates are no one-way communication exercises is the Regional Authority for the Guarantee and Promotion of Participation (*Autorità regionale per la garanzia e la promozione della partecipazione*). Public debates may be promoted by local authorities (provinces, municipalities), groups of citizens, schools, enterprises and other collective subjects. The proposals are assessed and screened by the above-mentioned Regional Authority, which also supplies venues, funds and logistical support. Such Debates must normally last no more than six months and must be amply inclusive so as to ensure that all points of view and interests have a fair chance to be heard. Among the criteria that the Regional Authority uses to select issues for the proposed public debates is whether the promoter has a direct involvement in the realisation of a given project. Institutional actors must accept a protocol according to which they promise to 'take into account' the result of the debate (Floridia 2007: 625).

turmoil, the changed partisan landscape and the reformed electoral laws had a deep impact on representative democracy.[7] The impact was felt particularly at the local level, where the new primacy of the executive over both its own governmental majority and the opposition clashed with an ingrained habit of governing by consensus. Most Trentino municipalities are very small: only twenty-three communes out of 223 (roughly 1 per cent) have more than 3,000 inhabitants while 52 percent of the municipalities have less than 1,000 inhabitants (Rapporto sulla qualità della democrazia in Trentino (henceforth Rapporto) 2008: 37). In this situation, face-to-face relations are very common and everyone has a natural stake in local government. In this social context, a government where the party that supported the elected mayor obtains two-thirds of the elected representatives (ten out of fifteen), nominates all the members of the municipal executive – and can therefore govern virtually alone – understandably strains the existing pattern of social relations and the existing political culture.[8] It also effectively prevents the opposition – and even the members of the governmental majority – from exercising their institutional watchdog function. The electoral reform, in other words, strengthened the electoral accountability of the chief executive, but weakened the institutional accountability of the mayoral office. In reality, only the municipal secretary (a non-elected career official) or the ombudsman can object to the mayor in his/her decisions.

The effects of party upheaval and electoral reform, thus, combined to render representative democracy less 'representative' and, potentially, also less 'accountable' in Trentino. Did it make it more 'responsive'? It would appear that since mayors (and the regional governor) are directly elected and considerably more powerful than before, they should also secure greater correspondence between societal preferences and governmental action. In the Trentino context, in which parties were weakened but associations remained strong, societal preferences could be still channelled through the latter. In Trentino (as in Tuscany) there is a well-founded practice of consulting with economic, social, cultural and religious associations prior to all major public decisions. And, indeed, associations do represent a potential channel for articulating a societal voice and a training ground for principled deliberation. However, in Trentino, more than elsewhere, the long tradition in consultation has created a relatively stable and closed circle of associations that are regularly consulted, leaving dissenting groups and the public at large voiceless; 'associationism appears to have created a new form of delegation (in this case through social, not political representatives)' (Rapporto 2008: 53).

---

7. The national reform of local elections is contained in law 25/03/1993, No. 31; the Trentino regional law, receiving and adapting the national law, is law 30/11/1994, No. 3.

8. This rule applies to municipalities with up to 5,000 inhabitants. For larger municipalities, the rule is slightly different but creates much of the same dynamic. In these larger municipalities, parties indicate which mayoral candidate they support. The parties supporting the winning candidate obtain 60 per cent of seats in the representative assembly and the mayor chooses the members of the local executives.

Trentino's 'corporatism' then appears more rigid and exclusionary than Tuscany's.

The regional government of Trentino has been accused by the municipal governments of excessively centralising decisions and to insufficiently involve local authorities in policy making. Apparently, as a way to streamline the consultation process and make it more effective, but also to rationalise local government and make it more cost-effective, Trentino passed a law creating so-called 'Valley Communities' (*Comunità di valle*). These are (second-level) public bodies made up of representatives of neighboring municipalities that can reasonably and effectively share the production and delivery of certain public goods. Their creation is mandatory and has been decided by the region Trentino (l.r. 16/06/2006, No. 3). According to this law, the Region Trentino retains legislative powers, while the administrative tasks are shared between the individual municipalities and the Valley Communities. Most mayors and local party leaders do not quite see the utility of a reform that creates yet another layer of government (of dubious representativeness and legitimacy) and de facto re-centralises the decision-making powers at the regional level (Rapporto 2008: 39).[9]

The reaction of the region Trentino to the political upheaval of the early 1990s and to the impact of the electoral reforms that ensued therefore appears somewhat different from that of Tuscany. Although both regions started from high levels of 'civicness', solid (red or white) political subcultures and a tradition of consultation with local associations, they reacted differently to the dual challenge of securing responsive and effective policies through representative democracy. Tuscany kept in place a consolidated system of multilevel consultation that involved not just associations, but also local governments, while opening itself up to experimentation with more innovative and interactive modes of governance. Trentino kept the conventional, and rather rigid, system of consultation with associations, while trying to rationalise and manage from above the relationship with the lower levels of government. It would thus appear that the greater ease with which political parties in Trentino regrouped under the new political and institutional circumstances induced its regional leadership to be less open to alternative ways of governance.

Also Trentino has experimented with new forms of consultation and deliberation that directly involve individual citizens. However, also in this case, the initiatives taken by Trentino were mostly of a top-down character (Rapporto 2008: 41). In part, this is confirmed by the rather extensive understanding of 'interactive participation' (which includes local referendums, opinion polls, public entertainment initiatives, etc.) that local public administrators used when answering questions about 'participatory democracy'. In reality, the only real instances of participatory democracy were considerably fewer and the authors of the *Rapporto* ended

---

9. Interestingly, Tuscany had also tried, in the 1970s, to reorganise its territory along functional areas that included several municipalities, each too small to perform anything but the most essential public functions. However, the experiment failed and the Provinces, which had been sidelined in the experiment, re-emerged as that intermediate level (between Region and Municipality) that could coordinate service delivery (Profeti 2010: 95–102). Trentino, being itself a Province, lacks this intermediate level, hence the attempt to create these Valley Communities.

up identifying only eighteen significant experiments. Of these, only six included citizens operating side-by-side with the conventional associations and civil society organisations, and only one was exclusively directed at citizens. Participatory budgets have been tried in Trentino, too, with the municipal council and government free to reject the proposals but forced to account for their rejection. The Strategic Plans for Trento and Rovereto, Trentino's two major cities, were particularly well constructed and involved lots of different associations and voluntary organisations reaching as many as 800 citizens.

Interactive participation may also have a conflictual character. In Trentino, there have been several instances of protest against regional and communal decisions, particularly regarding investment or infrastructural projects with a negative environmental impact. The general attitude of the regional and municipal governments, however, has been of general closure towards such truly bottom-up citizens' initiatives, even when they supplied scientific counter-evidence or alternative plans and not just a generic rejection of governmental proposals. The Rapporto (2008: 48) concludes:

> The debate, when it does take place at all, normally involves only institutional actors. Citizens' committees, civil society organisations, and informal groups are never explicitly involved, even when they are able to propose specific arguments and have a significant influence amongst the population.

In other words:

> Trentino seems reluctant to experiment with the new interactive modes of governance that have been internationally devised: its techniques appear often way too simplistic *vis-à-vis* the problems at hand.

(Rapporto 2008: 49)

Conclusion

The comparison between two regional Italian cases, Tuscany and Trentino, historically rich in social capital and endowed with well-established corporatist arrangements, though within different political subcultures, showed that whether and how participatory/deliberative democracy (interactive governance) is effectively experimented with depends in large part on its perceived relationship with representative and associative democracy. Participatory/deliberative forms of democratic policy making are not immediately embraced unless they appear to resolve a widely-felt sense of isolation on the part of regional and local governments, which not even well-established corporatist consultative arrangements manage to overcome. This, at least, is true in Italy, where the Napoleonic form of state – which has conventionally entrusted to the public administration decision-making and implementation of public policies – still bears the mark of its original imprint.

Truly interactive forms of governance, which invite into the policy-making process the citizenry at large and leave it to define the very problems to be tackled through public action, are still few and far between. They also depend closely on the type of metagovernance embraced by regional authorities. In regions like Trentino, where political representatives managed to weather the crisis of the 1990s and were unwilling to abandon existing corporatist channels, metagovernance is exerted through rather conventional consultation exercises and through the creation of yet another layer of representative institutions, which appears to create more problems than it solves. In regions like Tuscany, where the political class is well aware of the danger that the social capital once embedded in associational forms of participation and in corporatist channels of consultation might dissipate forever, participatory/deliberative forms of governance are pursued with greater commitment and metagovernance is exerted indirectly through an independent regional agency, whose task is to facilitate interactive governance.

Throughout Italy, attempts at interactive governance are multiplying (Bobbio 2004; Della Porta 2004), partly because some services cannot be delivered except with the active collaboration of the citizens, and partly because escalating costs and the declining quality of public services acts as an inducement to off-load some of these services on to voluntary associations, but particularly because democracy cannot properly work in the absence of a strong linkage between the represented and the representatives. These participatory/deliberative experiments produce mixed results that depend both on the commitment of the local political classes to reconnect with the citizenry and on their remaining trust in more conventional forms of participation (Fung 2004).

References

Almagisti, M. (2008) *La qualità delle democrazia in Italia. Capitale sociale e politica*, Roma: Carocci.

Andeweg, R. (2003), 'Beyond representativeness? Trends in political representation', *European Review*, 11 (2): 147–61.

Bagnasco, A. (1977) *Tre Italie: La problematica territoriale dello sviluppo italiano*, Bologna: il Mulino.

—   (1988) La costruzione sociale del mercato, Bologna: il Mulino.

Bagnasco, Arnaldo and Trigilia, C. (1984) Società e politica nelle aree di piccola impresa: il caso di Bassano, Venezia: Arsenale.

—   (1985) *Società e politica nelle aree di piccola impresa: il caso della Val d'Elsa*, Milano: Angeli.

Baldini, Gianfranco and Guido Legnante (2000), *Città al voto. I sindaci e le elezioni comunali*, Bologna: il Mulino.

Bobbio, L. (2004) 'A più voci. Amministrazioni pubbliche, imprese, associazioni e cittadini nei processi decisionali inclusivi', *Edizioni Scientifiche Italiane*, Napoli-Roma.

—   (2007), Amministrare con i cittadini. Viaggio tra le pratiche di partecipazione in Italia, Soveria Mannelli: Rubbettino.

Caciagli, M. and di Virgilio, A. (2005) *Eleggere il sindaco. La nuova democrazia locale in Italia*, Torino: UTET.

della Porta, D. (2004) *Comitati dei cittadini e democrazia urbana*, Soveria Mannelli: Rubbettino.

della Porta, D. and Piazza, G. (2008) 'Le ragioni del no. Le campagne contro la TAV', in *Val di Susa e il ponte sullo stretto*, Milano: Feltrinelli.

Floridia, A. (2007) 'La democrazia deliberativa, dalla teoria alle procedure. Il caso della legge regionale toscana sulla partecipazione', *Le istituzioni del Federalismo*, 5: 603–81.

Fung, A. (2004) *Empowered Participation: Reinventing Urban Democracy*, Princeton: Princeton University Press.

Gilbert, M. (1995) *The Italian Revolution: The End of Politics Italian Style?*, Boulder, CO: Westview Press.

Heinelt, H., Sweeting, D. and Getimis, P. (eds) (2006) *Legitimacy and Urban Governance: A Cross-National Comparative Study*, London: Routledge.

Hendriks, F., Lidstrom, A. and Loughlin, J. (forthcoming) *The Oxford Handbook of Subnational Democracy in Europe,* Oxford: Oxford University Press.

Kohler-Koch, B. and Eising, R. (eds) *The Transformation of Governance in the European Union*, London: Routledge.

Lijphart, A. (1999) *Patterns of Democracy: Government Forms and Performance in Thirty-Six Countries*, New Haven: Yale University Press.

Mansbridge, J. (2003) 'Rethinking representation', *American Political Science Review*, 97 (4): 515–28.

Marcussen, M. and Torfing, J. (eds) (2007) *Democratic Networks and Governance in Europe*, Houndmills, UK: Palgrave.

Pateman, C. (1970) *Participation and Democratic Theory*, Cambridge: Cambridge University Press.

Piattoni, S. (2006) 'Informal governance in structural policy', *Perspectives on European Politics and Society*, 7 (1): 56–74.

Piattoni, S. and Smyrl, M. (2003) 'Building Effective Institutions: Italian Regions and the EU Structural Funds', in J. Bukowski, S. Piattoni and M. Smyrl (eds) *Between Europeanization and Local Socities: The Space for Territorial Governance in Europe*, Boulder, CO: Rowman and Littlefield, 133–56.

Pierre, J. (ed.) (2000) *Debating Governance*, Oxford: Oxford University Press.

Pierre, J. and Peters, G. (2000) *Governance, Politics and the State*, Houndmills, UK: Macmillan Press.

Profeti, S. (2010) *Il potere locale tra politca e politiche. Il mosaico della governance nell'area vasta fiorentina*, Soveria Mannelli: Rubbettino.

Putnam, R. (1993) *Making Democracy Work: Civic Traditions in Modern Italy*, Princeton: Princeton University Press.

—   (2000) *Bowling Alone: The Collapse and Revival of American Community*, New York: Simon and Schuster.

—   (ed.) (2002) 'Democracies in Flux: The Evolution of Social Capital', in *Contemporary Societies*, Oxford: Oxford University Press.

Ramella, F. (2005) *Cuore rosso. Viaggio politico nell'Italia di mezzo*, Roma: Donzelli.

Rapporto sulla qualità della democrazia in Trentino. Partecipazione e Governance (2008) Trento: Provincia Autonoma di Trento.

Rhodes, R. A. W. (2000) 'Governance and Public Administration', in J. Pierre (ed.) *Debating Governance*, Oxford: Oxford University Press, 54–90.

Saward, M. (2000) *Democratic Innovation: Deliberation, Representation and Association*, London: Routledge.

Sirianni, C. (2009) *Investing in Democracy: Engaging Citizens in Collaborative Governance*, Washington, DC: The Brooking Institute.

Sørensen, E. and Torfing, J. (eds) (2007) *Theories of Democratic Governance*, Houndmills, UK: Palgrave.

Stoker, G. (1998) 'Governance as theory: Five propositions', *International Social Science Journal*, 50 (155): 17–28.

Tocqueville, A. de (1988[1848]) *Democracy in America*, New York: Harper Perennial.

Zittel, T. and Fuchs, D. (eds) (2007) *Participatory Democracy and Political Participation: Can Participatory Engineering Bring Citizens Back In?*, London: Routldge.

chapter eleven | democratic legitimacy criteria in interactive governance and their empirical application

Erik-Hans Klijn

Introduction – governance and democracy

Whatever 'governance' is, it is certainly aimed at involving stakeholders. The literature gives various reasons for the necessity of involving stakeholders and thus why (interactive) governance can be more effective than more classical forms of steering. In general, they fall into three categories (see for instance Kooiman 1993; Kickert *et al.* 1997; Pierre 2000; Sørensen and Torfing 2007):

1. stakeholders have to be involved because governments are dependent on their resources ('veto power' argument);

2. stakeholders are involved because they have specific knowledge and can enhance the quality of the problem definition or even more so the quality and innovative character of the solutions ('quality' argument);

3. stakeholders have to be involved to enhance the democratic quality of decision-making in modern network societies ('democratic legitimacy' argument).

Governance and representative democracy – friends or enemies?

The fact that governance processes involve a plurality of value judgments of many involved actors is almost undisputed (Osborne 2010).[1] This means that governance processes are also (but not only) forms to reconcile value differences, which inevitably connects them with the classical democratic institutions that are traditionally thought of as the institutions to carry out this function. A substantial part of the governance literature takes the value problem and the relation (or tension) between governance processes and democratic institutions as one of the core subjects (Hirst 2000; Klijn and Koppenjan 2000; Fung and Wright 2001; Sørensen 2002; Edelenbos 2005). Generally, many authors recognise tensions between the idea of representative democracy, with its more vertical accountability structure, and governance processes, which have a more horizontal and less clearly ac-

---

1. Governance networks will be used here as an indication of *more or less stable patterns of social relationships (interactions, cognitions and rules) between mutually dependent public, semi-public and private actors, that arise and build up around complex policy issues or policy programmes.* Governance, then, refers to the interaction processes that take place within those networks.

countability structure. This tension is confirmed by empirical research (Klijn and Koppenjan, 2000; Edelenbos 2005, Skelcher *et al.* 2005).

In the literature, we find four main positions about the relationship between governance processes and representative institutions (Klijn and Skelcher 2007):

1. *Incompatible position:* classical representational democracy is incompatible with governance processes because these are a threat to the position of democratic institutions. The authority of democratic institutions is 'hollowed out' by the involvement of other stakeholders. This position is found especially in more classical political science literature.

2. *Complementary position:* governance processes provide for additional links to society and can perfectly co-exist beside classical democratic institutions. They provide elected officials, information and accountability is shared, but political officeholders retain an important position.

3. *Transition position:* governance networks offer greater flexibility and efficiency and will gradually replace representative democracy as the dominant model in the network society.

4. *Instrumental position:* governance networks provide a means for democratic institutions to increase their control in a situation of societal complexity. By setting performance targets, elected office holders secure a dominant position.

The second and the fourth positions could be said to consider governance and democratic institutions as friends, while positions one and three consider them as enemies, or at least as opposites.

Interactive governance: democratic?

When it comes to interactive governance, the question of whether the processes are democratic is an important one. On the one hand they can clash with the classical institutions of representative democracy, but on the other hand the processes themselves should be democratic. This is the question of the democratic legitimacy of interactive decision-making. Criteria are required to evaluate the democratic character (or the 'democratic anchorage', see Sørensen and Torfing 2007) of decisions made in interactive processes.

Democratic legitimacy – towards an analytical framework

Determining those criteria that make decision-making democratic is more difficult that it appears because we can identify different models of democracy.

Models of democracy

MacPherson puts forward four different models of democracy, in the history of political philosophy, each stressing different core elements of democracy (MacPherson, 1979):

1. *Utopian model:* in which democracy is the will of the people expressed by the people. Democracy is the best way to serve the common purpose (by means of participation of individuals in the government) and the best way to develop individuals. Rousseau with his 'general will of the people' and Jefferson provide examples of this model.

2. *Protective model:* in which democracy is mainly understood as a protection of citizens by their governments. Important institutional features protect the freedom of individuals and their freedom against the state. Individual votes in this liberal model are an effective expression of the citizens' wishes. James Mill and Jeremy Bentham are proponents of this second model.

3. *Developmental model:* stresses the participation of citizens as both a good way to organise democracy, and develop and actively enhance the freedom of citizens. John Stuart Mill is the leading exponent of this model.

4. *Competitive model:* in which democracy is a mechanism for decision-making where political leaders compete to gain votes. One of the most prominent authors of this model is Schumpeter (1943).

Schumpeter criticised the classical model for holding unrealistic demands on participation and the way citizens are informed. His now famous definition of democracy is: 'that institutional arrangement for arriving at political decisions in which individuals acquire the power to decide by means of a competitive struggle for the people's vote' (Schumpeter 1943: 269). This idea of competition is later taken further by the pluralists (Dahl 1956; Truman 1956) who see democracy as a plurality of groups struggling for power. Downs (1956) presents the image of democracy as a marketplace where voters act rationally and choose a political leader and a programme, and parties and leaders try to maximise votes. Legitimacy in this model is connected to the procedure that is followed (the voting) and the fact that political office holders are accountable and can be dismissed at the next election.

If we look at MacPherson (1979), his model of democracy provides two competing ideas: the idea that democracy is an arrangement to reach (efficient) decisions and protect individual freedom and the idea that democracy embodies normative ideas and rules about how we should organise our society. This is a society where people actively take part in decisions, developing themselves and the society as a whole. He calls the two competing models 'protective' and 'developmental' democracy.

The same distinction is emphasised by Pateman (1970), who compares some of the classical theorists on democracy. Pateman mentions elections and responsiveness of political leaders to citizens, political equality and participation as major characteristics of democracy (Pateman 1970: 14). These characteristics can also be found in the four different models of MacPherson, although they receive different emphasis.

More recently, models of 'deliberative' democracy (Dryzek 2000; Hirst 2000; Held 2006) add other characteristics, especially the idea of open debate among involved stakeholders about solutions (see also Fisher 2003). The key to deliberative models of democracy is: 'the transformation of private preferences via a process of deliberation into positions that can withstand public scrutiny and test' (Held 2006: 237). Essential to most forms of deliberative democracy is that preferences are not fixed, but can change in a debate, or as Dryzek tells us: 'The only condition for authentic deliberation is then the requirement that communication induce reflection upon preferences in non-coercive fashion' (Dryzek 2000: 2). But then for this deliberation to be successful, another kind of core characteristic of democracy is introduced, which could be described as 'openness' or at least it has to do with a number of rules and practices that all are connected to the process of discussion, information, plurality of values, etc. Deliberative models of democracy stress that besides the fact that officeholders are accountable and can be replaced (the core of the protective models of democracy) and that democracy is about participation in decisions being made (the core of the developmental models of democracy), democratic legitimacy can come from the characteristics of the process (openness, flow of information, argumentation process, etc.).

Sources of democratic legitimacy

Democratic legitimacy could be said to originate from three sources, which, of course, are related, but which receive different emphasis according to model (Skelcher and Sullivan 2008):

1. *Accountability:* this is strongly emphasised by the more protective models of democracy whereby office holders are accountable for decisions and for the decision-making process. The office holders (is it clear who is accountable?) and the procedures that hold them accountable (voting to get them in and, more importantly, the means to get them out of office) and various rules that protect citizens are stressed.

2. *Voice:* how are citizens able to exercise voice and influence decisions? In this source of legitimacy, it is not the passive influence that is important, but rather the active ways in which citizens can participate in concrete decisions and the processes by which these are achieved that are emphasised. From the participation literature (Arnstein, 1971; Berry 1993; Young, 2000), one can make distinctions such as the depth of participation (the intensity and the influence of stakeholders) and the width of participation (how many stakeholders are allowed to participate (Berry *et al.* 1993), or one could distinguish levels of participation (Arnstein 1971).

3. *Due deliberation:* this source of democratic legitimacy is strongly connected to how the interaction and deliberation process is organised. Democratic legitimacy arises out of a deliberative process, guaranteed by fair procedures and agreement between actors, where they share knowledge, explore possible solutions and exchange value judgments. This does not require something like a power-free dialogue (compare Habermas (1981) and his '*herscheiftsfreie* discussion'). Dryzek (2000) tells us that people who would favour the Habermas ideal speech situation would be very vul-

nerable to criticism from a number of theoretical insights. He tells us: 'In a pluralistic world, consensus is unattainable, unnecessary, and undesirable. More feasible and attractive is workable agreements in which participants agree on a course of action, but for different reasons (Dryzek 2000: 170). Interestingly, this very much resembles ideas in the literature on governance networks on outcomes, packages of goals, etc. (Koppenjan and Klijn 2004). It is the institutional characteristics, such as fair entry, reciprocity, freedom of coercion, open information access and lack of manipulation, that are important here, but also the empirical manifestations of these principles.

Democratic legitimacy in governance networks

The first step has now been taken in our attempt to define some of the, more or less, accepted norms for democratic legitimacy. These norms are in general derived from the wide variety of democratic models that exist and are discussed by authors in the field. But the next point to address is how these norms or principles apply to governance networks.

Because in network-like situations we come up against some problems these principles are applied to 'measure' democratic anchorage. The first obvious problem is that there is no clear demos defined (Sørensen 2002). Networks often stretch themselves over different governmental layers (municipalities, countries or even national governments) and include several functional actors.

This certainly holds true in recent policy-making processes on water management – a case we examine below. Networks pose multilevel problems because rivers, safety problems and environmental issues are not restricted to one governmental level, which may result in a collision of authority between various groups among the 'demos'. That makes it difficult to establish the 'will of the people' within these networks (or what constitute the 'demos' to phrase it differently) (Sørensen 2002).

At the same time, we see a wide range of organisational and institutional arrangements that are added or partly replace the classical mechanisms of representational democracy (Skelcher et al. 2005). These mechanisms are aimed at increasing effectiveness (and thus increasing output legitimacy) by involving actors who have important resources and can provide knowledge and solutions, or they have to obtain support for solutions before they can be implemented.

Interactive governance thus asks for a reinterpretation of the classical criteria for measuring legitimacy. Sørensen and Torfing (2005), for instance, pose four questions that look at the democratic quality of networks:

1. Are networks controlled by democratically-elected politicians?
2. Do networks represent the interests, preferences and opinions of members of the different groups that are part of the network?
3. Are networks accountable to the territorially-defined citizenry?

4. Do networks follow democratic rules, i.e. a specific set of rules for conduct?

If we compare the four criteria of Sørensen and Torfing with the three sources of legitimacy elaborated on above, we see that number four very much resembles the source of good procedures, number two is related to what we have termed 'voice' (who actually participates) and numbers one and three are strongly related to what we have called accountability.

Others stress process rules (the fact that networks have open access, that decision procedures are known and clear, etc.) as important to the judgment how well networks are in terms of democratic anchorage (Koppenjan and Klijn 2000). This resembles some of the ideas from deliberative democracy models. The process rules could also include arrangements how to involve representational democratic institutions more explicitly in the decision-making in networks (Klijn and Koppenjan 2000). Table 11.1 gives an overview of the three proposed sources of democratic legitimacy and the differences in a representational context and a governance network context.

Table 11.1: Three principles in representative democracy and governance networks

	Classical representational democracy	**Governance networks**
Accountability	Accountability is simple and clearly demarcated (elected office holders).	Accountability is diffuse and spread among different actors (even if formal elected bodies are present).
Voice	Voice is clearly arranged by fixed procedures of voting (elections) or maybe formal participation processes (arranged by law and regulations). In general, active possibilities of voice are not that large in pure representational democracy.	Voice is complex because many actors involved and clear rules often are lacking. In principle, there are many opportunities for voice in networks, especially when actors use their dependency relations. Actual voice possibilities related to.
Due deliberation	Representational democracy is characterised by a limited set of clear developed rules for procedures. Even in the case of more deliberative democratic procedures, with instruments like referenda and citizens juries, these rules are clearly set out.	Networks are characterised by a wide variety of institutional rules coming from various sources (various public authorities, self-made rules, informal rules, etc.), and it is a crowded institutional space.

As can be seen from Table 11.2, most of the sources of democratic legitimacy in representative democracy are far more straightforward than in governance networks, where there is more uncertainty about how to use the sources of legitimacy. Part of the problem is that in governance processes, the *process* is very important and many different decisions are taken over a long period of time during which arguments and choices change. So, democratic legitimacy is a characteristic that can change during the time of the process.

Parameters for democratic legitimacy in networks

We have to translate existing criteria for legitimacy to judge the nature of legitimacy of network governance. The three elements of accountability, voice and good procedures remain in function but have to be reinterpreted or given new meanings to apply them in the situation of governance networks. Actually, most of these refinements will appear similar to the ideas suggested in the literature on deliberative democracy because, in essence, interaction processes in networks are discussions about values between different actors who are interdependent and need each other for achieving solutions. So although governance networks are not a demos or city-state in the classical sense of the word like a 'polis', they are a sort of community made up of interdependent relationships. The only difficulty is that they do not have such clear procedures and authority positions as the classical demos.

In classical democratic theories, most of the legitimacy stems from input notions such as: if you arrange the positions and accountabilities in advance, it does not matter much how the process afterwards is organised. Scharpf already argued that one can make a distinction between output and input legitimacy (Scharpf 1997: 153–54). Others such as Easton (1953), who understood politics as the authorised allocations of values, also emphasises the throughput of a system. This fits the idea of governance as a process that also needs legitimacy during that process and not only at the start (input) or at the end (output). From this perspective, we derive a third notion of legitimacy: the notion of throughput legitimacy. Actually, the deliberative democracy idea already introduces more throughput-like sources of legitimacy in the discussion. And this throughput seems an interesting thought in the context of networks in which the emphasis is on complex decision-making and interaction between the involved actors.

So we can distinguish between input, throughput and output legitimacy (Bekkers and Edwards 2006). When we combine the three elements of legitimacy (accountability, voice and due deliberation) with the three types of legitimacy (input, throughput, output), legitimacy questions for governance networks are formulated as in Table 11.2.

Table 11.2: Indicators of legitimacy

	Input legitimacy	Throughput legitimacy	Output legitimacy
Accountability	Who is accountable for the process to come to decisions? How are interactions between the participatory process and representational institutions secured? *Indicators*: formal authority of representative bodies and organised interfaces at the beginning	How is feedback in the process between process interactions and the actors that are accountable arranged? *Indicators*: arranged/organised feedback moments to formal representative institutions	Who is accountable for the final decision? How are representational institutions involved in the final decision-making stage? *Indicators*: formal organised authority for decision, actual involvement at the last stage
Voice	How is the involvement of stakeholders arranged at the beginning of the process? What are the depth and width of voice possibilities? *Indicators*: regulations on entry stakeholders, possible subjects stakeholders have a say about and level of decisions	What opportunities do actors have to participate in the actual process? *Indicators*: opportunities for voice (organised and invited) and actual participation (number of stakeholders, and intensity of participation)	In what way can participants' contributions be traced in decisions? Do the stakeholders involved support the decisions? *Indicators*: correspondence proposals with ideas stakeholders, satisfaction of stakeholders with result
Due deliberation	Is there equal access to information, debate, etc.? Are the procedures transparent, clear and understandable? *Indicators*: entry possibilities and limitations (and regulations about that), clear procedures	How are procedures applied during the process? Are actors satisfied with the transparency of the process? What is the quality of the debate? *Indicators*: satisfaction of actors with transparency, range of arguments brought forward (wide or narrow)	Are participants satisfied with the quality of the process? Are actors satisfied with the quality of the debate of the (end) proposal? *Indicators*: overall satisfaction actors with process, judgement of argumentation

We use this typology in the analysis of an example of complex decision-making that involves water management problems, in the case study of the Zuidplaspolder.

Interactive governance – Zuidplaspolder

The area called the Zuidplaspolder, between the cities Rotterdam, Gouda and Zotermer, in the west of the Netherlands came to existence in the nineteenth century. The initiative came from King Willem I, who also arranged the financing of the operation. Pumping out the water started in 1828 and was completed in 1839 when 4,600 hectares of new land was realised. Until the 1960s, the main function was agriculture. After that greenhouse culture became very important, but the area was increasingly urbanised as result of extensions of Rotterdam and Zoetermeer.

Water management problems are becoming more pressing, partly the result of global warming (and the need to be prepared for more quantities of water), and partly as a response to the growing need to store and transport water integral to the management and creation of more wetlands, which is on the political agenda. At the same time, environmental groups complain about the ongoing industrial and urban activities that are slowly resulting in an incremental loss of the ('green') characteristics of the original polder.

So the problems in this area typically have the character of a 'wicked' problem (Rittel and Webber 1973): there is more than one problem at stake and these problems are connected to each other, but also conflict with each other. There are many actors involved (both as problem owners and/or actors with indispensible resources) who not only have different perceptions of the problems, but also of the desirable solutions. And in a media-driven world, many of these actors try to involve themselves in the decision-making process, which in turn are really a struggle about which values should prevail in public policy (environmental values, transport values, urban extension, etc.) and different actors represent these different values at stake (Klijn 2008).

Governance network and rounds in the decision-making process

Under the initiative of the province, a governance network formed itself around the issue of reconstructing the polder. The province deliberately and actively tried to attract all the main stakeholders from the start in 2002. In that sense, the case is clearly an example of interactive governance. A large group of twenty-three stakeholders was involved in the decision-making process by means of a steering committee. There were actors from a number of environmental groups and agricultural organisations (and especially from the greenhouse firms that are present in the Zuidplaspolder) together with the involved municipalities and several central government departments (Ministry of Transport, Ministry of Housing and Ministry of Agriculture).

If we look at the decision process from 2001/2002 through to 2009 we can see three rounds in the decision-making process. Table 11.3 provides an overview of the process.

Table 11.3: Rounds in the decision-making process on the Zuidplaspolder

	Round 1: exploring a content (2001–2004)	Round 2: elaborating in a smaller arena (2004–2006)	Round 3: working to an implementation programme (2006–2009)
Involved actors	Wide group of actors, province of South Holland initiator and network managers	A smaller core of main actors (the 'steering group' that includes municipalities and province) and a wider group of actors (called the 'forum') less intensively involved	Same as round 2
Character of decision-making process	Strong exploring character, looking for innovative content ideas that can satisfy stakeholders' demands and create support for the project	More focused interaction in which the ideas of the first round are developed and specified	Emphasis on translation of ideas to formal legally-binding documents, less interactive character of the process and increasing of conflicts (because costs and benefits have to be finalised)
Important decisions	Start: initiative from central government and province for area. End: producing a main policy document (ISV, integrated structure vision), which sets the main goals and desires for the area	Realising more elaborated and specific policy documents (especially ISP) that operationalises the ideas in the ISV	Working on formal municipality planning and zoning documents (the so-called bestemmingsplannen) that have legally-binding status
(Network management) strategies	Open, aimed at searching content, looking for wide support and trying to combine different values. Management strategies aimed at exploring content and connecting actors	Open, strong attempt to guide and organise process (steering group, project group, many meetings and conferences) – securing support by maintaining connections and communicating ideas	Maintaining coalition but emphasis on possibilities to implement; lobbying for greater involvement of central government, more dominated by formal legal requirements of the process
Content choices	Attempt to combine need for more dwellings (urban expansion) with need to secure green areas, restructuring greenhouses and water management problems	Working out the possibilities for extra dwellings (which make the plan economically viable); at the same time, look more closely at possibilities of water storages and green areas	More emphasis on economic and political feasibility; stress on possibilities for implementation

First round: exploring possible options

The first round is very interactive. The process began in January 2002 with a large working conference, where all the stakeholders were present at the negotiating table. A covenant is agreed upon (signed on the 27th of February) in which the main goals for the area are mentioned, including the restructuring and, if possible, the replacement of the greenhouses.

This interactive character is reinforced by a document from the province (at the beginning of 2003), the initiator of the process, in which the communicative and participative character of the process is stressed and the importance of all stakeholders having equal access to all information and knowledge. Using the idea of the participation ladder, the document identified for each target group the means of involvement and the communication activities.

The actors work on a joint 'area map' in which for every sub-area the possibilities and impossibilities are shown. The main conclusions regarding the activities (completed in the autumn of 2003) were:

- new dwellings are possible, but not everywhere in the polder;
- a logical green structure is very important;
- use the cores of the old villages of the small municipalities in the Zuidplaspolder;
- improvement of the infrastructure is important to realise the ambitions;
- there is a need for new places to store water (retention areas).

Based on the area map, actors interact further and also discuss the establishment of a 'Land Bank' that buys strategic parts of the area for development. At the same time, however, private actors (developers) also buy significant sections of land (mostly from farmers) to provide themselves a strategic position in the decision-making process. The Land Bank is established in July 2004 and at the end of 2004 the involved actors agree on a first policy document (ISV), which contains:

- a new build environment – the ISV states that there is room for 15,000–30,000 new dwellings, 150–350 commercial areas and 200 hectares of extra greenhouses;
- a division of the area of the polder into three parts – a northern area suited for new dwellings and greenhouses, a southern area to be developed as green area (with some small areas for dwellings) also suitable for retention area and water storage, and a middle area where ecological and recreational functions would be established.

At the end of 2004, the project bureau organised a large working conference to discuss the main ideas of the ISV. All of the stakeholders attended, which was one of the explicit functions of this large conference. Over the following years, the project bureau uses large conferences to inform stakeholders, present the latest ideas and generally communicate with stakeholders.

Second round: refining the plan

The second round commenced with a large number of information meetings to communicate the ideas in the ISV to all stakeholders, but also to the citizens of the municipalities in the area.

At the same time activities proceeded to develop the preliminary ideas of the ISV in a more operationally-led way in a new document that had to function as the basis for the legally-binding documents that will be made by the municipalities (in the third round). The steering committee was reduced to the core actors (municipalities and province), while the other actors are a little less involved, but still active, in the process.

In June 2005, the project bureau again organised a large two-day conference in which the latest developments were discussed. On the first day, mostly citizens were contacted and on the second day it was politicians of the municipalities and province. The new document ISP (inter-municipal structure plan) was completed at end of 2005. The documents built on the three zones in the area and for the northern area there was a new development of greenhouses and development of infrastructure. The middle area also saw new dwellings projected and also a new green area was added. The south area was reserved for nature development and a limited number of high quality dwellings in green areas. The number of dwelling in this document was slightly reduced to 15,000 dwellings (compared with a maximum of 30,000 dwellings). The ISP was discussed in all the municipal councils and did not meet much resistance. Most of the comments have to do with the emphasis on a good infrastructure, the economic perspectives of farmers (being a significant voter group in some of the municipalities) and remarks about the financing of the whole project.

Third round: working to an implementation programme (2006–2010)

From 2006, the project bureau and involved actors dedicated themselves to elaborating the ideas in the implementation plans and legally-binding zoning plans (the so-called *bestemmingsplannen* that have to be made and authorised by the municipalities). In March 2006, the first ideas for revising the province's legal plans were presented. To prepare the discussion, provincial council members visit the area and are informed of the project. On 22nd June 2006, another large conference took place. Besides information sharing and a discussion about the green character and condition of the development of the area, several covenants between various partners were officially signed, giving the day a symbolic meaning.

At the end of the year, several plans and environmental studies were presented, especially about which of the southern part of the area should become a green area. Then another large meeting was held by the project group, which was dedicated to new innovative ideas (especially about environmental-friendly developments of the area). At the beginning of 2007, there was a political disturbance at the central government level (an MP in the national parliament criticised the development of the area because, geographically, it is one of the lowest points in the Netherlands), but the project group effectively disarms this. The remainder of 2007 was char-acterised by pressure-cooker decision-making about a number of documents and studies that are obliged before plans can receive a legal status at all. The new Minister of Housing and Environmental Affairs (a new cabinet was installed mid-2007) visited the area and gave support for the development.

At the end of 2007, central government, which was charmed by the ideas and the pace of the decision-making, was encouraged by the actors of the Zuidplaspolder to include the project in the Randstad Urgency project, a central programme of important projects that have special interest and support of the central depart-ments. The Ministry of Housing and Environmental Affairs became the coordinat-ing ministry and took a seat on the steering group of the project to show its interest and involvement. There was a discussion again about the number of dwellings to be realised in the area and the compromise is that the development started with 7000 new dwellings. The project bureau explicitly stated that this was only the first phase and that more could be built later. The new involvement of central government led to a promise in 2008 of 100 million euros for investment in the infrastructure and in environmentally-friendly projects.

Most of the legal documents were realised and accepted by the municipal councils in 2008 and the beginning of 2009. There was much attention paid to the organised sessions to inform citizens of the formal zoning plans (*bestemming-splannen*). In general, there were few complaints and legal objections. There was the first agreement with private developers to start building dwellings in 2010. These activities proved to be slightly difficult in 2010 owing to less favourable economic times and discussions about the amount of money to be reserved for environmental goals in the project. It was crucial to retain the support from various environmental groups for the development.

Democratic legitimacy in the Zuidplaspolder

How was democratic legitimacy achieved in the case of Zuidplaspolder? We deal with the three forms of legitimacy: accountability, voice and due process before we formulate a conclusion.

Accountability – securing democratic legitimacy by connecting democratic institutions

Table 11.4 shows that the representational institutions are intensely involved in the process of democratic legitimacy, mainly because the project bureau arranged it. It is especially the 'throughput legitimacy' that is important here. By means of special organised meetings, providing information and reports, the project bureau attempts to tie the municipal councils and provincial council close to the project's development. The 'output legitimacy' is mainly secured by classical forms of ac-countability because the councils have to agree on the documents. The 'input ac-countability' is slightly more complicated. Of course, in the first place we have the normal accountability rules of the politicians who initiate the process and are controlled by their councils. This is nothing new. But the involvement of the steering group with all the different stakeholders complicates matters, since these members can be held accountable for the actions of their organisations. An example is the agreement about environmental greenhouses. In the process, the province and the farmers' organisation (especially the greenhouse farmers) had to agree on realising environmentally-friendly greenhouses (using more sun heat, using additional energy for other purposes, etc.). Members of the farmers' organisation were especially keen on this, but it had to be acknowledged by organisation itself. Covenants were laid down to finalise the agreement and these could be seen, in turn, as means to create output legitimacy. Of course, these covenants in the main do not have any legal basis, which means that trust between actors is very important.

Table 11.4: Parameters for legitimacy in governance networks and interactive decision-making

	Input legitimacy	Throughput legitimacy	Output legitimacy
Accountability (How accountability is arranged, who is held accountable and, especially, how the connection to classical representational institutions is arranged)	– decision to start is mainly made by city aldermen and province, formal accountability, aldermen controlled by councils – classic – involvement of other stakeholders makes them accountable, if not formally then empirically – members in steering group accountable for their organisations' decisions	Feedback secured by: – regular meetings (twice a year) of municipal councils and province council – regular information provided by the project bureau – information through studies and reports **Conclusion:** active feedback to and organised information to city and county councils (+)	– municipal and provincial councils have to accept all main documents (ISV, ISP, and formal zoning plans) – using covenants as mutually-binding documents between actors **Conclusion:** classical forms of legitimacy well established (+, +/-)

Voice – involvement and support of stakeholders

In general the involvement of various stakeholders is fairly intensive. Citizens were more involved on an ad hoc basis, in the sense that the participation process was more geared towards (well) organised interest groups such as environmental and agricultural organisations. The covenants functioned as binding decisions between actors and as a communication of decisions to formal political institutions.

Table 11.5: Parameters for legitimacy in governance networks and interactive decision-making

	Input legitimacy	**Throughput legitimacy**	**Output legitimacy**
Voice (how participation of stakeholders is arranged)	– wide definition of stakeholders (width is large) – not all stakeholders are involved in the same intense way (citizens less so than some of the core interest groups such as environmental and agricultural organisations) – participation secured by steering group (well organised interest) and large conference and interactive sessions (generating ideas, criticisms and comments)	– stakeholders explicitly invited to participate (most strongly in first round) – involvement of stakeholders connected especially through documents (formal documents, but also through covenants and agreements that are made public) **Conclusion:** fairly intense interaction (+)	– many contributions, both from the area guide and in terms of general ideas – in what way can participants contributions be traced in decisions – stakeholders in general are satisfied about their participation possibilities **Conclusion:** much support from stakeholders for both process and content (+)

Table 11.6: Parameters for legitimacy in governance networks and interactive decision-making

	Input legitimacy	Throughput legitimacy	Output legitimacy
Due deliberation (how debate and argumentation process is structured)	– process relatively open for new arguments and information. Content was relatively open at the beginning – mostly equal access to information for stakeholders involved in steering group, less so for interested citizens **Conclusion:** good conditions for open dialogue (+)	– debate encouraged by wide arrangement of seminars, conferences and information collection (like the area guide), but also by formal requirements (e.g. environmental impact assessment) – quality of the debate relatively high. Much information available (through many studies are a guide, etc) though many conferences and seminars relatively much discussion about options **Conclusion:** adequate (+/-)	– participants are satisfied about the process quality – argumentation – strong emphasis on combining different values, area should be global warming proof (with good water quality storage and management), high quality dwellings and green areas, and restructuring of greenhouses. In general, much support and appreciation for the content of the plans **Conclusion:** relatively high output legitimacy (+)

This results in fairly strong support from most of the stakeholders for both the process and the content of the decision-making process. This can be clearly demonstrated by an event in March 2007 when the process was suddenly in the media spotlight. A Member of Parliament voiced strong criticisms against plans to realise 7,500 to 15,000 new dwellings in the area. A greenfield development building houses at the lowest point of the Netherlands made no sense, according to the MP, and should be reconsidered; the area should retain its green and agricultural character. The (national) newspapers immediately picked up the issue and the otherwise relatively technocratic project suddenly found itself under full public and media scrutiny. However the project organisation could by now draw on considerable support. Several actors involved in the Zuidplaspolder project countered these criticisms in unison, and said the MP was talking nonsense. These included the province (the project leader), the representative from the environmental movement (surprising, given that the MP was arguing *against* building new houses on agricultural land) and the chair of the water management board (*Dijkgraaf*), who would normally be quite sympathetic to some of the MP's arguments.

The responsible project leader of the province told the newspapers: 'Miss Vermey [the MP objecting to the project] can of course say what she wants, but it would have been wiser if she had looked at the history of the project. If she had done that, she would have seen that the developments in the Zuidplaspolder take the future climate changes into account' (Cobouw, 24th March 2007). The representative of the environmental organisation voiced her discontent even more strongly:

> The past years everywhere greenhouses and dwellings have been added incrementally. I rather prefer an integral plan than this unnoticed messing up of the area ... The past years we have been seriously engaged with this polder. Voicing protests now without knowing anything about the project is cheap politics.
>
> (Trouw, Thursday 29th March 2007)

Due deliberation

In general, the process fulfilled most of the requirements of due deliberation, although this held more for the involved stakeholders in the steering group than affected citizens in the various municipalities, who were clearly less involved and had less access to the information. Discussion and debate were encouraged through a large number of meetings and gatherings that proved to be of a fairly high quality, which meant the project group had a significant advantage over other actors because of greater access to information.

This results in a fairly high output legitimacy. In general there is strong support for most of the content of the policy from almost all the actors who also are fairly satisfied with the way the process and the argumentation

Case conclusion – interactive process with intensive involvement of democratic institutions

In general, there was a fairly open process, with a high quality of dialogue in the Zuidplaspolder project. If we use the criteria developed in the second section most of the criteria receives a positive score. One can say that the general participation was fairly intense, while the involvement of representational institutions was high and the quality of the debate was good. This resulted in strong support from the main stakeholders, even those who would normally be critical, such as the environmental groups. One can say that the consideration given to the three aspects of legitimacy – accountability, voice and due deliberation – in both input and throughput phases resulted in strong output legitimacy.

Conclusion: creating legitimacy and the effects on outcomes

Governance processes try to find solutions that satisfy various values that are at stake and represented in the governance network as seen in the case study. Creating democratic legitimacy is a crucial element of the governance process. That much attention is given to this dimension of governance must be seen as a very positive development.

In this chapter, we advanced criteria to judge that democratic legitimacy and applied them to a specific case. We developed criteria from the democracy discussion and the various types of democracy that emerged. But, of course, there can be debated whether these criteria represent the full range of possibilities. And depending on the preference for a specific conception of democracy, people will probably favour different criteria as important.

That also means that the criteria of democratic legitimacy can be used in a normative sense (these are the criteria that should be met) or as an empirical tool (which of the criteria are met and what are their effects). Normatively speaking, one can prefer one type of legitimacy, for instance the classic parliamentary accountability criteria, over others. That also means that one would judge them to be more crucial empirically than the others. However, one could also approach this problem empirically and ask which of the legitimacies, if present, contribute most to good outcomes (which can be measured by the time it takes to make decisions, the quality and innovativeness of decisions, etc.). This approach is a quite different from the preceding one. Given our earlier findings that stakeholder involvement is more important for reaching good outcomes than political involvement (Edelenbos *et al.* 2010), the expectation may be that the last two forms of legitimacy contribute more to outcomes in interactive governance than the first one. Interestingly, the criteria can fulfil a good function in both discussions.

And last but not least, the case study shows that democratic legitimacy in each of the three dimensions is primarily reached through very active network management. Even the classical representational accountability criteria were greatly enhanced by actively informing and involving elected politicians in the process. This seems to point at a more peaceful co-existence of representational democracy and networks than we often find in the literature. This also means that it is important to look at the design of decision-making in governance networks and secure rules that enhance democratic legitimacy in those networks. The criteria also provide a guideline to which type of legitimacy one can and would like to enhance. Agency is crucial also for democratic legitimacy.

References

Agranoff, R. and McGuire, M. (2003) *Collaborative Public Management: New Strategies for Local Governments*, Washington DC: Georgetown University Press.

Arnstein, S. R. (1971) 'Eight rungs on the ladder of citizen participation', in S. C. Edgar and B. A. Passett (eds), *Citizen Participation: Effecting Community Change*, New York: Praeger Publishers.

Bekkers, V. and Edwards, A. (2007) 'Legitimacy and democracy: a conceptual framework for assessing governance practices', in V. Bekkers *et al Governance and the Democratic Deficit: Assessing the democratic legitimacy of governance practices, Aldershot: Ashgate..*

Bekkers, V., Dijkstra, G., Edwards, A. and Fenger, M. (2007) *Governance and the Democratic Deficit: Assessing the democratic legitimacy of governance practices*, Aldershot: Ashgate.

Berry, J. M., Portney, K. E. and Thomson, K. (1993) *The Rebirth of Urban Democracy*, Washington DC: The Brookings Institution.

Dahl, R. A. (1961) *Who Governs? Democracy and Power in an American City*, New Haven: Yale University Press.

Downs, A. (1957) *An Economic Theory of Democracy*, New York: Harper.

Dryzek, J. S. (2000) *Deliberative Democracy And Beyond: Liberals, critics, contestations*, Oxford: Oxford University Press.

Easton, D. (1953) *A Systems Analysis of Political Life*, New York: Wiley.

Edelenbos, J., Steijn, B. and Klijn, E. H. (2010) 'Does democratic anchorage matter?', in *American Review of Public Administration*, 40 (1): 46–63.

Edelenbos, J. and Monninkhof, R. A. H. (eds) (2001) *Lokale interactieve beleidsvorming*, Utrecht: Lemma.

Fischer, F. (2003) *Reframing Public Policy: Discursive Politics and Deliberative Practices*, Oxford: Oxford University Press.

Held, D. (2006) *Models of democracy*, Cambridge: Polity Press.

Hirst, P. (2000) 'Democracy and governance', in J. Pierre (ed.) *Debating Governance: Authority steering and democracy*, Oxford: Oxford University Press.

Kickert, W. J. M., Klijn, E. H. and Koppenjan, J. F. M. (eds) (1997) *Managing Complex Networks: Strategies for the Public Sector*, London: Sage.

Klijn, E. H. (2008) 'Governance and governance networks in Europe: An Assessment of 10 years of research on the theme', *Public Management Review*, 10 (4): 505–25.

Klijn, E. H. and Koppenjan, J. F. M. (2000) 'Politicians and interactive decision-making: institutional spoilsports or playmakers', *Public Administration*, 78 (2): 365–87.

Klijn, E. H., Skelcher, C. K. (2007) 'Democracy and governance networks: compatible or not? Four conjectures and their implications', *Public Administration*, 85 (3): 1–22.

Koppenjan, J. and Klijn, E. H (2004) *Managing Uncertainties in Networks: A network approach to problem solving and decision-making*, London: Routledge.

Lowndes, V., Pratchett, L. and Stoker, G. (2001) 'Trends in public participation: part1 – Local government perspectives', *Public Administration*, 79 (1): 205–22.

MacPherson, C. B. (1979) *The Life and Times of Liberal Democracy*, Oxford: Oxford University Press.

Osborne, S. P. (ed.) (2010) *The New Public Governance: Emerging perspectives on the theory and practice of public governance*, London: Routledge

Pateman, C. (1970) *Participation and Democratic Theory*, Cambridge: Cambridge University Press.

Pierre, J. (ed.) (2000) *Debating Governance: Authority steering and democracy*, Oxford: Oxford University Press.

Rittel, H. and Webber, M. (1973) 'Dilemmas in a general theory of planning', *Policy Sciences* 4 (2): 155–69.

Scharpf, F. W. (1997) *Games Real Actors Play. Actor-centered institutionalism in policy research*, Boulder: Westview Press.

Schumpeter, G. A. (1943) *Capitalism, Socialism and Democracy*, London: George Allen and Unwin.

Skelcher, C., Mathur, N. and Smith, M. (2005) 'The public governance of collaborative spaces: Discourse, design and democracy', *Public Administration*, 83 (3): 573–96.

Skelcher, S. K. and H. Sullivan (2008), 'Theory-driven approaches to analysing collaborative performance', *Public Management Review*, 10 (6): 751–771

Sørensen, E. (2002) 'Democratic theory and network governance', *Administrative Theory and Praxis*, 24 (4): 693–720.

Sørensen, E. and Torfing, J. (eds) (2007) *Theories of Democratic Network Governance*, Cheltenham: Edward Elgar.

Wälti, S., Kübler, D. and Papadopoulos, Y. (2004) 'How democratic is "governance"? Lessons from Swiss drug policy', *Governance*, 17 (1): 83–113.

Young, I. M. (2000) *Inclusion and Democracy*, Oxford: Oxford University Press.

chapter twelve | the role of citizen forums in local development planning in switzerland

Nico van der Heiden and Paul Krummenacher

Introduction

The political decision-making process in Switzerland is characterised by a high level of direct democratic impetus. It is a longstanding tradition that the people have the last say in the political process. Direct democracy concerns both sanctioning political decisions ex post but also bringing new ideas into the political process. On the input side, this means that people can enter the political process with new proposals through initiatives; on the output side, there exist referenda that allow people to reject a proposal that has already passed the political process. These strong possibilities of direct democratic decision-making procedures are not only carried out at the national level, but also at all state levels in Switzerland.

Direct democratic impetus is particularly elaborate at the local level and especially in small communities, where one can often propose an issue at the local assembly (*Gemeindeversammlung*) without needing to formally deposit the demand beforehand. If a proposition finds a majority at the local assembly, the municipal council (*Gemeinderat*) has to go along with it. Most Swiss communities have a system whereby local politicians work only part-time under their public mandate (the so-called *Milizsystem*).[1] The fact that they have another job beyond their political role fosters contact with the broader public. Given the fact that almost one third of Swiss communities have less than five hundred inhabitants and more than half of Swiss communities have less than 1,000 inhabitants (Horber-Parpazian 2007: 237), we see close ties between the local political elite and the broader public, giving the latter numerous possibilities to directly engage in the political process. Governance in Switzerland has thus traditionally been – and still is – very interactive.

However, there are also arguments against this form of direct democracy at the local scale. The critique concerns the percentage of people participating in local assemblies. Hardly more than 10 per cent of the registered voters turn out for local assemblies. Usually, the percentage is even lower (around 2 per cent) and only in the case of very important decisions for the community, participation rates raise over 20 per cent. This has led to the critique that a very small minority can decide over a silent majority that does not use its possibility of direct democratic

---

1. This is not the case for larger cities, where at least part of the municipal council works full time.

impetus. Local assemblies are sometimes called a form of 'gymnastic club democracy' ('*Turnverein-Demokratie*', Schneebeli 2009), meaning that only the people still active in local sports clubs participate in local assemblies, whereas the large majority is absent in those assemblies. Why, therefore, should there be the need for an additional form of participation when not even those provided are used by the people? We would also suspect that it is not about the need for other (time-consuming) means to participate in local politics for the broader public when we see the increasing debate in medium-sized communities about replacing local assemblies by ballot votes or by parliaments.

It is thus particularly puzzling that over the last few years, public forums at the local level are mushrooming in Switzerland, especially in the policy domain of planning. The general idea of such a public forum is to openly debate an issue of local politics with the interested people from the community. One would suspect that the necessity for such new forms of local direct democratic decision-making procedures is much lower in countries that already have well-established forms of interactive policy making through direct democracy. Nevertheless, we can see this new form of participation emerging at the local level in Switzerland, as in other countries (see e.g. Crosby *et al.* 1986 for the USA, Dienel 1999 for Germany, Groenewald and Smith 2002 for South Africa or Klijn and Koppenjan 2002 for the Netherlands). The question this chapter seeks to answer is therefore: *why have such new forms of public inclusion emerged in a system with traditionally strong direct-democratic possibilities?*

The general feature of deliberative policy making, as stated by Klijn and Koppenjan (2002: 148) is therefore not true for the case of Switzerland:

> Through interactive policy making, an institutional regime of roles and rules, based on views of democracy that emphasise direct participation and interaction between government and citizens, is introduced into a system dominated by representational democracy in which decision-making power is concentrated in elected representatives and where the primacy of politics is an important feature.

Switzerland is a political system with a longstanding tradition of interactive governance between government and citizens. One of the main reasons for the introduction of more deliberate ways of policy making was to overcome the frustration of the many citizens who were not willing to participate in a political system that only marginally allows for inputs from the broader public. This reason might be invalid for Switzerland. However, one could also argue that the tension between deliberative policy making and representative democracy (Klijn and Koppenjan 2002: 148) is smaller in a country where politicians are already used to a high level of interaction with the broader public at different stages of the policy process. This would explain the diffusion of deliberative policy-making instruments in a direct democratic country such as Switzerland.

The aim of this chapter is to position the (at least for Switzerland) new phenomenon of 'deliberative planning' in the traditional (direct democratic) political decision-making process and to ascertain the reasons for its emergence. We take up Papadopoulos and Warin's (2007: 460) claim that 'the issue of the [...] coupling of new [deliberative] policy-making tools with the well-institutionalised processes of representative democracy (perhaps also in a country like Switzerland with direct democracy) has to be examined.' Before analysing the ways of deliberative planning in Switzerland, let us first turn to the theory of 'deliberation'.

Deliberative democracy

There are two strands of literature that deal with the increasing interaction between politics and the people. On the one hand, there is the bottom-up approach of social movements (Castells 1993). These social movements usually have a grass-roots democratic approach; they try to achieve their goals by opposing traditional politics and use alternative methods such as strikes or protests to attract attention and to achieve their goals (Hutter 2009). On the other hand, there is the idea of deliberative policy making going back to Habermas's (1992) notion of 'political deliberation'. Deliberative democracy can be defined as a 'normative democracy model, which sets on the persuasive power of systematic considerations and conclusions in public debates and on communication-oriented acting of the citizens' (Schultze 2002: 119, my translation).[2] The basic idea is to intensify the relationship between politics and the broader public through discourse. This participative element of democracy is seen as a more top-down approach to increase the range of people participating in the political process. Politics itself should establish and eventually institutionalise deliberative elements in the policy-making process. There is a lively debate about which approach (grassroots movements or deliberative policy making) is more purposeful (Jouve 2005) that we will not take up here.

Proponents of deliberative democracy see public forums as an important step that gives citizens the possibility to participate in the decision-making process (Lowndes 1995). Papadopoulou (2005: 10) argues that deliberation is aggravating democracy and that it gives back credibility to democracy. The basic idea here is that the input side of politics has shown a lack of democracy that could be overcome by instruments of deliberative democracy. Deliberation does not only involve, but 'empowers' citizens and therefore enhances democratic procedures (Fung and Wright 2001; Groenewald and Smith 2002: 37; Jouve 2005; Sørensen 1997).

Critics of deliberative democracy, however, see it as a possibility for politicians to achieve their goals by pretending to involve citizens in the decision-making process although decisions have been made long before (Wampler 2008). Blondiaux (2008: 74) summarises this critique thus: 'it is more about signalling the intention to let participate than to really let participate' (my translation). Critics of deliberative democracy point to the fact that there might be more top-down steering involved in these deliberative processes than openly admitted. Blakeley (2002: 86) states:

---

2. Although there is a strand of literature that deals with long-term trends of the evolution of democracy (Abrams 1983; Heinelt 2008; Skocpol 2003: 254 et seq.), I restrict myself here to the more recent, sometimes normative, debate on deliberative democracy because the evaluation of these new forms of democracy is an important part of my analysis.

mobilising citizens around a local government project [...] implies defining participation in a way that is congruent with that project as well as a certain degree of control over that participation, especially where it is seen to run counter to, or to jeopardise that project.

Politicians will, therefore, try to keep a certain control over the deliberation process so that it does not produce outcomes that are unintended by the political elite. Deliberative politics thus runs the risk to just 'shadow the local administration and becom[e] a sort of auxiliary of local government action' (Blakeley 2002: 87) and that in the end, deliberative policy making is nothing more than a window-dressing instrument for politicians (Papadopoulos and Warin 2007: 459).

The concept of the planning cell (Planungszelle, Dienel 1999) is the implementation of deliberative policy making in the domain of planning in Germany. Dienel (1999) argues that through the process of deliberation, the broader public gets a say in a traditionally technocratic policy field where the possibilities for input-legitimacy have been low. This chapter looks at the question of whether these premises are correct for deliberative planning processes in Switzerland. Let us now derive two hypotheses from the theoretical controversy above. I propose two contradictory explanations of how deliberative planning processes fit into our traditional understanding of public policy making. The positive one highlights the additional possibilities for the broader public to engage in the policy-process. The negative one emphasises the strategic use of deliberation as a means for the local elite to realise their goals.

Positive hypothesis: deliberative planning in Switzerland

We can argue that public forums bring a new form of input legitimacy to the system (Papadopoulos and Warin 2007: 450). They provide a possibility for people to express ideas that are generally excluded from the political decision-making process. In turn, this brings up new ideas that would not have been considered by the political system even if there are direct democratic instruments at hand. To launch an initiative is still a hurdle not many people are willing to consider even at the local level, where it should be particularly easy. To put forward the argument at the local assembly needs certain political courage. However, public forums provide a platform where even people who would not consider launching an initiative can speak up and express their ideas. In this line of argument, public forums would thus strengthen the input legitimacy of the political system (Papadopoulos and Warin 2007) even if it already contains strong elements of direct democratic inclusion. The hypothesis from the positive perspective on deliberative planning is thus:

H1: Public forums are an additional form of direct democratic influence in the political decision-making process and they provide new possibilities for interactive governance (bottom-up).[3]

---

3. See also Fung and Wright (2001: 18).

In this line of argument, one would also suspect that public forums substitute local parliaments to a certain extent. In the communities where there is no parliament (usually the smaller ones), the need for new forms of input possibilities is higher than in communities where the parliament assumes this role.

H1a: Public forums are more often used in communities without a local parliament.

The literature on deliberative policy making also stresses the importance of the question of who actually participates in these forums (Andersen and Hansen 2007; Hendriks 2006; Papadopoulos and Warin 2007; Sintomer and de Maillard 2007). If deliberative policy making increases the influence of the broader public, one would expect that people that otherwise do not participate in the political process would show up at the deliberation and express their opinion.

H1b: Public forums attract people that otherwise do not participate in the political process.

Negative hypothesis: deliberative planning in Switzerland

We could argue that these public forums do not meet the claims they promised. They are not devoted to the idea of bringing new ideas into the political process, but to the will of the traditional political players and the political establishment (Hendriks 2006). Political elites use public forums to legitimise already established decisions through a pseudo-inclusive process. The proposal of the political establishment, consequently, seems to be the result of a public debate and, as such, emerging from a bottom-up process. This increases the changes of the proposal in a later public vote. Whereas, if the proposal from the elite fails to pass the test of the public forum, the elite will not be blamed for the proposal as it was never officially announced as coming from the local elite. They use/abuse the deliberation process as a test for the direct democratic decision to come and also try to influence the decision in favour of their terms.

It might also be that public forums are just a form of 'me-too-ism'. This means that the increasing use of participatory instruments in local planning in other countries has lead to a policy diffusion process (Berry and Berry 1990; Gilardi *et al.* 2009). Local politics in Switzerland just does what their counterparts in other countries do. According to this view, deliberation is thus much less reflected in an actual need for the increase of interactive governance. It is rather 'doing what your neighbour does'.

This more negative approach to deliberative planning leads to the following hypothesis:

H2: Public forums are used by the political elite to legitimise already established decisions through a pseudo-deliberative process (top-down).

Klijn and Koppenjan (2002: 141f.) distinguish between three motives of politicians for the introduction of deliberative processes: creating support, improving the quality of policy formation and improving democracy as such. The first motive clearly has elements of a top-down use of deliberation. Politicians would only attempt deliberative processes to 'diminish the opposition to policy proposals' (Klijn and Koppenjan 2002: 145; see also McLaverty 1999: 23). The third motive is more devoted to the bottom-up idea of deliberation. The goal of this chapter is thus to see which motive is predominant in Swiss deliberative planning.

Before turning to the analysis of all public forums in Switzerland, we want to look at the forms that these deliberation processes can take and give an example of such a deliberative planning process at the local level in Switzerland.

Four types of public forums

In order to classify the deliberation forums in Switzerland, we distinguish four types of them (Holman and Devane 1999):

1. The 'Future Search Conference' (FSC) is the most open form of a public forum. The idea is that there is no given question beforehand, but that the people freely and openly debate the future of their community. There are no constraints on the policy areas for debate and no solutions are mentioned before the conference. The outcome, therefore, is highly unpredictable.

2. The 'Open Space Technology' (OST) has a more structured outline because the policy field that is going to be discussed is predefined. However, the OST is still a relatively open method of deliberation as there is no clear question that guides the discussion, possible solutions are not discussed beforehand and the results of the debate are rather unpredictable.

3. The 'World Café' (WoC) is quite similar to the OST. However, in this form, not only the policy area, but also the question to be discussed, is defined before the public forum takes place.

4. The 'Real Time Strategic Change' (RTSC) is the most structured of the four forms of public forum. There is a concrete problem that needs to be solved and the public forum is discussing predefined possible solutions.

5. Deliberative Planning in Horw

Horw is a mid-size community with about 12,000 inhabitants, situated next to the city of Lucerne, and it held a Future Search Conference (FSC) in 2006. The municipal council wanted to discuss its new development plan (*Entwicklungsplan*) with the inhabitants of the community. There was neither a policy crisis nor a polity crisis at the time in Horw. The municipal council wanted to deliberate with its inhabitants over the general development path of the community. There was thus no clearly predefined question for the deliberative process and the process was open concerning possible results of the FSC.

The municipal council gave Frischer Wind a mandate to hold the conference. The project leader from Frischer Wind met with the municipal council and they together selected the people who should participate as a sounding board (the so-called *Spurgruppe*). These people were selected to represent the main interest groups within the community. These people met several times in 2005 to discuss the deliberation. The members who formed the sounding board were responsible for contacting the inhabitants of Horw to motivate them to participate in the FSC. Additionally, the news was spread in the local newspaper and on the community's web page.

More than 200 people participated in the FSC that took place in January 2006. It started on a Friday afternoon and went on until Saturday evening. The mayor inaugurated the debate and presented the goals of the meeting. Thereafter, the participants discussed various questions about the development of their community in small groups of eight to ten people. They rotated from time to time so that the composition of each group changed several times. They went on to discuss the current strengths and weaknesses of Horw. The participants then discussed theses on the development of Horw that were prepared by the municipal council before the conference. Participants could, however, critically discuss the preset aspects and bring up new points. They then went on to develop an idea how Horw should look in 2020. From this, they filtered the most urgent issues at stake for Horw. The conference finished with concrete policy suggestions and changes as well as amendments for the development plan.

The municipal council took these guidelines and prepared a draft for the development plan. The participants of the FSC were then invited to participate in a follow-up conference in April 2006. This meeting was called the 'outcome conference' and the municipal council presented what each of them wanted to do in his/her policy domain to follow the guidelines that were developed by the conference. The participants could then again discuss changes and amendments to the development plan. This second conference was held on a Saturday morning.

The discussion in the two conferences was in Swiss German, which excluded the foreign population from the debate to a certain extent, although some of them participated. Young people were also clearly under-represented. Horw has a communal parliament and the members of the parliament were invited to participate in the conference, and many of them did so.

After this example deliberative planning in a Swiss community, let us now turn to the analysis of all the public forums we examined.

Data and methods

To test the contradictory hypotheses set out above, we analysed forty-eight public forums that have been taken place in Swiss communities over the last ten years. The data set is provided by Frischer Wind, a private consulting agency that specialises in organising and moderating discussions of large groups (*Grossgruppendiskussionen*). We looked at the following questions that are linked to the hypotheses mentioned above for all 48 public forums:

1. In which year did the public forum start?
2. Why was the public forum initiated? Was it a policy crisis (a project that had problems), a polity crisis (nobody comes to the local assembly and no

candidates for the local council), or was the goal deliberation per se?

3. Was the goal/question for the public forum given before it took place?

4. How many people participated in the public forums?

5. How are the people participating characterised? Are they rather people that participate in politics anyway or are they people that have previously not engaged in politics?

6. Who participated as the sounding board? Were these people from the city council, the local elite or the public at large?

7. Does the community, where the deliberative planning took place, have a parliament or not?

8. Which of the four types of public forum mentioned above (Future Search Conference, Open Space Technology, World Café, and Real Time Strategic Change) was used in the respective communities?

As well as the quantitative analysis of all 48 communities with a process of deliberative planning, we conducted qualitative expert interviews with the people in charge from Frischer Wind.

Deliberative planning in Switzerland

Top-down or bottom-up?

Looking first at the time dimension of deliberative planning processes in Switzerland, we would expect no correlation between place and time when the politicians come to the conclusion that deliberation per se is needed. If, however, we find a clustering in place and time where deliberation took place, this would support the 'me-too-ism' hypothesis. Looking at the year in which the public forums started, we can see that the first deliberative planning process accompanied by Frischer Wind took place in 2001. In an international comparison, this is clearly late as other countries have experienced deliberative processes already back in the 1990s (Klijn and Koppenjan 2002). We can also see a rather clear trend over time that shows an increase in two phases of the deliberative planning processes in Switzerland: soon after they were introduced, their number went up and remained steady until the second increase in 2007 (see Table 12.1).

Table 12.1: The increase over time of deliberative planning in Switzerland[4]

Year	2001	2002	2003	2004	2005	2006	2007	2008
Communities	1	1	5	6	5	4	11	11

---

4. In four cases, we were unable to determine the year in which the public forums started.

The time dimension is thus a first hint that policy diffusion might have led to the dissemination of deliberative planning processes in Switzerland. Looking at the geographical dimension of this diffusion, this notion gets even stronger. The dissemination of deliberative planning happened more or less in clusters. This means that the deliberative processes started in one community and then spread over to communities in the same area. Later, other clusters started. Policy-makers learned from other close-by communities about the instrument of deliberative planning. There are clearly aspects of 'me-too-ism' in the spreading out of this instrument in Switzerland.

Looking at the motives as to why the communities started a deliberative process, the bottom-up hypothesis would be supported if we find a lot of communities without a concrete problem that initiated the deliberation process. If however, most communities started deliberating only after a crisis, this would be a hint that this is more of a top-down process. We can see that almost half of the communities started a deliberative process with their inhabitants because there was a concrete policy crisis, e.g. the development of a new home for elderly people (see Table 12.2). Only in seven cases, did a crisis of the political system initiate the deliberation process. Nineteen communities discussed very broad questions concerning how their community should develop in their near future. These were the ones that had the clearest interest in the deliberation process as such, whereas in the other cases, the outcome was at least equally important as the process.

Table 12.2: The motives for deliberative planning in Switzerland

Motive	Policy crisis	Polity crisis	Deliberation as such
Communities	22	7	19

The results here are thus mixed. If we take additional information from the qualitative interviews into account, this picture changes slightly. As the project leaders admitted, even in the cases where there is no crisis as such, there was usually a concrete problem that led to the idea of a deliberation process. Only a few communal leaders introduced deliberative processes just for the sake of deliberation. We also assessed whether the deliberation process had a clear question at commencement. This would support the top-down hypothesis. As we can see in Table 12.3, this was the case in slightly less than half of the analysed deliberation processes. In the other twenty-six communities, the discussion was open and no clear question stood at the beginning of the process.

Table 12.3: Type of the deliberation process

Type of deliberation	Clear question	Open discussion
Communities	22	26

To determine whether the deliberative process is a new bottom-up instrument or rather a strategically-used instrument of politicians, we also need to know which of the four forms of deliberative planning was dominant for Switzerland. If there were a lot of Future Search Conferences (FSCs) with an open framework for the deliberation, this would support the bottom-up hypothesis. Alternatively, if the form of Real Time Strategic Change (RTSC) dominates with its clearly-defined setting, this would support the top-down hypothesis. The analysis shows that FSCs were the most used form of deliberation (see Table 12.4), 31 of the 48 communities under scrutiny used this open method of deliberation. Only 12 communities used the RTSC approach.

Table 12.4: Form of the deliberation process

Form of deliberation	FSC	OST	WoC	RTSC
Communities	31	0	5	12

There are thus twice as many communities that use the bottom-up approach as there are ones using the top-down approach. This was confirmed by the experts in the interviews. They approved that, although most communal leaders have a clear question in mind when approaching Frischer Wind to start a deliberating process, they nevertheless chose the more open form of a FSC. Real Time Strategic Change is, according to the project leaders, more a method that is used in deliberation processes in the private sector. Political processes tend to be more open.

It is not easy to answer the question whether deliberative processes are really a bottom-up process that adds an input-component to the Swiss political system or if they are rather a strategic instrument of the communal political elite to achieve their goals. There are indicators for both aspects and this was confirmed in the interviews. To see deliberative planning processes as a pure form of the democratic bottom-up process seems to be naive. Clearly, politicians have their interests and goals when they demand a consultancy agency to conduct a deliberative process in their community. Few communities started deliberating just for the sake of deliberation. There has to be a driving factor that brings politicians to the idea of deliberating and this could be a policy crisis or the anxiety of losing a later public vote. Local politicians do not come up with the idea of deliberation 'out of the blue'; they often learn from close-by communities that already use this instrument. There are thus in almost all cases strategic considerations involved in deliberation processes at the local level in Switzerland.

However, to describe deliberation as a purely strategic instrument used by the local elite to push through their own policy agenda would be misleading. Not only did the quantitative analysis show that many communal leaders entered the debate with the broader public without a clear-cut question, the majority of them also chose the most open form a deliberative process can take, as in the Future Search Conference. This implies a certain openness of the political elite to unexpected outcomes. This notion was confirmed by the qualitative interviews, where the project leaders pointed to the fact that they advised communal leaders that were not open to other solutions, as they had in mind not to start a deliberative process. This biases the dataset used here to a certain extent, as communities were excluded where communal leaders wanted to use deliberation as a means to push their policy goals through. This, however, happened only very rarely according to the interview partners. Deliberative processes at the local scale thus seem to emanate from a two-step development: communal leaders need a crisis and then an open question. The introduction of the deliberation has thus a starting point in a top-down first move. Thereafter, communal leaders leave the deliberation relatively open and accept solutions and answers they did not predict. The deliberation then takes up many aspects of a bottom-up approach.

Let us now turn to the two sub-hypotheses to shed a light on the question if deliberation is substituting the work of local parliaments and who actually participates in the deliberative processes.

A substitute for the local parliament?

Theoretical reflections that see deliberation as a new bottom-up process led us to hypothesise that it would be mostly communities without a parliament that would use this instrument. The input function in the political process is traditionally taken by the parliament. If such an institution is missing (as is the case for the majority of communities with less than 10,000 inhabitants in Switzerland), then the municipal council might use the deliberative process as a substitute for the parliament. As Table 12.5 shows, this seems to be true. An overwhelming majority of the thirty-seven communities that made use of a deliberative process did not have a parliament. Only seven with a parliament did so.

Table 12.5: Form of the local democratic process[5]

Local democracy	With parliament	With local assembly
Communities	7	37

This strengthens the bottom-up hypothesis. Deliberative debates can indeed substitute the missing local parliament in small communities. The municipal council in a community with a parliament seems to rely on the latter to assume that its decisions in the policy-making process are correct. If the control function of the parliament is missing, the municipal council is much more uncertain about the needs of the broader public. It can thus use the deliberative processes to strengthen the link between the municipal council and the broader public, whereas in communities with a parliament, the latter has a bridging function between them.

5.　In four cases, more than one community was involved in the deliberative process. These cases were excluded from the analysis here.

Who participates?

Unfortunately, no data is available about the composition of the deliberative body. We do not know the percentage of females, foreigners, young people or other demographic aspects. We do, however, know how many participated in the deliberative conferences: the range of the number of participants is between 37 and 200. On average, 108 people participated in the deliberation. The information gathered from the qualitative interviews confirmed the notion from the case study of Horw (see above) that young people and foreigners are under-represented in the deliberation process. Cook *et al.* (2007: 42) hypothesise that young people use the interne rather than public forums for political communication. Although the project leaders of the deliberation process encourage people that are otherwise not interested in politics, they admit that it is a difficult task and they are only marginally successful in doing so. In general, the notion that those who participate in the deliberation process are already interested in politics is correct. Through a careful selection of the sounding board and wide dissemination of the announcement of the deliberation process, a few people that otherwise do not show any interest in politics, do participate.

Rosenberg's (2007: 14) concern that social criteria might hinder the deliberative body as being fully representative is thus partly confirmed by the analysis of deliberative planning in Switzerland. It is indeed very difficult to get people to participate in deliberative processes that are at the social margins. This result is confirmed by investigations in other countries, where an over-representation of those that are already engaged in the traditional political process was noted in deliberative processes (Groenewald and Smith 2002; Klijn and Koppenjan 2002). Deliberative policy making in Switzerland has not brought many new people to the political table. The people participating in the deliberative process are not representative of the inhabitants of the community. Deliberation is more open than the traditional political process, but this additional openness (to foreigners and young people not able to vote) is hardly used by those to whom the offer is made. In small Swiss communities, only relatively few people participate in the local assembly and only a few more participate in the deliberation process. They are very often the same people.

Conclusion

Our quantitative analysis of 48 deliberative planning processes in Switzerland analysed what it is that motivates communities to start up citizen forums. The theoretical notion that it is about citizens trying to make their voices heard beyond simple ballot voting has to be rejected. The process of deliberation in Swiss communities has many top-down elements and the initiation to start deliberating mostly comes from traditional politics. Politicians start a citizen's forum because they see this instrument in other, close-by communities. There is thus a 'me-too-ism' aspect in communal deliberative bodies that explains their increasing use in Switzerland. Politicians, however, also seek legitimacy by using deliberative elements. They use citizen forums as trial balloons for their ideas and to present themselves as open to new ideas. However, most citizen forums have a specific crisis as the starting point and are not as open as they seem to be.

The positive hypothesis on deliberative policy making stated that this process is an advancement of democratic governance even in those countries where democracy is firmly established (Rosenberg 2007: 1). This is to a certain extent true even for direct democratic countries such as Switzerland, where the interplay between politicians and the broader public is already strong and interactive governance a common and established process. Introducing elements of deliberation into a direct democratic system thus adds a component instead of replacing one. It allows citizens besides their strong possibilities to vote on referenda and initiatives to participate in the early stages of the policy process. Rosenberg's (2007: 8) notion that 'given the broader conception of autonomy and equality, the emphasis on the design of institutions such as selection or referenda that allow individuals to freely pursue their personal interests by equally contributing to collective decision-making are regarded as inadequate' has thus some relevance for Switzerland. Citizens appreciate the possibility to engage early in the policy process and to deliberate. At the same time, this increases the acceptance of the choices made by the deliberating people also being accepted by those who failed to take part.

However, the analysis of deliberative planning in Switzerland revealed a close connection between the traditional political process and the new instrument of deliberation. They are more closely interlinked than one might have expected (Denters and Klok 2010). Future research should draw more attention to forms of deliberation that are initiated by and thereby closely attached to the traditional political process. Fung (2007: 160 *et seq.*) defines four types of deliberative processes: the educative form, the participatory advisory panel, the participatory problem-solving collaboration and participatory governance. For the Swiss deliberations under scrutiny here, we can see that deliberation takes place with and not against politics. In all the cases analysed, the initiation for a deliberative process came from politics. This guaranteed at the same time that the impact of the decisions taken by the deliberative assembly was immediate and that the voice of the citizens determined the policy agenda directly. Swiss deliberative planning processes are thus a form of participatory democratic governance and the strongest form of deliberation in the categorisation of Fung (2007).

However, this reveals a core problem of the relationship between politics and the public concerning deliberative processes. The closer the deliberative process is to the 'normal' political process, the better the chances that the decisions of the deliberative body will be transformed into the political system but, at the same time, the higher the chances that the deliberative process is biased by the goals of politicians. Because our focus in this chapter was on the political process, less can be said about the changes in policies that may be the result of deliberative forums. It remains an open question for future research as to whether deliberative forums have a concrete impact on policy outcomes and thus fit within the term 'interactive governance'.

References

Abrams, P. (1983) *Historical Sociology*, Ithaca, New York: Cornell University Press.

Andersen, V. N. and Hansen, K. M. (2007) 'How deliberation makes better citizens: The danish deliberative poll on the Euro', *European Journal of Political Research*, 46(4): 531–56.

Berry, F. S. and Berry, W. D. (1990) 'State lottery adoptions as policy innovations: An event history analysis', *The American Political Science Review*, 84 (2): 395–415.

Blakeley, G. (2002) 'Decentralization and Citizen Participation in Barcelona', in P. McLaverty (ed.) *Public Participation and Innovations in Community Governance*, Aldershot: Ashgate.

Blondiaux, L. (2008) *Le nouvel esprit de la démocratie. Actualité de la démocratie participative*, Paris: Seuil.

Castells, M. (1993) *The City and the Grassroots*, Berkeley: University of California Press.

Cook, F. L., Carpini, Delli, M. X. and Jacobs, L. R. (2007) 'Who Deliberates? Discursive Participation in America', in S. W. Rosenberg (ed.) *Can the People Govern: Deliberation, Participation and Democracy*, New York: Palgrave.

Crosby, N., Kelly, J. M. and Schaefer, P. (1986) 'Citizens' Juries: A new approach to citizen participation', *Public Administration Review*, 46: 170–78.

Denters, B. and Klok, P.-J. (2010) 'Rebuilding Roombeek: Patterns of citizen participation in urban governance', *Urban Affairs Review*, 45 (5): 583–607.

Dienel, P. C. (1999) 'Planning Cells: The German Experience', in U. Khan (ed.) *Participation beyond the Ballot Box: European Case Studies in State-Citizen Political Dialogue*, London: UCL Press.

Fung, A. (2007) 'Minipublics: Deliberative Designs and their Consequences, in S. W. Rosenberg (ed.) *Can the People Govern: Deliberation, Participation and Democracy*, New York: Palgrave.

Fung, A. and Wright, E. O. (2001) 'Deepening democracy: Innovations in empowered participatory governance', *Politics and Society*, 29 (1): 5–41.

Gilardi, F., Fuglister, K. and Luyet, S. (2009) 'Learning from others: The diffusion of hospital financing reforms in OECD countries', *Comparative Political Studies* 42 (4): 549–73.

Groenewald, C. and Smith, A. (2002) 'Public Participation and Integrated Development Planning in Decentralized Local Government: A Case Study of Democratic Transition in South Africa', in P. McLaverty (ed.) *Public Participation and Innovations in Community Governance*, Aldershot: Ashgate.

Habermas, J. (1992) *Faktizität und Geltung. Beiträge zur Diskurstheorie des Rechtes und des demokratischen Rechtsstaats*, Frankfurt: Suhrkamp.

Heinelt, H. (2008) *Demokratie jenseits des Staates. Partizipatives Regieren und*

Governance, Baden-Baden: Nomos.

Hendriks, C. M. (2006) 'When the forum meets interest politics: Strategic uses of public deliberation', *Politics and Society*, 34 (4): 571–602.

Holman, P. and Devane, T. (eds) (1999) *The Change Handbook: Group Methods for Shaping the Future*, San Francisco: Berrett-Koehler.

Horber-Parpazian, K. (2007) 'The Municipalities', in U. Klöti, P. Knoepfel, H. Kriesi, W. Linder and Y. Papadopoulos (eds) *Handbook of Swiss Politics*, Zürich: Verlag Neue Zürcher Zeitung.

Hutter, S. (2009) 'Globalisation and the Transformation of National Protest Politics: An Appetiser, in H. Kouki and E. Romanos (eds) *Re-Visiting Protest: New Approaches to Social Mobilization in Europe since 1945*, New York: Berghahn Books.

Jouve, B. (2005) 'L'empowerment entre mythe et réalités, entre espoir et désenchantement', *Géographie, Economie, Société*, 8 (1): 5.

Klijn, E.-H. and Koppenjan, J. F. M. (2002) 'Rediscovering the Citizen: New Roles for Politicians in Interactive Policy Making', in P. McLaverty (ed.) *Public Participation and Innovations in Community Governance*, Aldershot: Ashgate.

Lowndes, V. (1995) 'Citizenship and Urban Politics', in D. Judge, G. Stoker and Harold Wolman (eds) *Theories of Urban Politics*, London: Sage.

McLaverty, P. (1999) 'Towards a Model of Public Participation', in U. Khan (ed.) *Participation beyond the Ballot Box: European Case Studies in State-Citizen Political Dialogue*, London: UCL Press.

Papadopoulos, Y. and Warin, P. (2007) 'Are innovative, participatory and deliberative procedures in policy making democratic and effective?', *European Journal of Political Research*, 46 (4): 445–472.

Papadopoulou, T. (2005) 'Deliberative Demokratie und Diskurs. Eine Debatte zwischen Habermas und Rawls'. Online. Available http://tobias-lib. ub.uni-tuebingen.de/volltexte/2007/2578/pdf/PhD_complete.pdf (accessed 18 March 2010).

Rosenberg, S. W. (2007) 'An Introduction: Theoretical Perspectives and Empirical Research on Deliberative Democracy', S. W. Rosenberg (ed.) *Can the People Govern: Deliberation, Participation and Democracy*, New York: Palgrave.

Scharpf, F. (1970) *Demokratietheorie zwischen Utopie und Anpassung*, Konstanz: Universitätsverlag.

Schneebeli, D. (2009) '"Turnverein-Demokratie": Gemeindeversammlungen sollen weg', in *Tagesanzeiger*, 29 July 2009, Seite.

Schultze, R. (2002) 'Deliberative Demokratie': Schultze, R. and D. Nohlen (eds.) *Lexikon der Politikwissenschaft: Theorien, Methoden, Begriffe, Band 1*. München: Beck. pp 119–120.

Sintomer, Y. and de Maillard, J (2007) 'The limits to local participation and deliberation in the French "politique de la ville"', *European Journal of Political Research*, 46 (4): 503–29.

Skocpol, T. (2003) *Diminished Democracy: From Membership to Management in American Civic Life*, Norman: University of Oklahoma Press.

Sørensen, E. (1997) 'Democracy and empowerment', *Public Administration*, 75 (3): 553–67.

Wampler, B. (2008) 'When does participatory democracy deepen the quality of democracy?', *Comparative Politics*, 41 (1): 61–81.

chapter thirteen | democratic ownership through metagovernance? the action plan on organic food

Åsa Casula Vifell

Introduction

In 2006, the Swedish Ministry of Agriculture declared its intention to increase domestic consumption of organic food by 25 per cent before 2010 in an action plan produced by stakeholders active in the field. The plan was launched during a seminar with a surprisingly provocative title: 'Action Plan 2010 – steering document or desk-warmer?' Did the plan, in spite of its participatory intentions, fail to achieve the desired outcomes, or did a lack of real participation prevent it from success? Using the case of the Action Plan 2010, this chapter aims to enhance the understanding of the specific institutional form of action plans and their ability to ensure or hamper democratic governance.

The mechanisms for achieving legitimacy through representative structures at the central state level are often regarded as ill-equipped to deal with the complexity and size of today's societal problems. There have been a multitude of calls for more participatory and deliberative modes of governance as well as a number of experiments and theoretical exercises that have enriched the debate (Bohman and Rehg 1997; Hajer and Wagenaar 2003; Mol 2001; Fung and Olin Wright 2003). Environmental policy has been one of the areas to provide fertile ground for interactive governance and involvement of non-state actors. The Aarhus Convention's explicit focus on participation, as well as the UN environmental conferences that have been held since the 1970s, seem to have functioned as critical junctures for institutionalising a broad participatory approach at the international level (Betsill and Corell 2008). Outcomes, such as Agenda 21, have also supported more inclusive policy processes at all levels (Freeman, Littlewood and Whitney 1996; Eckerberg and Lafferty 1998; Feichtinger and Pregernig 2005). In addition, regulatory innovations such as multi-stakeholder dialogue, private regulation, labelling, informational governance and joint environmental policy making can be seen as other attempts to deal with the crisis of legitimacy of traditional top-down regulation (Boström and Klintman 2008; Cashore 2002; Hajer 2003; Skogstad 2003). The environmental policy field is thus a good choice for anyone interested in studying participatory modes of governance. The Action Plan 2010 targets an important Swedish environmental objective and deliberately set out to increase stakeholder participation.

Action plans – a reform routine

Modern society has been described as 'frantically reformative', putting continuous pressure on *organisations* to adjust current practices to the dream of improving the world or creating a more efficient *organisation* (Brunsson 2006). The aspirations of individuals within an organisation and the expectations held by those outside arguably create an ongoing demand for organisational reform since it is never actually possible to fully meet expectations for a better future. Although somewhat contrary to intuitive understanding, reforms may be understood as a routine activity. In addition, action or reform plans are often seen as fulfilling external demands by presenting a façade of compliance while the organisation's core practices remain the same (Meyer and Rowan 1977).

Reforms are often accompanied by certain assumptions about how the work should best be carried out. Action plans are such a reform method. Some even speak of the 'tyranny of methods' when describing how particular practices shape and define the content of policies (Bell 1994). I regard action plans as a form of metagovernance, understood as the governance of self-governing networks (Sørensen and Torfing 2007). The case of the Swedish organic food action plan is a key example of how contemporary reforms are framed and undertaken, and it may be regarded as a taken-for-granted tool for attempting to change outcomes and practices (Røvik 2000). Examples of working methods associated with action plans are the use of deadlines, steering groups and the output of a voluntary arrangement.

As part of the alleged erosion of traditional bases of political power in favour of network governance, scholars have paid increasing amounts of attention to various kinds of partnerships and short-term projects designed to deal with reforms (Glasbergen *et al.* 2007; Djelic and Sahlin-Andersson 2007). Some speak of a 'projectification' of society, where tasks are increasingly carried out by temporary ad hoc organisations or networks (Bell and Morse 2005; Casula Vifell and Soneryd 2010). Conducting policy within a project means working with a specific mindset as the participants are aware that it is a temporary constellation, and there is the adjacent difficulty in ensuring commitment once the project is completed. This chapter focuses on the particular project of the Swedish action plan on organic food created by stakeholders in the field.

Democratic ownership and metagovernance

Although it is widely recognised that networks need some kind of management to ensure societal gains, it is a delicate issue how a network should be managed without losing the benefits ascribed to its self-regulating features (Kooiman 1993; Sørensen and Torfing 2007). Inquiries into democratic qualities of network management are often linked to state actors and the role they play as metagovernors in ensuring representative links to the electorate (O'Toole 2007; Sørensen 2006). However, the issue of ensuring democratic legitimacy remains imperative even in networks or projects that are not headed by a state actor. This is a concern not only from a normative point of view, but also from the perspective of ensuring active commitment to the non-binding agreements that often constitute the output. An additional purpose of this chapter is, therefore, to develop a model for evaluating projects that makes use of the increasingly popular concept of *democratic ownership*. The concept is frequently employed by practitioners to denote processes creating stakeholder participation and commitment. There are a number of reasons for engaging in this debate.

Democratic ownership consists of two words that do not sit easily together as they stem from disparate theoretical traditions. Nevertheless, it is an increasingly popular buzz-word used by various organisations and policy initiatives. For example, the European Commission issues calls for proposals using the concept in its endeavour to develop legitimate modes of governance. Much like other powerful concepts such as 'justice', 'progress', 'modernisation' or the surge of new public management terms like 'performance measurement' or 'benchmarking', democratic ownership has positive connotations – in this case both democratic and economic benefits, which are hard to disagree with (Meyer *et al.* 1997).

In conclusion, since concepts have specific implications for how we view the world, moving a concept with a particular theoretical meaning from one context to another might lead to a situation where we find a divergence between conventional language and political reality (Czarniawska and Sevón 1996). However, whether or not political initiatives and policies live up to these values is an empirical question to be investigated in each case. The content of democracy and ownership needs to be defined and evaluated and not be taken for granted.

Democratic ownership is de facto linked to the trend of applying concepts from the enterprise sphere to the public sector. Turning patients into clients or citizens into consumers can be seen as attempts to lend more weight to economic efficiency, which the public sector has been criticised for lacking (Christensen and Lægreid 2001; Hood 1998). Modifying the meanings of concepts is not always a bad thing as it might help identify phenomena that would otherwise be ignored. However, it may also be the result of less conscious strategies or an unintentional adoption of a particular meaning. There are several examples of this type of conceptual displacement, where positive terms are linked to activities that cannot primarily be associated with such values (Garsten and Jacobsson 2004).

Another reason for engaging in conceptual discussions is that it can enhance our understanding of how concepts and ideas become filled with value and meaning as they travel between different locations (Czarniawska and Sevón 1996).

An overview of the literature on democratic ownership shows that although previously used to denote a certain type of co-operative ownership in the economic field, when applied to governance the term originated in development studies. It is commonly used to describe the receiving countries' control over aid resources (Alliance 2015 and Ministry of Foreign Affairs Denmark 2008; Witte, Reinicke and Benner 2004).[1] Scholars active in this field often work close to practitioners

---

1. There has been a lively debate on what the concept of ownership should mean and the two interpretations are presented as mutually exclusive. The first one is closely related to government

and take part in policy discussions within organisations such as the Organisation for Economic Co-operation and Development (see for example Molina 2007). Within studies of global governance, an adjacent strain of literature can be found that deals with stakeholder involvement and democratisation of decision-making (Bäckstrand 2006; Dingworth 2004). These studies speak of 'ownership' as producing democratic legitimacy and contributing to enhanced international policy making from the point of view of accountability and effectiveness. Another usage can be found in the literature on local participatory processes where stakeholders assume responsibility for projects (Feichtinger and Pregernig 2005). It is not possible to find any elaborate definitions of the term in any of these research streams, but democratic ownership as well as ownership in general seems to be achieved through actors assuming responsibility for developed policies and therefore the efficiency is ensured. Still, there is no discussion of criteria for participation in the processes preceding the policies. This is in stark contrast to research on participatory governance in general, which is primarily concerned with evaluating the fulfillment of democratic values in stakeholder participation (for some recent examples see Kissling, Nanz and Steffek 2009 and Jönsson and Tallberg 2010).

To summarise, the current usage of the term democratic ownership indicates that a more thorough consideration of participatory principles is needed to avoid incorrectly assigning positive connotations to political activities. A displacement can occur where concepts become accepted without reflection and efficiency crowds out democratic principles in the understanding of the concept of democratic ownership. The following section presents a tentative framework to evaluate how the term is used.

Evaluating action plans

The *fulfilment* of democratic values may be hampered or ensured by organisational features such as governance structures (Saward 1998), in this case, an action plan. Six aspects will be considered:

- scope;
- inclusion;
- transparency;
- responsiveness;
- role of the state; and
- anchorage.

---

ownership, which might reduce power imbalances and strengthen the national development in the donor-receiver relationship, but that does not contribute to building structures for overall democratisation in a developing country (Alliance 2015 2008). The second one is a plea for broadening the interpretation of democratic ownership to also include parliaments, civil society organisations and citizens and the structures for ensuring their participation in national development.

There are numerous possible yardsticks for an evaluation of this kind (Beetham 1994), but we chose these features because they build on ideas relating both to democratic participation and commitment.

Scope

If the formal mandate has already decided the content (in this particular case by a state actor), there is limited possibility for the participants to influence the project (Bell and Morse 2005). Hence, participation might serve no other purpose than legitimising someone else's decision (Cook and Kothari 2001). 'Owning' a process must mean that participants can help shape a project's agenda. They need to have the space to interpret the task's definitions and formulation, as well as the possibility to add new items to the agenda, to fulfill this criterion.

Inclusion

To be regarded as a democratic process, the narrow interpretation of democratic ownership as responsibility needs to be broadened to also include the input side of the process. Ensuring commitment is arguably also related to a participatory process where the project's governance bodies include actors concerned by the issue. We, therefore, need to answer questions about if and how the *inclusion* of stakeholders is ensured.

Transparency

Transparency allows the participants to have access to relevant documents and meetings. It also allows independent actors to scrutinise the process and ensure that those not directly involved may monitor those responsible for different activities. Important empirical questions to investigate include: Do the actors have access to relevant information? How are those beyond the project able to assess and/ or take part in the process?

Responsiveness

If the inclusiveness and transparency demands are fulfilled, the views put forward by participants or the scrutiny conducted by others must also be able to shape the project's content and activities. Questions to be looked into are if viewpoints are collected and taken into account.

Role of the state

Taking part in network governance where the state is also involved should not lead to co-optation (Cooke and Kothari 2001; Héritier and Eckert 2007). The associative democratic perspective might give us some guidance as how to conceive of the appropriate role of state actors (Hirst 1994). Although critical of representative models of government, the perspective proposes complements rather than alternatives to such structures. Accordingly, the role of the state should be limited to funding and ensuring policy implementation structures are in place. The regulation should consequently be thin and procedural and aim at guaranteeing project integrity.

Anchorage

Anchorage of the issue in the home organisations of those directly participating in the project is important for ensuring democratic legitimacy and commitment. If those at lower levels in the participating organisations are not aware of or do not feel attached to the ideas put forward in the voluntary plan, an implementation gap might occur as these staff are most likely responsible for carrying out the policy. Structures for information and communication between the project participants and their home *organisations* need to be in place to *fulfil* this criterion.

Collecting the data

The data consists of documentation of the process at hand. I have used material such as minutes and summaries from the stakeholder meetings about the action plan, as well as reports, articles and comments. In addition, we conducted in-depth interviews with central actors. Steering groups participants, including representatives from the government, the producers and the consumer groups were included, as well as a number of informants representing organisations participating in the periphery of the project. The latter were identified through the documents and participant observations. I interviewed a total of twelve individuals. The interviews lasted between 45 minutes and 1.5 hours and were recorded and subsequently transcribed. Two of the interviews were conducted by phone. Participant observations were carried out during hearings and seminars throughout the process.

The action plan

Organic food production has steadily increased in Sweden over the last two decades. This was particularly tangible the first five years after European Union accession in 1995 when the sector became eligible for targeted support. In 2007, the growth of the market for organic food products was estimated at 25–30 per cent, but shortages in the supply of certain products were still a persistent problem. The Action Plan 2010 was produced by organic food organisations that came together to increase both production and consumption. Producer and consumer organisations as well as labelling organisations and environmental non-governmental organisations (NGOs) participated alongside public agencies represented by the Swedish Board of Agriculture (SBA), and around 75 people were involved in the activities. At the state level, the organisations responsible for organic food production are the ministries for agriculture and environment, the SBA and, to some extent, the National Food Administration. Other agencies that provided advice to farmers converting to organic production were the Agricultural Divisions of the County Administrative Boards and the Rural Economy and Agricultural Societies.

In the field of organic food, action plans are a well-established method for policy development. In 1994, the Swedish Parliament (*Riksdagen*) aimed to increase organic production by 10 per cent before 2000. An action plan was to be the means of implementation. A subsequent plan focused on the years up until 2005. The SBA drafted the plans in conjunction with hearings with stakeholders. The rather poor implementation of these plans was attributed to a top-down process. When discussions concerning a third plan started, the Organic Forum,[2] a platform organisation for the organic food sector established in 2002, assumed responsibility for the plan, since other actors in the field showed a distinct lack of commitment. In the autumn of 2006, the Organic Forum initiated the Action Plan 2010, and it was finalised a little more than two years later.

The action plan is linked to environmental policy as it is related to several of the qualitative environmental targets around which the Swedish environmental policy is constructed. The mandate broadly stipulated that the plan should contribute to sustainable development by increasing organic food production and consumption. Environmental policy in Sweden has a strong tradition of stakeholder involvement and consensus-building between public and private organisations (Boström 2001). This potentially creates favorable conditions for governance processes with participatory characteristics. Although issues of non-transparent selection processes for consultations might be as problematic, the distinguishing features of state society can be said to be one of trust, inclusion and participation in both formal and informal arrangements. As for the issue of organic farming, the inter-organisational relations are also characterised by collaboration and interaction, and the Farmers Federation was one of the first organisations to join the organic labelling organisation, KRAV. However, there is also a clear division between conventional and organic farming and the debate and interactions between the representatives of these groups have been antagonistic. The division is also apparent within Royal Academy of Agricultural Sciences where the Organic Forum is housed. The issue of organic food is also placed in between agricultural and environmental policy, which is clearly mirrored in that conflict.

The project's organisation was based on discussions in a steering group and hearings for a wider set of stakeholders. The participating organisations were self-selected in the sense that anyone connected to the issue of organic food could join. Still, despite the fact that the project explicitly intended to include broad participation, some organisations representing closely linked issues did not take part. More specifically, the plan targeted organic agricultural products and, for instance, fish products – while clearly food – were not part of the plan (although the demand for

---

2. The Organic Forum (Ekologiskt forum) was established in 2002 to function as a meeting place for those interested in developing organic production and contributing to constructing Sweden's position within the EU. Organic Forum is partly financed by the Swedish Board of Agriculture and is located at the Royal Swedish Academy of Agriculture and Forestry.

such products increased while the project was active). In a seminar with external speakers, fish were discussed and launched as a topic for consideration, but project members did not pick up the topic. The reasons for excluding the issue seems to relate to the institutionalised idea that it was not part of the agenda since it was not included in previous plans produced by the SBA. A second reason is linked to the fact that the issue of aquaculture had been the subject of heated debate in Sweden. 'It was hard enough to get along without them', as one interviewee from the project steering group put it. Instead, the plan was created within the participatory framework already in place within the Organic Forum. This meant engaging in a network of participants that had previously met in different contexts concerning issues of agricultural policy and organic farming.

A number of well-known individuals were invited to form the steering group. As one of the interviewees describing the steering group selection expressed it: 'Sweden is a small country and everyone in the agricultural sector knows each other.' The organisations participating in the first steering group were the Swedish Association of Every Day Commodities, the SBA, the Swedish Society for Nature Conservation, the Swedish Federation of Farmers, the Ecological Farmers, KRAV and a representative from the Cooperative Union (COOP) who served as project manager. Although the financial compensation for participating was trivial, the Ministry of Agriculture allocated 150,000 krona to the Organic Forum for the action plan, and all those asked to join were willing to commit their own resources to the project.

The steering group appointed by the Organic Forum was then asked to invite relevant persons to participate in six synthesis groups[3] designated the task of knowledge gathering. This process was ad hoc and more people were included along the way as members suggested others. The synthesis groups were asked to produce reports for the steering group and some of the groups were 'better than others at staying on track,' as one informant from the steering group put it. Several of the groups drifted somewhat from their original mandate, but this was in the end considered as positive as it revealed some issues the steering group had not initially considered important. The steering group also invited a wider circle of actors to participate and comment during a hearing on the synthesis groups' activities. Joint knowledge production is often described as an important part of metagovernance as it shapes the content of interaction within a network (Ehrmann and Stinson 1999; Klijn and Edelenbos 2008). It could constitute an arena for defining concepts and for interpreting data within a project, and could, therefore, become decisive for determining what issues may or may not be included.

Several seminars/hearings were conducted at the Organic Forum and state actors as well as the participating organisations were asked to comment on the plan.

---

3.   There were six groups: primary production (*primärproduktion*), knowledge and competence building (*kunskap och kompetensuppbyggnad*), the industrial sectors (*branscherna*), private consumption (*privatkonsumtion*), large-scale households and restaurants (*storhushåll och restaurang*) and commerce and markets (*handel och marknad*).

But while some representatives in the steering groups informally discussed issues concerning the plan with other colleagues in their home organisations, they generally chose to speak only to those directly working on the issues rather than inviting all members to a general discussion. According to the interviewees, none of the steering group members had any organised model for gathering feedback from their home organisations or for communicating what was happening within the project. Neither did the project issue any guidelines for the intra-organisational contacts. Also, contrary to the traditional Swedish policy cycle, the final draft was not circulated among all concerned parties for comment. Since all relevant actors were believed to already be part of the process, the plan finalised by the steering group was considered to be a final product. However, the steering group's participants all stated that they did not receive much feedback throughout the process.

Resetting the stage

With less than a year remaining, the steering group was unable to finalise the action plan because of an inability to find common ground. It had been difficult to reach agreement on issues such as the role of market actors and the focus on the demand side, as not all participants believed these to be relevant. The producer organisations were accused of not recognising a major shortage of organic products when the demand was high and stable. The producers, on the other hand did not believe demand would remain stable over time, and were therefore unwilling to further develop these parts of the plan. It takes around two years to convert agricultural production from traditional to organic, and farmers who were unsure about whether they would receive a fixed contract for selling organically-labelled products believed they might not recover the costs of conversion, according to several interviewees.

Some participants also described the various representatives' ideological bases as too far apart to be able to have meaningful dialogue. Industry representatives distrusted some of the 'organic idealists' who had dealt with these issues for decades as they were thought to be naïve and too ideologically bound. The discussion eventually came to a dead end, but several steering group participants reported that the threat of another government plan was an incentive to find a solution. It thus became the final task of the group to create a new steering group to save the plan. As the participants were eager to produce a group that would overcome the challenges they had been unable to resolve, the task was an easy one. Organisations representing marginal or more extreme viewpoints were not included the second time as they were believed to have blocked the first group. Others thought to be less willing to compromise were also excluded from selection.

Some participants believed that certain members of the first group had very strong mandates from the organisation they were representing. This meant they were unable to change their positions even if other participants had put forth convincing arguments. The second steering group consisted of representatives from the city of Gothenburg, the SBA, the Dairy Producers (MILKO), the Farmers Federation, COOP and a project manager from the consultancy firm, Goodpoint.

The reconstitution of the project happened when less than a year remained and a demand to extend it was filed and approved by the SBA.

The second steering group started out with a preliminary meeting to assess the project's future. The conclusion was that although a lot of things had been done, the presentation and structuring of the plan's content remained intact. Interviewees cited a strong motivation to succeed and described the meetings as positive and decisive. The members of the second group did not have the same personal connections as did the first group, but the participants represented well-known organisations that were aware of differences and points of agreement. The steering group also held meetings with the synthesis groups, which presented their results. However, this second steering group was much more action-oriented and did not believe they had the time to include the synthesis groups' findings in the plan's actual content. In order to not let the gathered knowledge 'be a complete waste,' in the words of one informant, the reports were edited and added as an appendix to the printed plan.

The group's discussions were devoted to identifying the 'bottlenecks' in increasing organic production and finding ways to encourage participant organisations to take responsibility for the completed plan so it would not turn into a 'desk warmer'. One informant described the task as follows:

> It is important to make sure that everyone feels responsible for the implementation. One way of doing this is to make sure that they feel they own the issue. This does not mean that their participation in the process has had any real effect, but they should feel that they own the question and recognise the thoughts as their own. (Author's interview with steering group representative)

From talk to action?

Following the completion of the project, all informants described it as a success and depicted the work as strenuous but rewarding, as the project managed to finalise a plan involving so many stakeholders. Completing what had previously been a government task was seen as major achievement. However, while no criticism was directed towards the plan, the fact that it did not contain any financial commitments by the government seemed to be a disappointment and, furthermore, gave rise to questions about its effectiveness. Although the formal role of the state actors during the process was limited to contributing resources (funding, providing statistical data and expertise), one important constraint was that the plan was to be implemented without any additional state funding. This meant that even if the Organic Forum was free to organise and bring forward suggestions for solutions, these could only be financed by the actors themselves on a voluntary basis. As one interviewee put it, the role of the project was to 'conjure forth' the results without any financial support. None of the previous plans within the sector had included vast funding schemes, so this point was unrelated to the fact that the government was no longer in charge.

The plan's voluntary character and the fact that no money was provided to designate responsibility to certain actors, created the suspicion among the group that it was easy to accept the plan as there was no associated risk of forced compliance. As the plan was finalised, the issue of the evaluation therefore turned out to be the biggest point of contention. Finding an appropriate way to evaluate implementation was seen as essential to ensuring compliance among the participating organisations.

> Ownership is essential for the implementation and that is why the evaluation is so important. We need to check up on the organisations to see if they are doing their job. (Author's interview with steering group representative)

Initially, it was suggested that the labelling organisation, KRAV, should do the evaluation, but this was contested by some of the participants who did not see KRAV as 'objective'. It might have been a logical choice to use the SBA's experience and resources, but no such suggestion was put forward and the SBA representative in the group 'kept a low profile' as the agency had no desire to take on the assignment. Several of the informants expressed severe concern that the evaluation issue had not been resolved six months after the plan's completion, indicating that responsibility and commitment would not be achieved without such an arrangement. In February 2009, more than a year after the project ended, it was announced that the Organic Forum had formed a steering group for the evaluation, which was also to be conducted in the form of a project. Once again, the Organic Forum was in charge and the group consisted of eight representatives from both producer and consumer organisations and a project manager employed by the Organic Forum.

The group began by meeting actors in the field who had expressed a clear wish to initiate activities to enhance and encourage implementation among the participants. The evaluation project would report on the plan through newsletters, describing the development within the organic food sector, and was also tasked with encouraging actors to undertake necessary steps to implement the plan. The newsletter also described the responsibility of various actors in detail. For example the first issue covered an initiative by the Swedish Association of Every Day Commodities to issue a 'sell plan', signalling to producers that they would require larger volumes of products in the future in order to instil confidence between the actors. A follow-up seminar was also held in April 2010 to gather the participants and discuss progress and further commitments. After slow progress, the process thus seemed to have gained a new momentum. The fact that actors could see that others were active may have inspired others to assume responsibility as well.

However, the awareness of the plan outside the circle of those participating in the project seems low, and for those aware of the plan, it remains unclear how it would govern the practices of the involved organisations. A search through the websites[4] of the participating organisations reveals that less than a third of

---

4. The search included the websites of all organisations involved either in any of the two steering groups, the six synthesis groups or present at the final presentation of the plan. First, the wordings

them mention or link to the plan. Almost all of them discuss organic production/consumption and several present their own strategies, but without mentioning the action plan. COOP, the SBA, the Ministry for Agriculture and the Organic Forum are the only organisations to have published the document online. Interviews with representatives from participating organisations that were not themselves involved in the steering or synthesis groups also revealed low awareness of the plan.

Democratic ownership – a tentative evaluation

The following section takes us back to the question of whether or not the action plan project managed to create democratic ownership as defined in the developed framework.

Scope

The Swedish Government and Parliament formulated the action plan's targets, but the scope was broad and the participants could decide how the work should be organised, which topics to include and who to invite. However, there were limits on the kinds of suggestions that would be feasible as the plan provided no additional funding.

Furthermore, even though the formal mandate did not limit the inclusion of a broader set of issues, some topics were excluded. One example was an initial agreement that the plan only concerned traditional agricultural production and not, for instance, fish products. While the project was going on, the issue of ecologically-sound fish production became a politically hot issue. But there were no organisations representing the organic food industry in the project, which explains why the issue was never included in the plan despite the apparent window of opportunity raised by the public debate.

Inclusion

First, the action plan was intended be participatory and involve all interested parties concerned with reaching the plan's targets. Broad inclusion was part of the initial strategy as well as the final product and stakeholders from a number of sectors were involved. However, the network created around the project was built mainly on previous collaboration between actors already engaged in co-operation and negotiation. When it comes to the division of labour in the project, the reorganisation of the steering group provided evidence that some organisations needed to be excluded from the inner circle of decision-makers to achieve consensus. On the other hand, these organisations were still a part of the process, just not in the steering group that drafted the plan. The modes of interaction seemed to promote

---

'Action Plan 2010' and 'action plan' were typed into the search engine on the particular website. Secondly, a more qualitative search through online documents and subheadings was conducted.

broad participation and still retain decision-making power and at the same time maintain the support of involved actors. In addition, the many hearings, seminars and interactive participation at various levels seemed to help fulfil this criterion, but the work became less inclusive the closer the project came to its deadline.

Transparency

Ensuring transparency is important for the legitimacy of a process where not everyone can take part in the actual decision-making process. Furthermore, this is often a weak spot for network governance. The transparency of this project, however, was high. Several hearings and seminars, which were published on a website accessible to organisations in the field, were held throughout the course of the project. Minutes of meetings and progress reports were published on an ongoing basis, as were announcements for forthcoming meetings well in advance. The available material and documentation is rich and easily accessible. The synthesis groups and their initial discussions were also available. However, contrary to Swedish policy-making tradition, the final document was not circulated among concerned parties for comment. Finally, the evaluation project is linked to other websites that report on the development of organic production and consumption. However, the interaction within the steering group was not documented and the quest for a solution for the evaluation of the process was conducted informally, somewhat curtailing my overall positive assessment of the project's transparency.

Responsiveness

Responsiveness is the project's weakest link, as revealed by the actors' reasoning concerning the concept of ownership. To ensure implementation of the plan, the need to make actors feel responsible for the plan crowded out the notion that their comments would have any actual impact on the plan. Thus the empirical usage of the term 'ownership' does not seem to be linked to issues of democracy, but rather to issues of policy effectiveness. Still, the fact that the synthesis groups' mandate allowed new issues to be introduced was indicative of a more responsive outlook, but due to the reorganisation of the project and lack of time, the content of their work was not reflected in the plan.

Also, the fact that the discussions during seminars and hearings could be characterised as a one-way flow of information from the core group could also be said to be non-responsive, although the formal means for participation were in place.

Role of the state

If a participatory governance project is carried out in the shadow of hierarchy, where the state actors control the process in such a way that other participants are co-opted, the democratic qualities and level of ownership are severely challenged. Or rather, there might be too much ownership but not enough democracy. In the action plan process, the state was represented mainly by the *SBA*'s participation in both steering groups. Its role was to support the groups' activities through funding and providing statistics and other types of data from its own organisation or other state agencies. Other participants perceived the SBA representatives as very 'helpful' and 'wise'. Nothing indicated that difficulties encountered with the action plan were related to the interactions or relationships between private and public actors. Instead, the fact that the government was not at the steering wheel motivated other organisations to overcome differences to show they were able to complete the task without government interference. The fact that no funding was attached to the plan's implementation did, however, disappoint some participants, who believed this would have enhanced the fulfilment of the plan.

Anchorage

The task of drafting the plan was limited in time and its implementation was linked to the commitment of the participating organisations as a whole – not only of their representatives in the project. An analysis of the anchorage of the plan during the process indicates that such structures were weak and not formalised. The representatives in the steering groups at times discussed issues concerning the plan with other colleagues in their home organisations, but only informally. There was no opportunity for comments when the plan was finalised and presented since the process itself was considered to have been so broad and inclusive. However, from the point of view of making lower-level members of the organisations aware of the plan, such an opportunity might have improved commitment to implementation. There was, in general, little awareness of the plan outside the circle of actors working on the project.

Conclusion

The analysis shows that some of the features inherent in this type of project organisation are crucial for understanding why plans tend to fall short in delivering the expected outcomes, both in terms of effectiveness and the democratic qualities often ascribed to processes of participatory governance.

Using the concept of democratic ownership as yardstick, the evaluation criteria of inclusion showed that a project was able to involve a broader set of stakeholders than government actors. Since the particular organisation of the project incorporated different levels of engagement and participation, it was possible to include organisations with both radical and moderate views. A project working outside of hierarchies and across organisational boundaries can more easily create new levels of decision-making. In this case, the governance network to a large extent lived up to the positive expectations outlined in the literature. However, one might also conclude that the selection criteria for inclusion and the time spent deliberating relevant definitions and possible representatives of various interests was highly limited due to the time constraints of the project. Also, the synthesis groups' findings were never used, thus not benefiting from the joint knowledge developed there. All in all, this resulted in a situation where some actors and issues were kept out of the project, in turn narrowing the scope of the plan. The pre-existing conflict between conventional and organic farming was accordingly avoided as the plan was directed towards those already within the field. The focus on consensus to finalise the plan crowded out the attention to issues that – if solved – may have had a much larger impact on policy development.

As for the role of the state, which throughout the process proved to be more helpful than limiting, the lack of funding constrained what could be done. Instead, a redirection of existing resources within the participating organisations made anchoring the issue in the organisations extremely important. The failure of this part of the plan seems to hinge on the temporary character of the project and on the non-binding nature of an action plan. If a plan is decoupled from formal structures in each participating organisation, with no way to connect project activities to traditional activities and resources, it is unlikely to be incorporated afterwards. Furthermore, the project format means there is no forum to further engage the organisations once the plan is finalised. The fact that the evaluation was seen as crucial for the commitment of the actors also indicates that the process did not create a sufficient sense of ownership.

Finally, the use of action plans seems to have become a routine activity within the organic food field and with this comes a lack of commitment that follows the legacy of the former plans. The choice to use an action plan as a governance method can be seen as an example of rule-following rather than an active choice, where established ways of going about activities was pursued. The way new policy measures are packaged is important as certain meanings are attached to the different forms and, in this case, the choice of an action plan might also have carried with it the notion of a plan as 'desk-warmer'.

As for the usefulness of the concept of democratic ownership, first, the criteria revealed a mismatch between the theoretical understanding and the concept as understood by the actors in the studied project. In the empirical usage of 'ownership,' responsiveness and inclusion of new viewpoints and ideas were not part of the understanding. Instead, ownership could be translated into a responsibility to implement the plan and thus it became an issue of ensuring effectiveness. It was clearly expressed that this was not linked to democratic aspects of the concept, where such a commitment is brought about by involving stakeholders in creating the content of a project outcome for which they are to assume responsibility. Rather it had to do with creating the illusion that they had some degree of influence. There was thus a risk of too much ownership or co-optation of the participants. If we want the concept of democratic ownership to be part of a strategy for creating more legitimate forms of governance in Europe, we also need to know that practitioners and researchers talk about the same things. Strengthening ownership as understood by practitioners in the case of the action plan does not strengthen any important democratic values.

Secondly, the combination of the traditional democratic criteria of inclusion, transparency and responsiveness with criteria for commitment concerning scope, the role of the state and anchorage seemed to generate important conclusions for understanding how action plans function as a form of metagovernance. In that sense, the criteria might create a more balanced discussion on the use of action plans that goes beyond the traditional view of them as either as an effective and democratic solution or as window dressing responding to external demands for reform.

References

Alliance 2015 and Ministry of Foreign Affairs Denmark (2008). Online. Available http://www.democraticownership.org/ documentation/Concept-paper. pdf (accessed 22 December 2008).

Beetham, D. (ed.) (1994) *Defining and Measuring Democracy*, London: Sage.

Bell, S. (1994) 'Methods and mindsets: towards an understanding of the tyranny of methodology', *Public Administration and Development*, 14 (4): 323–38.

Bell, S. and Morse, S. (2005) 'Story-telling in sustainable development projects', *Sustainable Development,* 15 (2): 97–110.

Benner, T, Reinicke, W. H. and Witte, J. M. (2004) 'Multisectoral networks in global governance: Towards a pluralistic system of accountability', *Government and Opposition*, 29 (2).

Betsill, M. and Corell, E. (eds) (2008) *NGO Diplomacy: The Influence of Nongovernmental Organizations in International Environmental Negotiations*, Cambridge: MIT Press.

Bohman, J. and Rehg W. (1997) *Deliberative Democracy*, Cambridge: MIT Press.

Boström, M. (2001) *Miljörörelsens Mångfald*, Stockholm: Arkiv.

Boström, M. and Klintman, M. (2008) *Eco-Standards, Product Labelling and Green Consumerism*, Basingstoke: Palgrave Macmillan.

Brunsson, N. (2006) *Mechanisms of Hope: Maintaining the Dream of the Rational Organization*, Liber: Stockholm.

Bäckstrand, K. (2006) 'Democratizing global environmental governance? Stakeholder democracy after the World Summit on Sustainable Development', *European Journal of International Relations*, 12 (4): 467–98.

Cashore, B. (2002) 'Legitimacy and the privatization of environmental governance: How non-state market driven (NSMD) governance systems gain rule making authority', *Governance*, 15 (4): 503–29.

Casula Vifell, Å. and Soneryd, L. (2010) 'Organizing Matters: How the social dimension gets lost in sustainability projects', *Sustainable Development*, 18 (3). Cooke, B. and Kothari, U. (2004) *Participation the New Tyranny?*, London, New York: Zed Books.

Christensen, T. and Lægreid, P. (2001) *New Public Management: The Transformation of Ideas and Practice*, Aldershot: Ashgate.

Czarniawska, B. and Sevón, G. (1996) *Translating Organizational Change*, Berlin: De Gruyter.

Dingworth, K. (2004) 'The democratic legitimacy of public–private rule making: What can we learn from the World Commission of Dams?', *Global Governance*, 11 (1): 65–83.

Djelic, M. L. and Sahlin-Andersson, K. (2006) *Transnational Governance. Institutional dynamics of regulation*, Cambridge: Cambridge University Press.

Ehrmann, J. R. and Stinson, B. L. (1999) 'Joint fact-finding and the use of technical expertise', in L. Susskind, S. McKearnan and J. T. Larmer (eds) *The Consensus Building Handbook*, London: Sage.

Feichtinger, J. and Pregernig, M. (2005) 'Imagined citizens and participation: Local Agenda 21 in two communities in Sweden and Austria', *Local Environment*, (3): 229–42.

Freeman, C., Littlewood, S. and Whitney, D. (1996) 'Local government and emerging models of participation in the local agenda 21 process', *Journal of Environmental Planning and Management*, 39 (1): 65–78.

Fung, A. and Wright, E. O. (eds) (2003) *Deepening Democracy: Institutional innovations in empowered participatory governance*, New York: Verso.

Garsten, C. and Jacobsson, K. (eds) (2004) *Learning to be Employable: New Agendas on Work, Responsibility and Learning in a Globalizing World*, Houndmills: Palgrave Macmillan.

Glasbergen, P., Bierman, F. and Mol, A. P. J. (2007) *Partnerships, Governance and Sustainable Development*, Cheltenham: Edward Elgar.

Hajer, M. (2003) 'Policy without polity? Policy analysis and the institutional void', *Policy Sciences*, 36: 175–95.

Hajer, M. and Wagenaar, H. (2003) *Deliberative Policy Analysis: Understanding governance in the network society*, Cambridge: Cambridge University Press.

Héritier, A. and Eckert, S. (2008) 'New modes of governance in the shadow of hierarchy: Self-regulation by industry in Europe', *Journal of Public Policy*, 28(1):113–138.

Hood, C. (1998) *The Art of the State: Culture, Rhetoric and Public Management*. Oxford: Oxford University Press.

Johansson, K. M. and Tallberg, J. (2010) 'Explaining chief executive empowerment; EU summitry and domestic institutional change', *West European Politics*, 33 (2): 208–236.

Kooiman, J. (ed.) (1993) *Modern Governance: New Government Society Interactions*, London: Sage.

Lafferty, W. and Eckerberg, K. (eds) (1998) *From the Earth-Summit to Local Agenda 21: working towards sustainable development*, London: Earthscan.

Meyer, J. W., Boli, J., Thomas, G. and Ramirez, F. (1997) 'World society and the nation state', *American Journal of Sociology*, 103 (1): 144–81.

Meyer, J. W. and Rowan, B. (1977) 'Formal structure as myth and ceremony', *American Journal of Sociology*, 83 (2): 340–63.

Mol, A. P. J. *Globalization and Environmental Reform: The Ecological Modernization of the Global Economy*, Cambridge: MIT Press.

Molina, N. (2007) 'The Ownership Paradox', Paper presented at the OECD Global Forum on Development, 27–28 September 2007.

O'Toole, L. J. (2007) 'Governing Outputs and Outcomes of Governance Networks', in J. Torfing and E. Sørensen (eds) *Theories of Democratic Network Governance*, Basingstoke: Palgrave Macmillan.

Røvik, K. A. (2000) *Moderna Organisationer*, Stockholm: Liber.

Sahlin-Andersson, K. and Söderholm, A. (2002) *Beyond Project Management: New Perspectives on the Temporary-Permanent Dilemma*, Malmö: Liber.

Saward, M. (1998) *The Terms of Democracy*, Cambridge: Polity Press.

Steffek, J., Kissling, C. and Nanz, P. (2007) *Civil Society Participation in European and Global Governance: A Cure for the Democratic Deficit?* Basingstoke: Palgrave Macmillan.

Skogstad, G. (2003) 'Legitimacy and/or policy effectiveness? Network governance and GMO regulation in the European Union', *Journal of European Public Policy*, 10 (3): 321–38.

Sørensen, E. (2006) 'Metagovernance: The Changing role of politicians in processes of democratic governance', *American Review of Public Administration*, 26 (1): 98–114.

Sørensen, E. and Torfing, J. (2007) 'Theoretical Approaches to Metagovernance', in E. Sørensen and J. Torfing (eds) *Theories of Democratic Network governance*, Basingstoke: Palgrave Macmillan.

chapter	conclusions and perspectives
fourteen	*Jacob Torfing and Peter Triantafillou*

This edited volume has addressed some of the many ways in which interactive governance and policy making are unfolding in contemporary liberal democracies. The proliferation of diverse forms of interactive governance and policy making has not gone unnoticed by academics and the last decade has seen a rapid rise in the scientific literature on network governance and other forms of interactive policy making. While the research literature on interactive forms of governance is burgeoning, the role of metagovernance and the democratic implications of enhanced policy interaction have so far received rather scant attention. This volume has attempted to cover part of that lacuna. It has done so by, first, accounting for some of the diverse forms and functions of interactive governance. Secondly, it has addressed how interactive governance may be subjected to metagovernance and analysed the problems and the conditions that may lead to successful metagovernance. Finally, the volume has addressed the democratic challenges linked to the spread of interactive governance and discussed the potential of metagovernance in tackling these challenges.

Lessons learned

Part I of the volume has tried to grasp some of the diversity and scope of interactive governance and policy making in liberal democracies. While these studies in no way amount to a comprehensive mapping of the manifold ways in which interactive governance is unfolding, they do touch on some significant features. At least two tentative conclusions may be drawn from this part.

First, *interactive governance does not operate in a vacuum, but is often more or less directly linked to other forms of governance.* Lewis' and Considine's study of the employment service frontline in Australia and Great Britain shows the co-existence and interrelatedness of three distinct forms of governance: procedural, corporate-market and network. Network governance seems to function in a more fluid, less coherent and probably also less institutionalised way than the other more established types of governance. However, while advisers do engage in networks that might be useful to them in placing clients into work, this comes second to the importance of meeting the targets and knowing the rules. Esmark's study of the impact of the European Employment Strategy (EES) on national institutions and procedures in the area of employment policy further sheds light on the interlinking between different forms of governance. In a situation where the jurisdiction over employment services remain at member state level, the EES has tried to influence member state policies by supplementing hierarchical steering with interactive governance in which a range of stakeholders are urged to participate. Again, interactive governance is supplementing rather than supplanting other forms of governance in a particular policy area.

Secondly, *the functioning and effectiveness of interactive governance seems to thrive best when two institutional conditions are fulfilled*, namely when a need for policy innovation has been articulated and recognised and when facilitating institutions are present. The study of the employment services in Australia and Great Britain indicates that networking is used more by policy advisers when they are faced with new demands, as it is highest in contexts (countries and times) with the greatest system volatility. Interactive governance, then, may be particularly advantageous and proliferate in specific conditions of volatility leading to the articulation of demands for policy innovation. Fotel's survey of a Nordic regional governance network show that interactive forms of governance may also thrive under more stable political conditions. Her study indicates that historically-entrenched institutions are important for the effective functioning of network governance. Here it may not be enough, nor even desirable, to have a historical tradition of tripartite negotiations in policy making if that implies that all other political actors are excluded. Instead, the institutional legacy should rather be attuned to dialogue and interactions between a wide range of both state and civil society actors. Likewise, the range of responses by the British, Danish and French Governments to the EES' attempt to expand the inclusion of stakeholders in domestic employment policy processes testifies to the importance of historically-entrenched institutions.

Part II of this volume examined the conditions under which, and the mechanisms by which, metagovernance produces a particular result. We may distil at least three crucial insights. First, with regard to its object, *metagovernance may be particularly suitable in coordinating the interrelations between different governance forms*. Meuleman's study showed that first-order metagovernance of networks should be accompanied by another 'second-order' form of metagovernance that enables policy-makers to change the combination of different governance styles (hierarchy, market and networks). This may ensure that the potentials of each type of governance are better utilised and eventual contradictions between these different governance styles may be tackled by changing the overall governance mix. Such second-order metagovernance would have been relevant in the case of employment policy service delivery described in the previous Part I. Here we saw that hierarchy and market often seem preferable to local bureaucrats because of existing incentive systems even if these created undesirable and unintended side effects. In such cases, the suggestion that policy-makers adopt a second-order mode of metagovernance with a view to obtaining a more optimum mix of policy forms seems to provide a suitable way forward.

This leads us to the question of the subject of metagovernance, i.e. *who may adequately act as metagovernors*? The existing literature on metagovernance more or less unanimously points to public authorities, which are seen to have the capacity and the legitimacy to take up such a task. While there are many solid arguments for making the state act as metagovernor, Baker and Stoker's analysis of the regulation of the British nuclear industry shows that despite the government's claim to nodality, its ability to exercise authority, deploy treasure and organisational resources, its capacity for metagovernance is limited. Political conflicts, international pressures, legal requirements, limited resources and organisational complexities all serve to impede the state's capacity to metagovern. Yet this case is a least-likely one and their findings cannot be immediately transferred to other settings. Accordingly, more work needs to be undertaken to specify the conditions under which the state has the capacity to function as an effective metagovernor. At least some of this work is carried out by Koppenjan, Kars and van der Voort in their study of the way in which metagovernance is deployed in a case of Dutch physical planning. This case may also be considered, if not a least likely one, then at least a case in which the conditions in many ways are not very conducive for metagovernance. Nonetheless, their study shows that elected representatives were actually able to align their steering attempts with those of the executive council and in this way prove *co-metagovernance*. By doing so, they may succeed in influencing the process, giving it a political direction and holding network actors accountable. In short, the research on metagovernance should probably be attuned less to most likely cases in which one single actor (the state) has the capacities to bring about desired changes, but more to less – and perhaps even least – likely cases in which (perhaps) two or more actors work together to metagovern and lend legitimacy to a networked policy process.

Finally, we should pay more attention to the *instruments available for metagovernance and their effects on policy objectives*. Existing research on the effectiveness of metagovernance tends to focus rather narrowly on policy-making processes and outputs. However, Triantafillou's analysis of the effect of deploying performance measurement techniques in the attempt to metagovern the Australian and Danish employment policies shows that such techniques seem to entrench particular policy objectives, namely a 'work-first' approach. While the performance-measuring regimes in both countries were launched to focus more on outputs and outcomes, they actually seem to lead to an increased policy emphasis on process standards. Now, such effects on policy objectives may be intended and very legitimate. However, if performance-management regimes (or other policy instruments) seeking to metagovern policy outputs create a strong path dependency and make such policy goals virtually impossible to change, metagovernance may actually create more democratic problems than they solve.

This leads us to the democratic implications of interactive governance, which is the topic of Part III. The studies in this section all go to show that what is at stake is not a process of replacing representative ideals and forms of policy making with interactive ones, but making them supplement one another in a more or less productive fashion. Accordingly, a key challenge is to understand *how and why interactive and participatory forms of governance can link up productively with representative ideals and forms of democracy.* Ideally speaking, participation and representation should complement each other and thereby contribute to the democratic strengthening of policy making. Yet the studies in this volume show that such a positive arrangement is not easy to achieve and certainly does not come by default.

Several factors seem to influence how representative democracy and interactive ideals and forms of policy making are interlinked. One set of factors promoting such a link between representative and interactive forms of governance has to do with features of *the political system*. Piattonis' study of the relationship between representative institutions and interactive forms of governance in Italy shows that even strong economic incentives to look for new, more cost-effective ways of delivering public services may not be enough to make headway for truly participatory forms of governance. In a political context dominated by Napoleonic forms of state and corporatist forms of policy making, the political classes are reluctant to commit themselves to new forms of interactive governance as demonstrated by the case of Trentino. In contrast, Edelenbos and van Meerkerk's study of local democracy in a Dutch municipality bears the mark of a political system much more familiar and supportive in linking representative and participatory ideals of governance, though even here there are difficulties due to different institutional logics at play. Van der Heiden and Krummenacher's study of innovative forms of citizen participation and deliberation in local Swiss politics also testify to the importance of the political system. Switzerland has a long and firm tradition for direct democracy through local referendums, which has constituted a significant complement to representative forms of policy making. In this system, deliberative citizens' forums in urban municipal policy making are a novelty. Nonetheless it has been supported, on the one hand, by politicians who believed deliberation would help legitimise their policies and, on the other hand, by citizens who believed – correctly or not – that they may actually influence the policy process. Accordingly, while the political system matters by being more or less conducive to linking representative and participatory forms of governance, it does not constitute a determining factor. Piattoni's study shows that in the region of Tuscany – as in contrast with the case of Trentino – the political class recognised the danger of dissipating social capital, which was once embedded in associational forms of participation and in corporatist channels of consultation. It therefore decided to commit itself to participatory and deliberative forms of governance.

Apart from the general features of the political system and its policy-making traditions, we may note a set of *local political factors*. As mentioned above, Edelenbos and van Meerkerk's study testifies to the difficulties of linking representative and participatory forms of governance even in a conducive political environment like the Netherlands. Yet they show that trust, informal bridging networks and boundary spanning may support the establishment of a strong connection between the participatory and representative institutions. Together these factors facilitate a process of interaction through which existing institutions slightly change or evolve by interacting political actors. While trust, informal bridging networks and boundary spanning may seem like plausible factors, they do not help us understand how interactive governance may emerge in cases where such factors are not present. Here Erik-Hans Klijn's study of how a Dutch case of agricultural land management is discussed and develops is enlightening. He shows that relatively high levels of accountability, voice and due deliberation were less the result of trust and spontaneous action, and more the result of a carefully designed network management of the policy process.

This leads us to the third and final feature, namely *the role of metagovernance in aligning representative and interactive ideals and forms of governance.* True, we may have political situations and environments, like the Dutch, where such alignment may arise more or less easily, yet such a political environment is hardly representative and, as Klijn's study shows, even in the Netherlands such alignment may need firm steering in the form of metagovernance. Vifell's study of the Swedish Government's plan to increase organic food production implied the development of an association of stakeholders within the food industry and public agencies that engaged in a joint project and developed an action plan. By deliberately supporting an inclusive framework, the government successfully facilitated the development of an interactive policy network that included organisations with both radical and moderate views. Yet as also indicated by Vifell's study, metagovernance is not without problems. First, in order to avoid antagonist conflicts and policy deadlocks, politicians were metagoverning the policy process in ways that narrowed down of the scope of policy interests articulated. Marginal or simply less dominant political interests may, therefore, be excluded as a result of the metagovernance of the policy process. Secondly, the study also shows that sustainable or durable linking of representative and interactive forms of governance hinges on the metagovernor to make the outcome of the latter feed into the former. In other words, unless the participants in the interactive governance processes believe that the policy suggestions they produce will somehow feed into the representational system and thereby into the authoritative allocation of values and resources, they are unlikely to remain engaged.

In sum, there is absolutely no guarantee that interactive forms of policy making will lead to more democracy irrespective of the ideals used to measure this. Linking interactive and representational forms of policy making is necessary not only to honour a wider array of democratic norms (from participation over deliberation to representation), but also to ensure effective policy making. As indicated by several studies in this volume, metagovernance may provide a partial answer to this need of linking representative and interactive forms of governance and realigning their at times conflicting relationship. Yet, as some of the studies also show, metagovernance may come with a number of political costs such as the exclusion of certain policy goals and interests. Therefore, we need more research not only into the conditions under which interactive policy making may be domesticated by metagovernance in order to allow it to feed into established representational systems, but also the political implications of such measures.

Advancing the interactive governance paradigm

The empirical studies presented in this volume help us to better understand some crucial aspects of how interactive forms of policy making are organised, how interactive governance is metagoverned, and the democratic problems and merits of bringing together public and private actors in interactive governance arenas that contribute to the production of public policy. Nevertheless, despite the growing attention to interactive governance in this and a growing number of scholarly books and research articles, the interactive governance paradigm continues to be under-developed, at least when compared to the more established research on representative and bureaucratic government and the use of markets in public governance.

In the remaining part of this concluding chapter we shall discuss how to further advance the interactive governance paradigm. As such, we shall argue that a further advancement of the interactive governance paradigm requires a clarification of the role of the State, the development of a micro-foundation, the articulation of a galvanising myth, a problem-driven dialogue between relevant theories that facilitates cross-fertilisation, a renewal of the methodological toolbox and some new kinds of empirical studies. Let us briefly consider these six requirements in turn.

Role of the state in interactive forms of governance

The role of the state in modern governance is a controversial and much debated issue. Neo-liberal critics recommended deregulation, privatisation and contracting out, whereas neo-statists have opted for reforms of the public sector that aim to make it more efficient, flexible and responsive while preserving the bureaucratic virtues of fair, predictable and impartial decision-making based on explicit and transparent rules. However, the ideological battles about the role and the size of the state tend to overlook the fact that markets require a lot of governance to function properly and that state institutions are embedded in a dense network of interaction with other state institutions, corporate market actors and a plethora of civil society organisations. The state is still there and it is not walking alone. The recognition of the embeddedness of the state has given rise to a numerous ideas about 'the regulatory state', 'the facilitating state' and 'the enabling state'. While these ideas aim to approach the new role of the state from a state theoretical perspective, we shall here focus on the role of the state from an interactive policy making perspective.

Today public organisations are not only engaged in horizontal and vertical interaction with other political authorities, but also participate in networks and partnerships in which the responsibility for public governance is shared with a host of private actors. The apparent loss of sovereignty has led some others scholars to conclude that we are witnessing a 'hollowing out of the state' that makes way for 'governing without government' (Milward and Provan 2000; Rhodes 1997). Other scholars go in the opposite direction and claim that interactive governance is merely a new tool in the box of strong bureaucratic states that sometime aim to exchange resources with private actors in order to be able to govern more effectively (Bell and Hindmoor 2000). Supported by the empirical studies in this volume, we believe that the somewhat extreme views about either the demise or the exaltation of the state are equally problematic. The state continues to play a huge role in governance and its mutual dependence on other actors prevents it from exercising traditional forms of command and control. Instead of siding with one of the polar extreme views of the state, we should rather focus on how embedded states are metagoverning different governance arenas and, in turn, are transformed by their relationship with these arenas.

The state plays a crucial role as metagovernor and, as indicated in Part II, this role tends to involve both a reflexive and contextual choice about which combination of governance modes to rely upon and strategic attempt to facilitate, manage and direct processes of interactive policy making as well as the use of market-based competition. As we have also seen in the empirical studies, the public metagovernance of interactive policy arenas can play a crucial role in enhancing effective governance and in bringing out the democratic potential. However, as Baker and Stoker show in Chapter 6, metagovernance may also fail to bring about desired outcomes.

Metagovernance is an important task for governments that are operating in networked policy settings and it allows governments to insist on the primacy of politics, although metagovernors must allow some room for self-regulated action and therefore cannot revert to the old command and control scheme. However, if metagovernance permits governments to initiate and influence, if not control, interactive policy processes, we should not forget that state institutions are transformed by their relationship with interactive policy arenas. Not only will they occasionally be forced to adopt, or at least take into account, policies that have been negotiated in relatively autonomous policy arenas, but the role as metagovernors also tend to transform the state. The ability to metagovern interactive policy arenas requires the development of new reflexive and monitoring capacities and new soft tools of 'guidance' to replace the old tools based on hierarchical 'imposition'. It also requires the devolution of competence to middle managers and street-level bureaucrats who have the day-to-day contact with the various partners in networks and partnerships, and this should probably be balanced by new forms of centralised monitoring and coordination in order to ensure some overall policy cohesion and avoid a complete 'Balkanisation' of the state.

In case a tentative agreement on the role of the state should emerge in the scientific community – something that is rather unlikely given the different normative and theoretical orientations of the scholars – some crucial tasks remain. As such, we need more research to determine when and how governments choose to rely on interactive governance, what kind of metagovernance tools are used and with what effects, and how successful are different state institutions in building a capacity for metagoverning interactive forms of governance.

Towards a micro-foundation of interactive governance

Advancing the interactive governance paradigm does not only call for macro-level reflections about the precise relationship between state and society, but also raises the question of the micro-level foundation of interactive governance research. Studies of public governance tend to build on more or less explicit assumptions about human agency and these assumptions, we will argue, are often coloured by the implicit view of how governance is produced. Hence, if interactive governance provides a new perspective on an emerging reality, it throws up the question of how to account for the micro-foundation of this particular governance style.

The micro-foundation of many theories of governmental rule tends to see human action as a result of normative integration and institutional constraints and thus portrays actors as value-based rule followers. This comes as no surprise as governmental actors operate within clear and highly institutionalised authority structures in terms of representative government institutions and public bureaucracies. At the top of the political system, there is highly institutionalised competition between politicians and political parties that is based on different ideological definitions of the common good. Further down and at the bottom of the hierarchical political system, we find public bureaucrats acting within institutional settings that prescribe rational, impartial and rule-bound action, and define a set of professional norms and roles that leave minimal space for discretion and free action. Bureaucracy was originally perceived as a well-lubricated machine in which politicians and, in particular, public bureaucrats constituted the cogwheels. Anthony Downs (1957) added problems to this image by emphasising the rational games played by vote-maximising political parties, and the theories of street-level bureaucrats advanced by Michael Lipsky (1980) insisted that civil servants have room for developing strategies for coping with the conflicting pressures that they are facing. However, whereas Downs' rational choice theory seems to transgress the idea of rule-bound action, Lipsky's street-level bureaucrats merely present us with a limiting case since the frontline administrators are not making rational choices between different pressures and alternative actions, but merely aim to protect themselves in a complex and confused situation.

The advancement of New Public Management (NPM) has brought us far into the land of rational choice theory. The reforms of NPM aim to expand the role of competition and rational decision-making by bringing in market actors and recasting public bureaucrats as strategic managers and incentive-driven actors. NPM's micro-foundation is provided by Principal-Agent theory, which distinguishes between a superior political authority (the Principal) and a subordinate administrative unit (the Agent) and assumes that both parties need each other in order to carry out public governance tasks. The Principal-Agent problem arises because the two parties have different preferences and objectives and because the Agent will be tempted to exploit various information asymmetries to advance the Agent's own interests in terms of better working conditions and furthering of particular professionals norms and values (Miller 2005). The Principal's response to the opportunistic action of the Agent is an increased use of sticks and carrots, and maybe even an occasional sermon (Bemelmans-Videc, Rist and Vedung 1998). The argument is based on Rational Choice theory, which assumes that individuals calculate all the possible consequences of different options and choose the one that maximises their utility in relation to a set of pregiven and perfectly ranked objectives (Moe 1984). The strict assumptions about full information and decision-making capacities have been relaxed by theories of bounded rationality, which constitute the limiting case of the logic of consequential action on which NPM is founded (Simon 1997).

The research on interactive governance is not only offering a different understanding of how public policy is produced, but also highlights the need for a new micro-foundation that is different from those associated with the traditional forms of government and the new market-based NPM reforms. Hence, the relatively weak institutionalisation of interactive governance hinders a strong normative socialisation and prevents institutional rules and norms from fully determining the action of social and political actors. This might widen the space for opportunistic action on the part of the actors involved in interactive governance, especially the private actors who come from a world that is foreign to the public ethos that is supposed to public governance. At the same time, the strategic, cognitive and institutional uncertainties – which pervade interactive governance – call for the construction of rules, norms, values and role images that can ensure that the perceived interdependencies among the operationally-autonomous actors are matched by stable forms of horizontal collaboration. This demand will narrow the space for opportunistic action considerably and, at least partly, replace it with a reflexive mode of action that is based on an attempt to provide matching answers to questions such as: Who am I in relation to the other actors? What is at stake in this interactive policy process? And finally: What kinds of rules, norms and behaviours will help to facilitate resource exchange. The result is a micro-foundation that combines a certain amount of rule following and opportunistic behaviour with a considerable amount of reflexive action, which support the creation of ground rules and behaviours that are conducive for enhancing collaboration in the face of diverging interests and conflicting identities. More research is required to further justify the link between interactive governance and such a 'mixed motives' micro-foundation, but the link has already been established more or less explicitly in the scholarly literature (March and Olsen 1995).

Is there a galvanising myth of interactive governance?

Whether – for better or worse – the proliferation of interactive forms of governance will continue, and become a taken-for-granted way of governing complex, horizontal and wicked policy problems, depends to a large extent on the creation of a galvanising myth, or storyline, which can provide a narrative and normative support of interactive forms of governance (Stoker 1998). New governance practices must not only produce desired results, but must also appear to be the right way of doing things in light of the overall social and political predicament and the prevailing value system.

Governing through traditional forms of top-down government has been a tremendous success when measured in terms of its global reach, robustness and endurance. The explanation of this success is not only that the government model has proved its value by delivering social, economic and cultural growth and development, but also that it has been supported by a galvanising myth that, since John Locke, has been compatible with the core values of liberal democracy. The first part of the galvanising myth of government aims to answer the question of why we should adopt the government model. The answer to this question has been that government provides an effective and feasible response to the need for unifying cultural, economic and political territories in a way that facilitates sovereign rule on the basis of the rule of law and the respect of basic individual rights.

The second part of the government myth provides an answer to the question of how we should organise government; the simple and persuasive answer being that government combines representative political institutions that drive decision-making with a public bureaucracy that is responsible for implementing policy decisions in accordance with clear and explicit rules.

The final part of the government myth is concerned with the democratic justification of government that became increasingly important after the American and the French revolutions in the end of eighteenth century. The government myth is particularly convincing on this point since majoritarian decision-making is simultaneously a mechanism for producing clear and effective policy solutions and for ensuring democratic legitimacy through the pivotal role that the people's elected representatives play in the decision-making process. Hence, if the prescribed institutional procedures are followed, all decisions about how to govern society and the economy will, per definition, be democratic.

The government myth is still going strong, despite an increasing number of associated problems. It is extremely robust exactly because it provides a number of simple, idealised and persuasive answers to the fundamental questions of how to provide a stable and democratic rule. Against this background, it is clear that the proliferation of the interactive form of governance is most often seen as an option of last resort. Interactive governance is invoked when traditional forms of government, or the market alternative, fails to solve the problems, either because policy reforms requires the mobilisation of specialised forms of knowledge and broad ownership, or because one or more actors aim to influence policy decisions by building alliances, exchanging resources and creating arenas for joint decision-making. For interactive governance to be seen as more than a last resort option and to obtain the prominence and legitimacy, which it is already enjoying in certain countries and policy areas, it will need to be based on a galvanising myth that is just as strong and persuasive as the government myth.

A galvanising myth of interactive governance cannot be crafted by academics. Although the credibility and authority of academics is generally high, their role in shaping social and political ideas is relatively small. Hence, if a myth supporting the development and consolidation of interactive governance is going to emerge, it will be a result of political debates and battles in which key decision-makers, international campaign institutions, mass media, social scientists, etc. advance different and slightly totalising ideas. However, the recognition of the limited impact of academics does not mean that we cannot speculate about whether such a myth could possibly be constructed. Embarking on such a speculative venture is, per definition, a risky business, but we believe that the ongoing research can provide some of the building blocks to construct a galvanising myth in support of interactive governance.

One way forward would be to see if it is possible to answer the same three kinds of questions that the government myth has answered so well. The first question is: why do we need interactive governance? The answer here is that growing interdependence between different actors, sites and domains calls for exchange and coordination facilitated by interactive forms of governance. The recognition of interdependency fundamentally alters the policy-making process since the chains of delegation and control associated with government cannot cope sufficiently with the need for mutual exchange and pooling of knowledge, resources and ideas. The interactive form of governance provides a suitable solution to this problem of interdependency because it brings together public and private stakeholders who have an interest in collaborating exactly because of their interdependence.

The next question concerns how to organise interactive governance. Here, we still face real problems when attempting to provide a simple answer. In the absence of uniform models and clearly identifiable best practices, various scholars point to the need for flexible and context-sensitive designs of interactive governance. The range of actors, the interactive arena, the ground rules, and the mechanism for consensus-oriented decision-making will depend on the precise circumstances and tasks at hand. That being said, public forums, governance networks, partnerships and quasi-markets based on relational contracts might provide some ideal-typical institutional arrangements that can help to guide our thinking about how to organise and institutionalise interactive governance. Indeed, in a certain sense, there seems to be widespread appreciation in postmodern times that there is 'no one size fits all' and that we often need tailor-made designs of governance processes.

The final question about the democratic justification of interactive policy making is also difficult to answer. What spring to most people's mind when thinking about the democratic implications of interactive governance are illegitimate exclusions, opaque processes and the lack of accountability. We are so used to thinking about democracy in terms of representative democracy that we often fail to recognise the democratic potential of interactive governance. However, as it has been argued in recent governance research (Warren 2009), interactive governance may be justified by its ability to realise one of the key principles in democratic thinking, namely that those who are affected by a particular decision should have a say in the decision-making process. Interactive governance by its very definition calls for more extensive participation in the policy-making process. Now, while the scope for this participation both in terms of interests and actors is a politically-contested issue, such participation may ultimately lead to the empowerment of groups that are normally not involved in policy making. Interactive policy making can be viewed as democratic in so far as it realises this crucial principle of participation. In a certain sense, governance and democracy result from the very same process since interactive policy making aims to find solutions to wicked problems while permitting those who are affected, or care about a particular problem, to be involved in solving it. This does mean that interactive forms of governance are always effective and democratic, nor that 'governance-driven democracy' (Warren 2009) can stand alone. However, there might be enough democratic justification of interactive governance to argue that it can provide a useful supplement to existing forms of representative democracy.

These bold reflections are not meant as a normative defense of interactive governance, but merely an attempt to show that interactive governance may in the future be supported by the creation of some kind of galvanising myth, which will help it to develop beyond its present scope and status as a default option. However, there is no doubt that the future development of interactive governance is contingent upon a number of factors. Hence, instead of talking about a unified future of interactive governance, we should rather talk about different future scenarios where interactive governance and policy making play a more or less prominent role.

Theoretical dialogue and cross-fertilisation

The study of interactive governance and policy making is under-theorised and there is no commonly accepted theoretical framework for studying policy interaction at different levels and in different areas. We are not saying that the empirical studies are without theoretical foundation, but are merely claiming that the theoretical foundation is weak and underdeveloped and that so far there have not been any successful attempts to bring the different theoretical approaches together in an integrated framework. In many ways, this situation reflects the general predicament in the social sciences. Only, the situation is a little worse in the field of interactive policy making because the general interest in theory building and development of theoretically-informed hypotheses seems to be low in the international research community. As such, there are very few attempts to develop the theoretical underpinning of interactive governance studies and integrate different theoretical and empirical insights into a set of testable hypotheses (for a good exception, see Ansell and Gash 2007)

However, the prospects for a theoretical advancement in the field of interactive governance research are good. At least, there are a number of theoretical perspectives to draw upon. Some of them were highlighted in the introduction. Hence, there are several theoretical approaches to the study of interactive governance and metagovernance that are drawing on insights from the new institutionalism. Moreover, there are a number of recent contributions within democratic theory that are helpful and elucidate the democratic implications of policy interaction. Finally, systems theory (Esmark and Triantafillou 2009), complexity theory (Koliba, Meek and Zia 2010), theories of reflexive law (Teubner 1986) and certain strands of post-structuralism (Deleuze and Guattari 1987) also offer crucial insights into the intricacies of interactive policy making.

It would not make sense to try to bring all these different theoretical perspectives together in a unified theory about interactive governance and policy making since the analytical assumptions behind the different theoretical contributions are not compatible. Alternatively, what we should aim at the creation of a problem-driven dialogue between relevant theoretical perspectives in order to explore the potential for cross-fertilisation. A problem-driven approach to theory building provides an excellent tool for selecting, comparing and combining different theoretical strands with a view to understanding particular problems and puzzles by supplying useful perspectives, concepts and arguments (Howarth and Glynos 2007). Bringing together different theoretical perspectives in an attempt to shed light on relevant problems will most often produce new insights and new analytical frameworks that can be used by other researchers and help to advance this field of study.

Methodological renewal

The usual way of studying interactive forms of governance is to conduct a case study based on a variety of qualitative methods such as document analysis and research interviews. This choice of method is justified by the need to study processes in a particular context, the presence of complex causalities between many different variables and the need to interpret the actions and interpretations of a plethora of social and political actors. However, there is a need to expand the methodological toolbox (Bogason and Zølner 2007). As such, it is a positive sign that a growing number of political scientists have begun to use more anthropological methods, such as observation studies, diary writing, focus group interviews and Q-method, in order to identify and decipher the way that actors involved in policy interaction perceive their roles as well as the roles of other actors within a particular institutional context.

Another way to expand the methodological toolbox is to attempt to bridge the gap between the qualitative method associated with the analysis of policy networks and the quantitative methods associated with Social Network Analysis. There is a lot to gain in terms of cross-fertilisation by bringing these two separate research avenues together and combining them in the study of how different patterns of interaction are sustained by particular perceptions and discourses and how they impact on policy making.

Empirical challenges

Single-country case studies of interactive policy making are helpful in falsifying established knowledge, testing new concepts, and generating new hypotheses. But there is also an inherent limit to such a study, which constitutes the backbone of this particular research field. In the future, we need to supplement the single case-study approach with multilevel case studies, which look at policy interaction that cuts across the local, regional, national and transnational levels, and comparative case studies, which aim to test and modify hypotheses and theoretical propositions through a comparison of cases across countries and policy areas. There is already a promising development in this direction, as some of the chapters in this edited volume attest, but we need to move further along this road. The proposed expansion of the scope of the empirical case studies of interactive governance will be highly demanding in terms of the collection and analysis of empirical data. Process tracing at a single level in a single country can be tough enough, and the inclusion of several countries and several levels makes it much harder. Meeting this challenge will probably require an intensification of research collaboration and teamwork both within and across research departments.

References

Ansell, C. and Gash, A. (2007) 'Collaborative governance in theory and practice', *Journal of Public Administration Research and Theory*, 18 (4): 543–71.

Bell, S. and Hindmoor, A. (2009) *Rethinking Governance: Bring the State Back In*, Cambridge: Cambridge University Press.

Bemelmans-Videc, M.-L., Rist, R. C. and Vedung, E. (eds) (1998) *Carrots, Sticks and Sermons*, New Brunswick: Transaction Publishers.

Bogason, P. and Zølner, M. (eds) (2007) *Methods in Democratic Network Governance*, Basingstoke: Palgrave-Macmillan.

Deleuze, G. and Guattari, F. (1987) *A Thousand Plateaus: Capitalism and Schizophrenia*, London: Continuum.

Downs, A. (1957) *An Economic Theory of Democracy*, New York: Harper.

Esmark, A. and Triantafillou, P. (2009) 'A macro-level perspective on the self and others', in E. Sørensen and P. Triantafillou (eds) *The Politics of Self-Governance*, London: Ashgate.

Howarth, D. and Glynos, J. (2007) *Logics of Critical Explanation in Social and Political Theory*, London: Routledge.

Koliba, C., Meeks, J. W. and Zia, A. (2010) *Governance Networks in Public Administration and Public Policy*, Boca Raton, FL: CRC Press.

Lipsky, M. (1980) *Street-Level Bureaucracy: Dilemmas of the Individual in Public Services*, New York: Russell Sage Foundation.

March, J. G. and Olsen, J. P. (1995) *Democratic Governance*, New York: Free Press.

Miller, G. (2005) 'The political evolution of principal-agent models', *Annual Review of Political Science*, 8(1): 203–25.

Milward, H. B. and Provan, K. G. (2000) 'Governing the hollow state', *Journal of Public Administration Research and Theory*, 10 (2): 359–79.

Moe, T. (1984) 'The new economics of organization', *American Journal of Political Science*, 24 (4): 739–77.

Rhodes, R. A. W. (1997) *Understanding Governance*, Buckingham: Open University Press.

Simon, H. (1997) *Administrative Behaviour*, New York: Free Press.

Stoker, G. (1998) 'Governance as theory: Five propositions', *International Social Science Journal*, 50 (155): 119–131.

Teubner, G. (ed.) (1986) *Dilemmas of Law in the Welfare State*, New York: Walter de Gruyter.

Warren, M. E. (2009), 'Governance-driven democratization', *Critical Policy Studies*, 3(1): 3–13.

index

161, 162, 163
  private providers and 152
  see also under Australia; Denmark;
    European Union; United
    Kingdom
'empowered participatory governance'
  (EPC) 16
Engineering and Physical Sciences
  Research Council (EPSRC) 124
environmental policy 101, 104, 243
  Aarhus Convention 243
  Agenda 21 243
  interactive governance and 243
  UN and 243
  see also case study Sweden, Action
    Plan 2010
Esmark, A. 19, 263, 274
Esping-Andersen, G. 54
Estrin, S. 113
Etzioni-Halevy, E. 15, 16
European Commission 79, 95 n.2, 245
European Council 9, 78, 79
  EU Treaty Reform and 9
European Employment Strategy (EES)
  19, 75, 77–8, 79, 80, 81, 83–4,
  85–8, 263
  Broad Economic Policy Guidelines
    (BEPGs) and 79, 81, 82, 87
  National Action Plans (NAPs) and
    77, 78, 84, 86
  national polity changes analysis
    75–7, 79
    document analysis of 77
  National Reform Programmes
    (NRPs) and 77, 78, 81, 82, 84,
    87
  procedural and sustantive norms of
    77–8
  Open Method of Coordination
    (OMC) 6, 75, 76, 77, 78, 79,
    80, 81, 87
  social dialogue and 78–9, 80, 82,
    84, 88
  stakeholder inclusion 79, 83–4, 264
European Union (EU)

Amsterdam Treaty 78, 79
employment policy 19, 75, 78, 79,
  81
  see also European Employment
    Strategy
energy policy 113, 117
interactive policy making in 5, 6
Lisbon Treaty 79, 87
Maastricht Treaty 78
structural funds policy 54
Europeanisation studies 75–6, 88
Evans, P. 112

Farrell, H. 184
Featherstone, K. 75
Feichtinger, J. 243, 246
Fidell, L. S. 35 n.2
Finland 19
  regional network governance study
    19, 51, 54, 55–64, *68*
  state structure 54, 56, 62
    external regulation and 63
    Regional Management
      Committees (RMCs) 57
Finn, D. 32
Fisher, F. 207
Floridia, A. 193, 196, 197 n.6
Folke, C. 172
Fotel, T. 54, 57, *65, 264*
Foucault, M. 11, 151
  regime of practice, notion of 151
France
  Chertier Report (2006) 86
  Confédération Française Démocra-
    tique du Travail (CFDT) 86
  Confédération Générale du Travail
    (CGT) 86
  employment policy 75, 85–7
    Europeanisation of 75
    private interest organisations
      and 75
  European Employment Strategy
    (EES) 86
    CDSEI, creation and role of 86
    social dialogue and 86, 87

287

139, 140, *141*, 142–3, 144
metagovernance and 138, 142–5, 265
Provincal Council (PC), role 135–6, 138-
Provincial Executive (PE) 135–6, 140, 141, 142–3, 144, 145
swine flu epidemic 1997 134, 137, *141*
White Paper 'Reconstruction's Move' 2001 135, 136, 137–8, 139, *141*
provincial dual system and 134, 135–6
Soil Protection Act (1987) 103
state consensus model 103
ZLTO 139–40, *141*
Zuidplaspolder, interactive governance case study
decision-making process 213, *214*, 215–17
democratic legitimacy and 217–21
Ministry of Housing and Environmental Affairs and 217
water management problems in 213
network governance 19, 29–32, 34–7, 40–1, 53, 95, 95, 96, 130, 209, 244
academic focus on 96, 131, 263
as a combined style 101, 102–4
as personal priority 39, 40, 41
democratic legitimacy and 209–13, 222–3, 244–5
democratic ownership and 247–8
democratic quality of 130, 209–10, 244
effectiveness analysis of 51, 52–4, 56, 61, 63–4, 209
attitude surveys and 56
conflict resolution and 53
Nordic governments analysis 51,

54–70
three-dimensional model of 51–3, 63
employment policy and 30, 31, 40–1
see also under Australia; United Kingdom
failure and weaknesses of 52, 97, 98, 99, 104
democracy and 97, 98
hierarchical governance and 99–100, 104, 105
ideal types (modes) study 31–2, 34–41
factor analysis 34–7
market governance and 100, 102, 104
metagovernance, role of 29, 51, 53–4, 62, 63, 130, 134, 244
public/private partnerships and 53, 59, 63
regional performance and 51, 54, 63
regulation of (metagovernance) 29
representative democracy and 130, 133–4, 136, 222–3
elected politicians, role of 129, 134, 135, 136, 144–5
metagovernance strategies 134–5, 144–5
sources of legitimacy 210–11, 222–3
see also Netherlands, The, agricultural reconstruction case study
research and 29–30, 41, 51–2, 60, 131
steering, function of 131, 132, 133, 145
'Steering with frameworks' research 135
values of 100
see also under Denmark; Finland; Norway; Sweden
networks